From the library of

SOPHENE

Published by Sophene 2023

Matthew of Edessa's Chronicle was translated
into English by Robert Bedrosian in 2017.
This edition is Volume I of III.

A searchable, digital copy of the English translation can be accessed at:

https://archive.org/details/ChronicleMatthewEdessa

www.sophenebooks.com
www.sophenearmenianlibrary.com

ISBN-13: 978-1-925937-70-1

ԺԱՄԱՆԱԿԱԳՐՈՒԹԻՒՆ
ՄԱՏԹԷՈՍԻ
ՈՒՌՀԱՅԵՑՒՈՅ

ՀԱՏՈՐ Ա.

ՏՊԱՐԱՆ
ԾՈՓՔ
Լոս Անճելըս

MATTHEW
OF
EDESSA'S CHRONICLE

IN THREE VOLUMES OF CLASSICAL ARMENIAN
WITH AN ENGLISH TRANSLATION BY
ROBERT BEDROSIAN

VOLUME I

SOPHENE BOOKS
LOS ANGELES

This translation is dedicated to the memory of Matti Moosa,
visionary historian.

GLOSSARY

Acolyth (**ակողութ**), a commander of the imperial bodyguards.

(A)sparapet (*[ա]սպարապետ*), commander-in-chief.

Azat (**ազատ**), a nobleman.

Azatagund (**ազատագունդ**), a military corps, unit or regiment composed of azats.

Catapan (**կատապան**), a senior Byzantine military rank.

Curopalate (**կուրապաղտ**), a senior Byzantine court rank.

Dahekan (**դահեկան**), a unit of mass, or a corresponding unit of currency.

Domesticus (**դեմեսդիկոս**), a term denoting a broad range of Byzantine officials.

Kentenarion (**կենդինար**), a unit of mass, or a corresponding unit of currency.

Marzban (**մարզպան**), an Iranian administrative title.

Nakharar (**նախարար**), a hereditary class of Armenian feudal lords and highest ranking nobles (see Naxarar in the Encyclopedia Iranica).

Protosphatharius (**պրոտոսպաթար**), a senior Byzantine court rank.

Shinakan (շինական), a peasant or rustic.

Spasalar (**դասպասալար**), an Islamic title for a military commander or officer.

Telarches (տեղիար), a commander of a regiment.

Vardapet (**վարդապետ**), a high-ranking and learned member of the Armenian clergy.

TRANSLATOR'S PREFACE

The *Chronicle* of Matthew of Edessa is a valuable source for the history of the Middle East in the 10th-12th centuries. Matthew's work describes the period from 952 to 1129. Appended to it is a continuation by Gregory the Priest, which describes events from 1137 to 1162. Western scholars have used the *Chronicle* primarily for its unique information on the Crusades. It contains, additionally, invaluable information on Byzantium, the Arabs, Saljuqs, Persians, and especially the Armenians, both secular and clerical, both lords and louts. Along with this, Matthew describes such diverse phenomena as urban mobs, siege warfare, and confessional disputes, and he presents a welter of remarkable material of interest to many disciplines, including folklore and anthropology. Curiously, the *Chronicle* also may be of some value to the history of astronomy, as it seems to describe, under different dates, the social impact of the supernova of 1054. This astounding phenomenon, which was visible for two years, was the background of a series of prophecies related by our author.

Matthew wrote his work in three parts, over many years. Part I was written during an eight-year period (1102-1110), and Part II was written during a fifteen-year period (1110-1125). Then, for ten years, Matthew wrote nothing, expecting that others would continue the work. Seeing that this did not happen, he wrote Part III, probably during 1136-1137. Part I covers the period from 952 to 1052; Part II, from 1053 to 1102; and Part III, from 1102 to 1129.

Nothing certain is known about Matthew's life. Only in one place does he speak of himself, as "I, Matthew, a priest from Edessa." From his worldview it is clear that he was a God-fearing Christian (that is, an anti-Chalcedonian, eastern Orthodox Christian). He is not unswervingly loyal to any individual, and criticizes secular and clerical folk, Christians and Muslims of different persuasions. Acts of noteworthy cruelty and kindness are recorded by him without particular bias.

The city of Edessa (Ur'ha/Urfa), whose medieval history is an important focus of Matthew's *Chronicle*, played a major role in the development of Armenian literary culture. It was a cosmopolitan center of Syrian, Armenian, and Jewish culture from remote antiquity, and later was influenced somewhat by Greek Hellenism. To the north was the city of Melitene, and to the west was Sophene, cradles of Armenian culture. While it is conventional to regard Armenian settlement in and around Cilicia—which Matthew describes—as a specifically *medieval* phenomenon, this is not the case. An Armenian population has been documented as residing in the area from at least the fourth century. In fact, the renowned historian of fourth-century Armenian events, P'awstos Buzand, himself probably hailed from Faustinopolos or Podandus/Bozanti, just north of the Cilician Gates.

Events of the 10th-12th centuries vastly increased the Armenian population in this area. There were several causes for this. First, since the early 10th century, the Byzantine empire had been following a policy of annexing the lands of Armenian grandees in eastern Asia Minor. Armenian kings and nobles were coaxed or compelled to leave, and received, in exchange, territories in western areas, that is, in Cappadocia, northern Syria, Cilicia, and also in northern Mesopotamia. The Seljuk raids and invasions of Asia Minor, beginning in the 1020s, were a second important stimulus for Armenian emigration to Cilicia. Many prominent lords, with their gentry and their bishops, left the area. The bulk of the population, however, could not or would not leave, and so remained. Matthew chronicles all this: the Byzantine annexations, the movement of the Armenian population, the Saljuq invasions, the Byzantine reactions, the Crusades, the Cilician Armenian kingdoms and regional statelets. He describes events in the Caucasus, among the Georgians and Aghuans, and mentions the Armenian statelets by the Caspian Sea.

At the time Matthew was writing—as well as before and after—Armenians of various faiths and speaking numerous languages, lived in a vast stretch of territory, from Georgia in the north, through eastern, central, and western Asia Minor, western Persia, northern Mesopotamia, the Levant, and Egypt. They were Christians and Muslims of various persuasions, some pre-Christian and non-Christian elements (such as pagans, sun-worshippers, Zoroastrians, and Jews), as well as "heretics" or sectarians (such as the Paulicians and Tondrakians), some of the latter with ties to other radical movements of the day. At the time Matthew was writing—as well as before and after—large Armenian noble families, "dynastic condominiums," as Cyril Toumanoff calls them, functioned in place of (or alongside) political states. Some, like the Pahlawunids (and the Bagratids before them), controlled territories and enterprises throughout the Middle East as well as the Catholicosate of the Armenian Church. The Church itself often served as a surrogate or ghost state among the Armenians, in the absence of political states.

Matthew speaks of the "House of the Armenians" throughout his work (as he collectively styles these *Christian* communities). In addition, he is an invaluable source for the *Muslim* Armenians, whose descendants continue to live in the same areas occupied by their Christian and non-Christian ancestors.

Unfortunately, no critical edition of Matthew's *Chronicle* exists, as yet. The preferred edition of the Classical Armenian text was published in Vagharshapat (Ejmiatsin) in 1898.[1] This is the text we have translated below, minus two lengthy sections mostly of doctrinal interest. Prior to the publication of the 1898 edition, Matthew's *Chronicle* already had been translated into French by Dulaurier.[2] Since then, the *Chronicle* also has been translated into Turkish (1962), and modern Armenian (1991). The first full English translation was by Dostourian.[3,4] Regrettably, this publication's reliability is compromised by a fair number of errors in translation. For example:

- Volume I (p. 35): "Ashot, *shahnshah* of the illustrious Armenians" should be "Ashot, *shahnshah* of Greater Armenia" [Hayots' metsats' is a geographical term].
- Volume I (p. 47): "for it was seven years" should be "for it was seven months".
- Volume I (p. 47): "We chased him and defeated..." should be "we would have chased and defeated…"

Beyond such errors in translation, there are some questionable techniques employed, such as translating the same word variously. For example, Dostourian sometimes translates Armenian *k'aghak'* ("city"), as "town," even though Matthew uses one and the same word. Again, though *aylasgi* ("foreigner") and *ano're'n* ("impious") usually refer to Muslims, and *Tachik* usually refers to "Arabs" and/or "Muslims" in Matthew's work and elsewhere in the Armenian sources, this is not always the case, especially at the beginning of the invasions. Furthermore, the presence of Armenians of different persuasions, often on multiple sides of the various conflicts, also makes automatic equations of this nature dubious. For such reasons, we prefer to be literal in our translation. Otherwise, the translator is adding a layer of possible misunderstanding, where it does not exist in the original text.

Our decision to translate Matthew was not, primarily, related to correcting errors. Rather, there were several additional reasons. For one, we want to have copyright-free, searchable versions of the Armenian historical sources online. Considering that for some periods, these Armenian sources are almost the only contemporary sources for the history of neighboring countries as well, having them online and searchable is a good way to more thoroughly integrate their information into the study of world history. Our second and principal reason for translating Matthew is personal: we enjoy this activity greatly. Each of the Armenian sources has its own luster, like a radiant, magical gem. They are enchanting, and if you hold them up and turn them, you will see different and unexpected facets each time. Matthew, although he disparages his own abilities, is a fine stylist. His *grabar* is straightforward, his prose is graceful and pleasurable to read, at times seeming almost like modern Armenian. Thus, a personal enjoyment of historical literature—enjoyment of a work's composition, style, and vocabulary—is involved. A third reason is our enthusiasm for the challenges involved in putting such material online, which can transform online books into wonderful platforms for study.

In 2009 an important publication appeared by Tara Andrews.[5] This outstanding work (the author's Ph.D. dissertation) is the best available in a Western language describing many aspects of the *Chronicle* and its continuation, including a history of the manuscript tradition and an insightful discussion of Matthew's themes. The author's aim is to describe and demonstrate a methodological framework for creating a critical edition (there are some 35 known manuscripts of Matthew's *Chronicle*). She has modified and created computer software to help with this daunting task, and tests the method with translations of four excerpts: the first prophecy of Yovhanne's Kozer'n, (1029/30); the second prophecy of Yovhanne's Kozer'n (1036/7); the author's prologue to Book 2; and the author's prologue to Book 3. Andrews' approach and virtuoso computer skills augur well for philology in general and for Armenian studies in particular.

—

Readers who like human duplicity with a medieval patina will find much to savor in Matthew's compilation. One need only change the clothing styles, the types of weapons, and the declared motives, and the general historical processes chronicled by Matthew could be transferred to our own day. Even the places and the peoples are the same. Those interested in studying this period would do well to begin with the 12th-century *Syriac Chronicle of Michael Rabo*, the great patriarch of the Asori/Assyrians or Syriacs/ Syrians, translated into English by our colleague, Dr. Matti Moosa.[6] Event by event, Moosa, in his detailed footnotes, describes other sources (including Matthew) and how they agree and disagree. An extract, covering the same period as Matthew's *Chronicle*, may be read online and/or downloaded from Internet Archive in various formats[a]. Another valuable Armenian primary source for the 11th century is Aristake's Lastivertc'i's *History*, which describes the Saljuq invasions and the dislocations they caused. A third Armenian source of particular interest is the 13th-century *Chronicle* of Smbat Sparapet. Smbat actually used Matthew's *Chronicle* extensively in the early part of his own compilation, and made corrections to it—providing us with a rare example of medieval Armenian philology.

For information on early Armenian settlement en route to Cilicia, see Dédéyan;[7,8] for Cilicia, see Der-Nersessian;[9] for aspects of the Saljuq invasions and domination, see Bedrosian.[10] For the Muslim Armenians and a view of the complex texture of medieval Middle Eastern culture, see the important works of Dadoyan.[11-14]

---

a With the search terms "*The 10th-12th Centuries from Michael Rabo's Chronicle," and also "The Late 12th century from Michael Rabo's Chronicle,"* and an English translation of the medieval Armenian version "*The Chronicle of Michael the Great, Patriarch of the Syrians.*"

BIBLIOGRAPHY

1. Matthew of Edessa. (1898). Chronicle. Armenian. Adamean, M. M., & Ter-Mikayelean (Eds.). *Matt'e'os Ur'hayets'i, Zhamanakagrut'iwn*. Vagharshapat.

2. Dulaurier, É. (1858). *Chronique de Matthieu d'Edesse (962-1136) avec la Continuation de Grégoire le prêtre jusqu'en 1162*. Paris.

3. Dostourian, A. (1993). *Armenia and the Crusades: Tenth to Twelfth Centuries. The Chronicle of Matthew of Edessa*. Belmont.

4. Dostourian, A. (2013). *Armenia and the Crusades: Tenth to Twelfth Centuries. The Chronicle of Matthew of Edessa (2nd Edition)*. Armenian Heritage Press: Belmont.

5. Andrews, T. L. (2009). *Prolegomena to a Critical Edition of the Chronicle of Matthew of Edessa, with a Discussion of Computer-Aided Methods Used to Edit the Text*. Oxford University.

6. Moosa, M. (2014). *The Syriac Chronicle of Michael Rabo (the Great): A Universal History from the Creation*. Beth Antioch Press.

7. Dédéyan, G. (1986). Le peuplement arménien aux frontières de la Cilicie aux IVe-Ve siècles. In D. Kouymjian (Ed.). *Armenian Studies in Memoriam Haig Berberian* (pp. 215-227). Lisbon.

8. Dédéyan, G. (1996). *L'Arménie et Byzance*. In Byzantina Sorbonensia. Paris.

9. Der Nersessian, S. (1969). The Kingdom of Cilician Armenia. In K. M. Setton & R. L. Wolff (Eds.) *History of the Crusades, Volume II: The Later Crusades, 1189-1311* (pp. 630-659). University of Wisconsin Press.

10. Bedrosian, R. (1979). *The Turco-Mongol invasions and the lords of Armenia in the 13-14th centuries*. Columbia University, New York, NY.

11. Dadoyan, S. B. (1997). *The Fatimid Armenians, Cultural & Political Interaction in the Near East*. New York.

12. Dadoyan, S. B. (2011). *The Armenians in the Medieval Islamic World, Paradigms of Interaction in the Seventh to Fourteenth Centuries, Volume 1 (7th-11th centuries)*. New Brunswick.

13. Dadoyan, S. B. (2013). *The Armenians in the Medieval Islamic World, Paradigms of Interaction in the Seventh to Fourteenth Centuries, Volume 2 (7th to 14th centuries)*. New Brunswick.

14. Dadoyan, S. B. (2014). *The Armenians in the Medieval Islamic World, Paradigms of Interaction in the Seventh to Fourteenth Centuries, Volume 3 (13th to 14th centuries)*. New Brunswick.

MATTHEW OF EDESSA'S CHRONICLE

VOLUME I

I.

1. Իսկ ընդ աւուրսն ընդ այնոսիկ եւ ի ՆԱ թուականին Հայոց եղեւ սով սաստիկ ի բազում տեղիս. բայց յաշխարհն հարաւոյ յերկրին Տաճկաց եղեւ նեղութիւն մեծ եւ առաւել քան զամենայն ի Միջագետս. եւ ի խստութենէ սովոյն տագնապ եւ տատանումն լինէր ի բազում տեղիս եւ եւս ի հռչակաւոր մայրաքաղաքն յՈւռհա, զոր կանգնեաց Տիգրան արքայ Հայոց: Եւ կացեալ սովն յայնմ աշխարհին զամս եւթն, եւ անթիւ լինէր կոտորածն յերեսաց սովոյն այն. եւ յաշխարհին Տաճկաց լինէր անցումն մեծ եւ ի քրիստոնէից անթիւք մեռան յերեսաց բարկութեան սովոյն: Եւ զկնի երկու ամի եկեալ մարախ յայնմ գաւառի որպէս զաւազ ծովու եւ ապականեաց զերկիրն: Եւ սաստկանայր սովն առաւել. եւ զայրացեալ բազմաց եւ անողորմ գազանաբար յարձակեալ՝ զմիմեանս ուտէին, եւ իշխանքն եւ մեծամեծքն ընդօք եւ մրգօք կերակրէին. եւ եղեւ անցումն անասնոց. բազում գեւղք եւ գաւառք անմարդաբնակ լինէին եւ այլ ոչ շինեցան մինչեւ ցայսօր ժամանակի:

Դարձեալ ի թուականութեանս Հայոց ՆԷ ամին զօրաժողով լինէին ազգն Արաբկաց յՈւռհա եւ յամենայն Եդեսացւոց աշխարհն եւ ահագին բազմութեամբ անցեալ ընդ մեծ գետն Եփրատ եւ եկեալ ի վերայ ամուր քաղաքին, որ կոչի Սամուսատ: Եւ ելանէր ի պատերազմ զօրապետն Հոռոմոց, որում անուն ասէին Պառակամանոս, այր զօրաւոր եւ քաջ. եւ ի դուռն քաղաքին բախէին զմիմեանս, եւ յաւուր յայնմիկ հարին Տաճկունք զզօրսն Հոռոմոց եւ արարին կոտորած մեծ առ դրան քաղաքին. եւ յետ աւուրց ինչ առաւ քաղաքն Սամուսատ, մերձ ի քաղաքն յՈւռհա:

I.

1. In those days, in 401 of the Armenian Era [A.D. 952], there was severe famine in many places. However, in the land to the south, in the country of the *Tachiks* [Arabs], there was great suffering—more than in all the rest of Mesopotamia. With the worsening of the famine came turmoil and agitation in many areas, especially in the renowned metropolis of Edessa, which had been constructed by Tigran, king of the Armenians. Famine lasted in that land for seven years, and those who died from it were without number. There was great mortality also in the land of the Tachiks and countless Christians died from the wrath of the famine. Two years later locusts—as many of them as the sands of the sea—came to that district and polluted the country. Meanwhile, the famine grew even more devastating. Many [people] became enraged and, mercilessly, like beasts, attacked, [slaughtered,] and devoured one another. As for the princes and grandees, they dined on legumes and fruit. [The area] became devoid of animals, and many villages and districts became depopulated, and they have not [re]built [these places] to the present day.

In 407 of the Armenian Era [A.D. 958] the nation of the Arabs massed troops at Edessa and throughout the land of Edessa and, with an enormous multitude, they crossed the great Euphrates River and came against the fortified city named Samosata. There arose against them in battle the military commander of the Romans [Byzantines] who was called [the] *Paracoemomenus*, a brave and powerful man. [The two armies] clashed with each other at the city gate and, on that day, the Tachiks beat the Byzantine troops and there was great killing by the city gate. After some days the city of Samosata, which is close to the city of Edessa, was taken.

Իսկ ի թուականութեանս ազգիս Հայոց ի ՆԸ ամին զօրաժողով արարեալ թագաւորն Հոռոմոց Ռամանոս եւ գայ ի վերայ Տաճկաց. եւ անցեալ ընդ համատարած ծովն Ովկիանոս, եւ նաւովք անցանէր ի մեծ կղզին, որ ասի Կրիտ. եւ սաստիկ պատերազմաւ առեալ զնա ի զօրացն Եգիպտոսի, վասն զի զամենայն կղզիքն եւ զամենայն ծովեզերեայց աշխարհն Արաբկաց ազգն ունէին զամս չորս հարիւր: Յայսմ ամի կոտորեցին զօրք Հայոց զՀամտուն զօրապետն Տաճկաց:

Յամի թուականութեանս Հայոց ի ՆԺ զԱնաւարզա եւ զՀալապ էառ Արապիկն ի թագաւորէն Միրայ եւ անթիւ արար զկոտորածն, առաւել քրիստոնէից քան իւրեանց ազգին:

Յայսմ ամի ժողով արար զօրապետն Հայոց զմարզպետական գունդն քառասուն եւ հինգ հազար արանց քաջաց, զատ ի յարքունական գնդէն. եւ ժողովեցան ամենայն իշխանքն աշխարհաց տանն Հայոց առ սուրբ հայրապետն Անանիա, վասն զի տացեն զօծումն թագաւորութեան որդւոյն Աշոտի Գագկայ ըստ առաջին օծման հարցն իւրոց, վասն զի չեւ եւս էր նստեալ յաթոռ թագաւորութեան տանն Հայոց եւ ոչ էր եդեալ թագ ի վերայ գլխոյ իւրոյ:

2. Հարկաւորեալ կոչեցին զամենագովելին զՏէր Յովհաննէս կաթուղիկոսն Աղուանից աշխարհին, եւ քառասուն եպիսկոպոսունք ընդ նմա. եւ մեծաշուք իշխանութեամբ կոչեցին զՓիլիպպոս զթագաւորն Աղուանից՝ զայր աստուածային եւ զսուրբ, զորդին Գողազգակայ որդւոյ Վաչագանայ, որք էին թագաւորք Աղուանից աշխարհաց:

In 408 of the Armenian Era [A.D. 959] Romanus, king [emperor] of the Byzantines, massed troops and then came against the Tachiks. Crossing the vast Ocean Sea [the Mediterranean] he went by ship to the great island named Crete. After a fierce battle, he took it from the forces of Egypt, for all the islands [in those parts] and the land of the coast had been held by the nation of the Arabs for four hundred years. In the same year, the forces of the Armenians defeated Hamdun, the military commander of the Tachiks.

In 410 of the Armenian Era [A.D. 961] the Arabs took Anazarbus and Aleppo from the king of Egypt and made a countless slaughter, more of Christians than of their own people.

In the same year the military commander of the Armenians convened an assembly of 45,000 valiant men of the marzpetakan brigade, separate from the royal brigade. And all the princes of the Houses of the land of the Armenians assembled by the blessed patriarch Anania[1] to anoint to the kingship Gagik, son of Ashot, in accordance with the earlier anointing of his fathers. For up to this time [Gagik] had not sat on the throne of the kingdom of the House of the Armenians, and a crown had not been placed on his head.

2. Of necessity, they invited the most praiseworthy Lord Yovhanne's, Catholicos of the land of the Aghuans, and forty bishops with him. With magnificent splendor they invited P'illipos, king of the Aghuans, a spiritual and blessed man. [P'illipos] was the son of Goghazgak, son of Vach'agan, [from a line] which had been kings of the land of the Aghuans.

1 *Patriarch Anania:* Catholicos Ananoia I Mokats'i, 946-968.

Եւ յայնմ աւուր եղեւ ժողով ահագին եւ մեծ ի քաղաքն յԱնի, որ եղեւ այժմիկ թագաւորանիստ քաղաք Հայոց: Եւ յայսմ ամի օծաւ որդի Աշոտի Գագիկ արքայ յօծումն հարց իւրոց եւ նստաւ ի գահոյս առաջին թագաւորացն Հայոց ազգիս, եւ լինէր ուրախութիւն մեծ ամենայն տանն Հայոց, վասն զի տեսին նորոգեալ զաթոռ թագաւորութեան աշխարհիս Հայոց՝ ըստ առաջին հարցն: Եւս առաւել լինէին ուրախ յաղագս քաջութեանն Գագկայ, վասն զի էր կորովի եւ այր պատերազմող: Եւ յայնմ աւուր լինէր հանդէս զօրաց նորա հարիւր հազարաց վառելոց ընտիր արանց ի մարտ պատերազմաց անուանեաց եւ քաջ կորովեաց. վասն զի որպէս զկորիւնս առիւծուց կամ որպէս զձագս արծուեաց յուզէին զօր պատերազմին: Եւ լուեալ զայս ամենայն շուրջակայք եւ ամենայն թագաւորք ազգաց՝ Ափխազաց եւ Յունաց, Բաբելացւոց եւ Պարսից, տուրս եւ սէրս հանդերձ պատուական ընծայիւք յուղարկէին ի փառաւորութիւն Հայոց թագաւորութեանն: Եւ յայնժամ զթագաւորն Աղուանից զՓիլիպպէ եւ զկաթուղիկոսն զՏէր Յովհաննէսն, զեպիսկոպոսունսն եւ զզօրսն, որ եկին զհետ թագաւորին եւ հայրապետին, եւ յուղարկեցին մեծամեծ տրօք եւ սիրով յաշխարհին Աղուանից, որ էր աթոռ սուրբ առաքելոցն Թադէոսի եւ Բարդուղիմէոսի, որք են նահապետք առաջինք Հայոց Մեծաց:

Իսկ զկնի անցանելոյ երկուց ամաց մեռաւ թագաւորն Հոռոմոց Ռոմանոսն, եւ մնացեալ լինէր երկու որդիք, Վասիլն եւ Կոստանդին՝ որդիք Ռոմանոսի ծերոյն: Եւ եղեւ յամի ՆԺԲ թագաւորեաց Նիկիփոռ ի վերայ տանն Յունաց. եւ էր այր բարի, սուրբ եւ աստուածասէր, լցեալ ամենայն առաքինութեամբ եւ արդարութեամբ, յաղթող եւ քաջ ի վերայ ամենայն պատերազմաց, ողորմած ի վերայ ամենայն հաւատացելոց Քրիստոսի, այցելու այրեաց եւ գերեաց, դարմանիչ որբոց եւ տնանկաց:

On that day an enormous, massive assembly took place in the city of Ani, which was then the royal city of the Armenians. And it was in this same year that Gagik, son of Ashot, was anointed with the same anointing as his fathers and sat upon the throne of the first kings of the Armenian people. There was great rejoicing throughout all the House of the Armenians, since they were seeing renewed the throne of the kingdom of the land of the Armenians, as it was under the first fathers. They were made even happier by the valor of Gagik, for he was a capable, military man. On that day he conducted a review of his troops—100,000 select armed men, renowned for their martial abilities, robust and brave. They resembled lion cubs or eaglets roused into a force for combat. When all the surrounding [folk], and all the kings of the [neighboring] peoples—the Abkhazes, Byzantines, Babylonians, and Persians—heard about [the coronation of Gagik] they sent their affection and money, including precious gifts, to glorify the Armenian kingdom. Then [the Armenian court] sent home to the land of the Aghuans with very magnificent presents and great affection P'ilippe', king of the Aghuans, and the Catholicos, Lord Yovhanne's, the bishops and troops which had accompanied the king and the patriarch. [Aghuania] was the throne of the blessed Apostles Thaddeus and Bartholomew, who also were the first [Christian] patriarchs of Greater Armenia.

Two years later, the elderly Emperor Romanus of the Byzantines died [A.D. 963] leaving two sons: Basil and Constantine. In 412 of the Armenian Era [A.D. 963], Nicephorus [II, Phocas 963-969] ruled over the House of the Byzantines. He was a good man, holy and pious, full of all virtues and justice, triumphant and valiant in all battles, merciful toward all believers in Christ, a visitor of widows and captives, a comforter of orphans and the poor.

Սա ժողով արարեալ աՀագին բազմութեամբ եւ անցեալ ընդ Համատարած ծովն Ովկիանոս՝ գայ ի վերայ Տաճկաց, մոմռեալ որպէս զառիւծ սաստիկ պատերազմաւ, եւ խաղայր նախ յաշխարՀն Կիլիկեցւոց եւ մեծաւ յաղթութեամբ առնոյր զՀռչակաւորն զՏարսոն քաղաք: Եւ անցեալ էառ զԱտանա եւ զՄսիս եւ զականաւորն զԱնաւարզա եւ աՀագին եւ սաստիկ կոտորած էած ի վերայ ազգին Տաճկաց մինչեւ ի դուռն Անտիոքայ քաղաքին: Եւ դարձաւ թագաւորն Նիկիփոռ մեծաւ յաղթութեամբ եւ անթիւ գերեօք եւ բազմաւ աւարաւ գայ մտանէ ի թագաւորաբնակ քաղաքն ի Կոստանդնուպօլիս. եւ զորդիսն Ռոմանոսի զՎասիլն եւ զԿոստանդինն առ իւր պաՀէր ի պաղատանն մեծաւ պատուով եւ փառաւորութեամբ:

Դարձեալ ի թուականութեանս Հայոց ՆԺԸ ոմն մաՀապարտ, որ եւ յարգելական կղզւոջն կայր, որում անունն կոչէին Չմշկիկ, գաղտ յուղարկեալ առ նա անօրէն եւ պիղծ թագուՀին, որպէս թէ Հրամանաւ թագաւորին, եՀան զնա ի կղզւոյն եւ եբեր ի Կոստանդնուպօլիս առանց գիտելոյ թագաւորին, եւ ի ծածուկ արար ընդ նմա դաշինս սպանանել զՆիկիփոռ թագաւորն, եւ խոստացաւ լինել նմա կին, եւ նստուցանել զնա յաթոռ թագաւորութեանն: Եւ Հաւանեցաւ առնել զՀրամանս անօրէն թագուՀւոյն: Եւ սուրբ թագաւորն Նիկիփոռ նստեալ կայր ի գաՀոյն իւր ի ժամ երեկոյին եւ վառեալ մոմեղինօք ընթեռնոյր զաստուածային կտակագիրսն: Եւ եկեալ թագուՀին շաղապատէր զթագաւորաւն եւ զթուրն, որ կայր մօտ առ նա, փոկակապս արարեալ պնդագոյն եւ ելեալ գնաց առ չարախորՀուրդն իւր. եւ ձեռօքն իւրովք տայր զթուրն մաՀաբեր ի նա՝ առ ի Հեղուլ զարիւն արդարոյն:

He massed troops and, with an enormous multitude, crossed the great Ocean Sea [the Mediterranean] and came against the Tachiks, growling like a lion [anticipating a] great battle. First [Nicephorus] went to the land of Cilicia and, in great triumph, took the renowned city of Tarsus. Then he went and took Adana and Msis [Mamistra], and the famous Anazarbus, inflicting massive and severe destruction on the nation of Tachiks as far as the gate of the city of Antioch. Then Emperor Nicephorus returned to the city of Constantinople, the royal residence, in great triumph, with numberless captives and much booty. As for the sons of Romanus, Basil and Constantine, [Nicephorus] kept them with him at the palace in great honor and glory.

In 418 of the Armenian Era [A.D. 969] there was a certain man named Tzimisces, who had been condemned to death and was living on an island. The impious and obscene empress secretly sent to him—as though it was at the emperor's order—and had him removed from the island and brought to Constantinople. [This was done] without the emperor's knowledge. She secretly made a pact with him to slay Emperor Nicephorus, and she promised to become his wife and seat him on the imperial throne. [Tzimisces] agreed to effect the wicked empress' command. And [so it came about that while] the blessed Emperor Nicephorus was seated on his throne one evening, reading the Bible by candlelight, the empress came in and embraced him. [At the same time she secretly] secured the strap holding the sword which was close to him [to prevent him from defending himself later on]. Then she went to her wicked co-conspirator and, with her own hands, gave him the fatal sword with which he was to shed the blood of this innocent man.

Եւ եկեալ Չմշկիկն եւ ծածկաբար ի ներքս վազեաց ի սենեակ թագաւորին: Եւ տեսեալ զնա թագաւորն՝ ասէ ցնա. «Ո՛ւն կատաղեալ, աստ զի՞նչ ուզես»: Եւ քաջապէս յարուցեալ թագաւորն յուզէր զթուրն, եւ տեսեալ զի սաստկապէս պնդեալ էր, յայնժամ Չմշկիկն յարձակեցաւ ի վերայ թագաւորին եւ անխնայ գազանաբար խողխողէր զամենաբարի արքայն եւ հերձեալ զնա յերիս մասունս. եւ սպանեալն սուրբ թագաւորն ծածկեալ լինէր ի մէջ արեանն իւրոյ եւ աւանդէր զհոգին ի Քրիստոս դառն մահուամբ: Եւ տեսանէին զի այծեայս զգեցեալ էր թագաւորն մերկուց ի վերայ մարմնոյն ծածկեալ ծիրանեօք եւ արիւնն սփռեալ ցայտէր զերեսօք սպանողաց զայրն Աստուծոյ. եւ զմարմին նորա թաղեցին մօտ առ սուրբ թագաւորացն յարժանաւոր գերեզմանի: Եւ նստաւ յաթոռ թագաւորութեանն Յունաց անօրէն Չմշկիկն եւ տիրեալ էառ զԿոստանդնուպօլիս եւ զամենայն սահմանս աշխարհին Հոռոմց արար ընդ իշխանութեամբ իւրով. եւ զորդիս Ռոմանոսի թագաւորին փախոյց ի յանօրէն թագուհւոյն ի Վասակաւան ի Յանձիթ գաւառին. տարան զՎասիլն եւ զԿոստանդինն առ Սպրամիկն՝ մեծ Մխիթարայ մայրն, զի մի՛ դեղ մահու տացէ նոցա թագուհին եւ սպանանիցէ զնոսա: Եւ յաղագս անիրաւ մահուանս այս կայր ի մեծի տրտմութեան թագաւորն Չմշկիկ անհանգիստ վիրաւորեալ ոգւով:

3. Իսկ ի վերանալ թուականութեանս Հայոց ի ՆԾԻ մեռանէր Գագիկ արքայն խաղաղական մահուամբ: Եւ եղեւ հակառակութիւն եւ աղմուկ մեծ ի մէջ երկու որդւոց թագաւորին Գագկայ՝ ընդ Յովհաննէս եւ ընդ Աշոտ:

Tzimisces came and secretly ran into the emperor's chamber. When the emperor saw him, he cried out: "What do you want here, you mad dog?" The emperor, bravely getting up, reached for his sword and saw that it was firmly bound. And then Tzimisces attacked the emperor and mercilessly, like a wild beast, stabbed this most goodly monarch, cutting him into three parts. Thus did the blessed emperor surrender his soul to Christ, dying a bitter death, covered with his own blood. With the blood of this man of God spattered and glistening on their faces, the murderers saw that the emperor was wearing a goat's hair shirt against his skin, concealed under the [imperial] purple [garments]. They buried his body in a worthy cemetery, close to the [other] blessed emperors. Then the impious Tzimisces sat on the throne of the Byzantine empire. He ruled Constantinople and put under his sway all the borders of the land of the Romans. As for the sons of Emperor Romanus, [Tzimisces] had them removed from the wicked empress. [The sons,] Basil and Constantine, were evacuated to Vasakawan in the district of Handzit', to [the care of] Spramik, mother of the great Mxit'ar, so that the empress would not poison and kill them. Because of this unjust murder [of Nicephorus], Emperor Tzimisces lived in great sorrow, his soul wounded and uneasy.

3. At the end of the year 420 of the Armenian Era [A.D. 971], King Gagik died a peaceful death. There was discord and a great clamor between the two sons of King Gagik, Yovhanne's and Ashot.

Յովհաննէս աւագ էր քան զԱշոտ եւ իմաստուն եւ հանճարեղ յոյժ, բայց մարմնովն տարտամ եւ հեղգ եւ թուլամորթ ի պատերազմունս եւ անկիրթ. իսկ Աշոտ կրտսեր էր, այլ էր արի եւ քաջ եւ զօրաւոր, անպարտելի եւ յաղթող ի պատերազմունս: Բայց բռնակալեաց Յովհաննէս զաթոռ թագաւորութեանն Հայոց. եւ Աշոտ շրջէր զօրօքն եւ աւար հարկանէր զբազում տեղիս եւ նեղէր զքաղաքն Անի. եւ գընացեալ առ Սենեքարիմ թագաւորն Վասպուրականի, առ որդին Ապուսահլի՝ որդւոյ Աշոտոյ, որդւոյ Դերենկանն, որդւոյ Գագկայ՝ Արծրունի ազգաւ, որդիք Ադրամելէքայ արքային Ասորեստանեայց:

Եւ առեալ Աշոտ զօրս ի նմանէ եւ անցանէր առ Գուրգէն թագաւորն Անձեւացեաց եւ խաղայր զօրօքն եւ գայր հասանէր ի լեառն Վարագ եւ մտանէր ի վանք սրբոյ Նշանին Քրիստոսի. եւ երկրպագեալ առաջի աստուածընկալ Խաչին Աստուծոյ եւ պատկերի սրբուհւոյ Աստուածածնին եւ տուեալ յոսկւոյն Արաբացւոց ընծայ սրբոյ Նշանին երեսուն հազար դահեկանս՝ զոր եհան ի Բաղդատ քաղաքէն, զոր էր պարգեւեալ նմա խալիփային, եւ արար զայն Աշոտ պահարան սրբոյ Նշանին եւ զարդարեաց զնա ականբք եւ մարգարտօք. եւ ինքն զօրօք բազմօք հասանէր ի թագաւորանիստ քաղաքն յԱնի: Եւ իբրեւ լուաւ Յովհաննէս զգալն Աշոտոյ եղբօրն իւրոյ, հրամայեաց փող պատերազմի հարկանել, եւ ինքն ի գահոյսն անշարժ նստեալ կայր, վասն զի անհմուտ էր պատերազմի. եւ դրդեալ քաղաքն Անի՝ ելանել ի պատերազմ ընդ Աշոտոյ քառասուն հազար հետեւակաց եւ քսան հազար ձիաւորաց:

Although Yovhanne's was Ashot's senior, wise and very brilliant, physically he was unsteady and weak, cowardly in battle and unschooled [in military matters]. Meanwhile, though his junior, Ashot was brave, courageous, and powerful, triumphant and unbeatable in battle. Nonetheless, Yovhanne's forcibly took the throne of the kingdom of the Armenians. Ashot circulated around with the troops, looting many places and harassing the city of Ani. Then he went to Senek'erim, king of Vaspurakan, to the son of Apusahl, son of Ashot, son of Derenik, son of Gagik of the Ardzruni line, who were descendants of Adramelik', king of Assyria.

Getting troops from him, [Ashot] continued onto Gurge'n, king of the Andzewats'is, advancing with his forces to Mount Varag. There he entered the monastery of Surb Nshan[2] of Christ, and prostrated himself before the Cross which had received Christ and the picture of the blessed Mother of God. He also gave as a gift to [the monastery of] Surb Nshan 30,000 *dahekan*s of Arab gold, which the caliph had bestowed on him in Baghdad. Ashot also had a reliquary made for the [fragment of the] Holy Cross, and adorned it with gems and pearls. Then, with many troops, he went to the city of Ani, the royal residence. Now as soon as Yovhanne's heard about the coming of his brother Ashot, he ordered that the trumpets of war be sounded—though he himself remained immovably seated on the throne, as he was unskilled in battle. The city of Ani was roused to fight against Ashot, with 40,000 infantry and 20,000 cavalry.

2 *Surb Nshan:* "the Holy Cross".

Եւ յանժամ մի ոմն իշխան ի զօրաց թագաւորին Վրաց՝ ի դեսպանութիւն եկեալ առ Յովհաննէս արքայ. վասն զի մայրն Յովհաննիսի եւ Աշոտոյ դուստր էր Վրաց թագաւորին Գէորգէ՝ Կատրամիդէս թագուհին. եւ ասէր իշխանն Վրաց ընդ թագաւորն Յովհաննէս. «Ո՛վ արքայ Յովհաննէս, հրամայեա զի ցուցանիցեն ինձ միայն զԱշոտ, եւ ես ձերբակալ արարից զնա եւ կապանօք բերից զնա առաջի քո»: Վասն զի այրն այն էր այր քաջ եւ անպարտելի ի պատերազմ. եւ ասէր Յովհաննէս թագաւորն ցայրն այն. «Ահա այր հզօր է Աշոտ, դու զիա՞րդ կարես ածել զնա առաջի իմ»: Եւ ասէր իշխանն Վրաց. «Ի ձիոյն առից զնա կենդանի»: Ասէ ցնա Յովհաննէս, եթէ «Զկորիւն առիւծու մի՛ արհամարհիցես՝ մինչեւ տեսանիցես»: Եւ յորժամ ճակատեցան ընդ միմեանս, իշխանն որ յԱփխազաց, որպէս զարծուի ընթացեալ ի ձայն բարձր յուզէր զԱշոտ եւ ասէր. «Ո՛վ է Աշոտ, յառաջ եկեսցէ»: Եւ լուեալ Աշոտ եղեւ զայրացեալ իբրեւ զինձ. եւ յուզեալ զմիմեանս ընթանային առ իրեարս. եւ իշխանն Վրաց զնիզակն եդեալ ի վերայ Աշոտոյ, իսկ Աշոտ իբրեւ զկայծակն ի ներքոյ անցանէր եւ հարկանէր զնա պողովատովն ի վերայ սաղաւարտին եւ զերկաթապատ մարմինն պատառեաց մինչեւ ցատինսն եւ հանդերձ միջօքն յերկիր ընկենոյր: Եւ եղեւ յաւուր յայնմիկ սաստիկ պատերազմ. եւ դարձուցին զքաղաքն ի փախուստ, մինչ զի փախուցեալքն ոչ ժամանէին մտանել ի քաղաքն, այլ յԱխուրան գետն անկանէին. եւ դարձաւ Աշոտ մեծաւ յաղթութեամբ: Եւ յետ աւուրց ինչ խորհեցան Բագրատունիքն եւ Պալհաւունիքն եւ այլ ամենայն ազատագունդ զօրքն հայկազանց առնել խաղաղութիւն ի մէջ Յովհաննիսի եւ Աշոտոյ: Եւ յայնժամ սուրբ հայրապետն Պետրոս եւ իշխանքն ամենայն եկին առ Աշոտ եւ մեծաւ երդմամբ նստուցին զԱշոտ դրուց աշխարհին՝ թագաւոր ամենայն տանն Հայոց, եւ Յովհաննէս նստցի թագաւոր ի քաղաքն յԱնի. եւ եթէ մեռցի Յովհաննէս, Աշոտ լիցի թագաւոր ամենայն տանն Հայոց: Եւ յայնժամ եղեւ խաղաղութիւն ամենայն աշխարհին Հայոց:

At this juncture, a certain prince from the forces of the king of Georgia [Iberia] had come on an embassy to King Yovhanne's. For the mother of Yovhanne's and Ashot was Queen Katramide', daughter of the Georgian King Giorgi.[3] The Georgian prince said to King Yovhanne's: "O, King Yovhanne's, just order them to point out to me Ashot and I shall arrest him and bring him before you in fetters." For [the speaker] was a brave man, invincible in battle. But King Yovhanne's said to that man: "Behold, Ashot is mighty. How can you lead him before me?" And the Georgian prince said: "I shall take him from his horse, living." Yovhanne's responded: "Don't judge a lion's cub until you've seen it." Now when [the two sides] were drawn up for battle with one another, the prince, who was [an] Abkhaz, called out in a loud voice, like an eagle's, seeking Ashot: "Who is Ashot? Let him come forward." When Ashot heard this, he became as furious as a leopard. Having thus antagonized one another, they approached each other. The Georgian prince threw a lance at Ashot who, quick as lightning, ducked. [Ashot] struck him on the helmet with a steel sword and cleaved [the man's] armor-clad body down to the chest, and it fell to the ground with the entrails. There was a fierce battle on that day and the city [forces] were put to flight—to the point that those fleeing did not have time to reach the city. Rather, they fell into the Axurean River. And Ashot turned back in great glory. After some days there conferred together the Bagratunis, Pahlavunis, and all troops of the Armenian nobility in order to make peace between Yovhanne's and Ashot. And then the blessed patriarch Petros[4] and all the princes arose and went to Ashot and, with a solemn vow, seated Ashot as king of all the House of the Armenians outside the gates [of Ani], while Yovhanne's would sit as king in the city of Ani. Should Yovhanne's die, Ashot would become king over the entire House of the Armenians. Then there was peace throughout the land of the Armenians.

---

3 *King Giorgi:* George I, 1014-1027.

4 *Petros* I Getadardz, 1019-1058.

4. Յայնմ ժամանակի նստաւ Աբաս ի Կարս թագաւորական իշխանութեամբ՝ հրամանաւ ազգապետին իւրոյ Գագկայ Հայոց արքային, եւ Գուրգէն՝ յԱղուանից աշխարհին, վասն զի յազգէ Հայոց թագաւորացն էին եւ կային ի հընազանդութիւն տանն Շիրակայ: Իսկ թագաւորն Աշոտ ոչ ժամանեաց բնաւ մտանել ի քաղաքն յԱնի մինչեւ ցօր մահուան իւրոյ:

Իսկ յայսմ աւուրս Ապիրատ ոմն, որ էր մեծ իշխան Հայոց, որդի Հասանայ, սա վասն Աշոտոյ միաբանութեանն, զոր ունէր յառաջագոյն, երկուցեալ ի թագաւորէն Յովհաննիսէ, ապստամբեալ փախեաւ ի նմանէ եւ գնաց ի Դուին քաղաք առ Ապուսուար զօրավարն Պարսից, եւ երկոտասան հազար ձիաւորք ընդ նմա. եւ Ապուսուար մեծարեալ զնա բազում աւուրս: Յայնժամ մատեան առ Ապուսուար չարախօսք ոմանք եւ ասեն, եթէ «Այսպիսի այր յաղթող եւ զօրաւոր եւ զօրօք բազմօք եկեալ է առ քեզ, կորուստ գործէ քեզ եւ ամենայն տանս Տաճկաց»: Յայնժամ ոխս առեալ ամիրային ի սիրտ իւր, եւ գաղտ յայլ զօրացն ի զրոյց սիրոյ կոչեաց զԱպիրատն եւ ի ծածուկ կորոյս զայնպիսի այր քաջ, հզօր եւ անուանի ի մէջ ամենայն աշխարհին Հայոց:

Իսկ իշխան ոմն Սարի անուն, որ էր զօրավար մեծ իշխանին Ապիրատին, առեալ զկին եւ զորդիս նոցա եւ զհեծելազունդ զօրսն եւ գնաց ի քաղաքն յԱնի. եւ թագաւորն Յովհաննէս կարի յոյժ ապաշաւէր զանիրաւ մահն Ապիրատին Հայոց իշխանին: Եւ որդեաց նորա Ապլջահապայ եւ Վասակայ եւ Սարէ եւ ամենայն զօրացն տայր թագաւորն Հայոց գաւառս եւ զիշխանութիւնս:

4. In that period Abas[5] sat in Kars enjoying royal authority by order of his clan head, Gagik, king of the Armenians, and Gurge'n was [ruling in] the land of the Aghuans. They belonged to the line of the Armenian kings and stood in obedience to the House of Shirak. As for Ashot, he never managed to enter the city of Ani until the day of his death.

Now in these days there lived a certain man named Apirat, son of Hasan, who was a great prince of the Armenians. He was afraid of King Yovhanne's because of his own earlier alliance with Ashot. And so he rebelled and fled from him, going to Apusuar, general of the Persians, in the city of Dvin, and taking 12,000 cavalry along with him. Apusuar exalted him for many days. Then some slanderers approached Apusuar and said: "Such a victorious and powerful man has come to you with many troops. He will work harm against you and against the entire House of the Tachiks." Then [desire for] vengeance took hold of the emir's heart. Unbeknownst to the other troops, [Apusuar] called Apirat to him, as though for a friendly chat, and then secretly did away with this man, who was so brave, mighty, and renowned throughout all the land of the Armenians.

Now there was a certain prince named Sari, who was general to the great Prince Apirat. [Sari] took [Apirat's] wife and children and the cavalry force, and went to the city of Ani. King Yovhanne's greatly lamented the unjust death of Apirat, prince of the Armenians, and the Armenian king gave districts and authority to his sons, Apljahap and Vasak, as well as to Sari and all the troops.

5 *Abas I,* 984-1029.

Յայսմ ժամանակի զօրաժողով արարեալ թագաւորն Դելումաց եւ յանկարծիւս գայր հասանէր ի Նիգ գաւառն Հայոց՝ մերձ ի յամուրն Բջնի։ Եւ Վասակ ասպարապետն Հայոց սիրեցեալ որդւովն իւրով Գրիգորիւ եւ այլ փառաւոր ազատօքն նստեալ կայր մեծաւ ուրախութեամբ. եւ հայեցաւ Վասակ ի յառապարս ճանապարհին, եւ ահա գայր այր մի ի շտապս ընդ հետեւակագնացս ճանապարհին. եւ տեսեալ Վասակայ՝ ասէր. «Գուժաբեր է այրն»։ Եւ հասանէր այրն ի դուռն բերդին Բջնոյ, ձայն աղաղակի բարձեալ՝ ասէր. «Գերեցաւ ամենայն գաւառն Նգաց»։ Յայնժամ գոչեաց որպէս զառիւծ քաջ զօրավարն Վասակ, եւ յարուցեալ զգենոյր զգեստ երկաթապատ, եւ զկնի նորա եւթն այր ազատ, եւ ըստ պատահելոյ ժամուն այլ հեծելազօրք զկնի նոցա։ Եւ կազմեցան ազատքն զկնի Վասակայ. եւ սլանայր քաջ եւ աղէկ անունն Փիլիպպէ, ընդ նմին եւ Գորգ եւ Չորտուանէլ եւ այլք ոմանք. եւ այսոքիկ արք քաջք եւ յաղթողք ի պատերազմունս. եւ ոչ կարաց Վասակ համբերել սրտին, մինչեւ զօրքն ժողովէին, վասն զի կային ընդ ձեռամբ նորա արք իբրեւ հինգ հազար. եւ առ հպարտութիւն զօրութեան իւրոյ հինգ հարիւր արամբ յառաջեալ որպէս զառիւծ ի Նգաց գաւառին, եւ յանձն արարեալ զտուն իւր եւ զամուրն Բջնի որդւոյ իւրում Գրիգորի։ Եւ հասանէր Վասակ ի վանք մի. հաղորդեցան ինքն եւ ամենայն զօրքն եւ խոստովանեցան զմեղս իւրեանց բարի խոստովանութեամբ, որ ի Քրիստոս Յիսուս։ Եւ ի ճանապարհին հանդիպեալ ի գեւղ մի եւ տեսին, զի այլազգիքն կոտորեալ էին զամենայն գեւղն առ հասարակ, եւ զօրք այլազգեացն պատեալ էին շուրջ զեկեղեցեաւն եւ զհաւատացեալսն որք ի ներքս կային կոտորէին զնոսա յանխնայ սրով։

In this period the king of the Delumk' [Daylamites] massed troops and unexpectedly arrived in the Nik district of Armenia, close to the fortress of Bjni. Now it happened that Vasak, *asparapet* of the Armenians, was seated in great merriment [in Bjni] with his beloved son, Grigor, and other glorious nobles. Vasak chanced to look out over the rocky road when, behold, he saw a man approaching on foot in a great hurry. Seeing him, Vasak said: "That man is bringing bad news." When the man reached the gate of the fortress of Bjni, he cried out loudly: "The entire district of Nig has been taken captive." Then the brave General Vasak roared like a lion and rose up, donning his iron coat of mail. Seven nobles also did so, and other cavalry began arriving. The nobles ranged themselves behind Vasak. Then the brave and illustrious P'ilippe' flew to his side, as did Gorg and Ch'ortuane'l and some others. These men were brave and triumphant in battle. However, Vasak could not restrain his heart until the troops arrived, for he had under his hand some 5,000 men [altogether]. Through pride in the strength of 500 of his men [who were with him at the time], he advanced to the district of Nik, like a lion. He entrusted his House and the fortress of Bjni to his son, Grigor. When Vasak reached a monastery, he and all his troops took communion and confessed their sins, with a goodly confession in Jesus Christ. En route, they came upon a village and saw how the foreigners had destroyed that village completely. Moreover, the foreigners' troops had surrounded a church and mercilessly were killing with their swords the believers who were inside.

Եւ տեսեալ զայն քաջին Վասակայ, ձայնիւ գոչեաց որպէս զառիւծ, եւ յարձակեցաւ ի վերայ զօրաց այլազգեացն. եւ կոտորեցին զնոսա արս երեք հարիւր, եւ մնացեալքն փախստականք լեալք անկանէին ի զօրսն այլազգեաց: Եւ ապա շարժեալ գային բազմութիւն բանակին Հայոց ի վերայ զօրացն այլազգեաց եւ իբրեւ անչափ անթիւ տեսանէին զբազմութիւն զօրացն այլազգեաց, յայնժամ միաբան զմահ առաջի եդեալ սկսան արիանալ ի պատերազմին եւ որպէս զգայլս ի մէջ այծեաց եւ կամ որպէս զարծուիս յերամս ձագուց, այնպէս արիաբար գնացին ի մէջ պատերազմին եւ զբազումս խոցեալ դիաթաւալ յերկիր ձգէին: Յայնժամ ախոյեան մի ելեալ ի զօրացն այլազգեաց սեաւ խափշիկ եւ այր քաջ, որ եւ Եւթն գայլ կոչէին զնա, վասն զինչ որ եօթն գայլքն ի յոչխարսն եւ ի ջոկս նոցա գործէին, սա եւս առաւել ի մէջ զօրաց պատերազմին: Եւ ահա գայր խափշիկն իբրեւ զսեաւ ամպ որոտալով, որ բոց հատանէին ի վերայ զրահից նորա, եւ ձայն տուեալ եւ յանուանէ յուզէր Վասակ: Հայեցաւ քաջն Եմրան, եւ ետես զնա, զի ահա գայր որպէս զլեառն մրրկեալ, դարձաւ առ Վասակ եւ ասէր. «Ահա այր անպարտելի եւ քաջ, որ այլ չէ ծնեալ ի վերայ երկրի»: Եւ ասաց Վասակ. «Ո՛վ առիւծդ եւ քաջդ Եմրան, վասն է՞ր զարհուրեցար ընդ տեսիլ նորա. ահա ես ելից ընդդէմ նորա եւ տաց նմա զպարգեւքն, զոր ետ Դաւիթ Գողիաթու՝ հայհոյչին Աստուծոյ»: Յայնժամ հասանէր գազան այրն այն, ռումբ եղեալ քաջին Վասակայ, որպէս զի առցէ զնա ի ծայր գեղարդեանն իւրոյ. եւ ի շտապս լեալ Վասակ ի ներքս դիմեաց եւ պողովատ թրովն ի վերայ սաղաւարտին քահեաց եւ յերկուս հերձեաց զխափշիկ քաջն, որ եւ մասունք մարմնոյն յերկիր անկանէին. եւ հաստատեցան ի պատերազմն եւ յանհնարին գործոյն: Եւ ի սաստկանալ մարտին եւ ի բազմանալ խոցուածոց սուսերացն՝ պակասեաց քաջն Եմրան, վասն զի յանհուն եւ յանհնար պատերազմէն ի միմեանց մոլորեալ եղեն դասք ազատացն, որ եւ զիրերաց մահ ոչ կարացին տեսանել:

When the brave Vasak observed this, he roared like a lion and attacked the force of the foreigners, killing three hundred of them. The rest were put to flight, fleeing back to the [main] army of the foreigners. Moving forward, the multitude of the Armenian army came upon the troops of the foreigners and saw the uncountable, limitless multitude of the foreigners' troops. At the sight of this, [the Armenians] together chose death before life and began to take courage for the battle, like a wolf among goats or like an eagle among a flock of chicks. Thus did they bravely go into battle and pierced and felled many of them. At that point there arose from the troops of the foreigners a champion, a dark-skinned Qipchaq, a brave man whom they called Seven Wolves. He was so called because he did more [damage] in warfare among the [enemy] troops than did seven wolves attacking a flock of sheep. And behold, the Qipchaq approached like a thundering black cloud, with sparks flashing on his coat of mail, and he called out, seeking Vasak by name. The brave Emran, seeing the man approaching like a turbulent mountain, turned to Vasak and said: "Behold this invincible and valiant man, the likes of which this world has never seen." Vasak replied: "O you brave lion, Emran, why are you terrified at the sight of him? Now watch how I will rise up against him and give him the kinds of gifts that David gave to Goliath, who had cursed God." And then that beast-like man arrived and hurled a projectile at brave Vasak, intending to pierce him with his lance. But Vasak quickly ducked down. Then, with a steel sword, he struck the crest of his [opponent's] helmet and sliced that brave Qipchaq into two parts which fell to the ground. And thus [the Armenians] were fortified for battle by this unbelievable feat. As the battle grew fiercer and the number pierced by swords grew greater, the brave Emran was not present, since the ranks of *azat*s had strayed from each other in the immense and impossible battle and were not able to see one another's deaths.

5. Յայնժամ դարձաւ քաջն Վասակ միայնացեալ եւ գնայր իբրեւ զառիւծ զայրացեալ ընդ մէջ զօրաց այլազգեացն անցանէր եւ էր ձանձրացեալ ի մեծի պատերազմին եւ դիմեալ ելանէր ի լեառն, որ կոչէր Սերկեւելոյ, եւ ի բազում հալածանաց պատերազմին նստեալ ընդ հովանեաւ քարանցն, եւ տեսեալ զնա շինականացն որ փախուցեալ էին: Յայնժամ մի ոմն նմանեալ Կայենի սպանողին, եկեալ գտանէր զնա, զի ննջէր ի վշտացն. ուժգին բախեաց զնա եւ ընկէց ընդ բարձրութիւն քարին. եւ այսպէս կատարեցաւ քաջն Վասակ Պալհաւունին:

Դարձեալ այս ինչ գործեցաւ ի Հայոց թուականութեանն՝ յամին ՆԻԱ, վասն զի զօրապետն Հոռոմց Դեմեսլիկոսն, որում անուն Մլեհ ասէին, ելեալ բազում զօրօք գայր ի վերայ Տաճկաց եւ ի տեղիս տեղիս յաղթեաց նոցա օգնականութեամբն Քրիստոսի. եւ գայր հասանէր ի քաղաքն Մելտենու եւ բազում չարչարանօք նեղեալ զքաղաքն արգելեալ ի հացէ եւ ի ջրոյ եւ այնու հաւանեցուցանէր զքաղաքն Մելտենի եւ յարուցեալ գնայր մեծաւ ուրախութեամբ իջանէր ի վերայ Տիգրանակերտ քաղաքին, որ անուանեալ կոչի Ամիթ, ի վերայ Տգլատ գետոյ: Եւ զօրքն Տաճկաց ելեալ ի պատերազմ ընդ զօրսն Հոռոմց եւ արարին սաստիկ պատերազմ մերձ առ դուրս քաղաքին Ամթայ եւ զօրքն Տաճկաց դարձան ի փախուստ առաջի զօրացն Հոռոմց եւ բազում կոտորածս եղեալ ի նոցանէ մտին ի քաղաքն. եւ զօրքն Հոռոմց բնակեցան առ ափն գետոյն, ի տեղին, որ կոչի Աւսալ, մերձ ի քաղաքն երկու նետընկէցս:

5. Then brave Vasak, who had become isolated, turned about and, like an enraged lion, cut through the midst of the foreigners' troops. [Vasak] had wearied from the great battle and went up onto the mountain named Serkeweli, where he sat himself down under the protection of some rocks, suffering from the many harassments of warfare. Some peasants who had been put to flight saw him. Then one of them, like the murderer of Cain, came up and saw him sleeping, [exhausted] from his wounds. He struck him forcefully and threw him down from a high rock. Thus perished the brave Vasak Pahlawuni.

This next [event] occurred in 421 of the Armenian Era [A.D. 972]. [In that year] the military commander of the Byzantines, the *domesticus* who was called Mleh, arose with many troops and came against the Tachiks. And here and there he defeated them, with the aid of Christ. [Mleh] arrived at the city of Melitene and harassed the city with numerous torments, preventing [the entrance] of bread and water. Thereby did he manage to convince the city of Melitene [to surrender]. Then [Mleh] arose and went with great joy to descend upon the city of Tigranakert, which was called Amida, [situated] on the banks of the Tigris River. The forces of the Tachiks arose to do battle with the Byzantines, and there occurred a fierce battle close to the gates of the city of Amida. The troops of the Tachiks, after sustaining many casualties, turned and took to flight before the troops of the Byzantines, and were able to enter the city. Then the Byzantine troops encamped by the banks of the river at a place called Awsal, [just] two arrow shots distant from the city.

Եւ յետ սակաւ աւուրց աստուածաաստ բարկութիւնն շարժեցաւ յերկնից, եւ ահա ելանէր հողմն ուժգնակի, մինչեւ ի սաստկութենէ գոչմանն շարժէր երկիրն եւ ի բռնութենէ հողմոյն հող երկրին ի վեր հոսեալ տարածէր ի վերայ զօրացն քրիստոնէից. եւ թանձրացեալ փոշին ծածկէր զմարդն եւ զանասուն եւ զամենայն կարասի նոցա ի գետ անդր լնոյր, եւ ի փոշւոյն խաւարեալ կուրանային մարդ եւ անասուն, եւ յաստուածաաստ բարկութենէ փոշւոյն փակեալ մթացան ամենայն աչք ի լուսոյ. եւ եղեն պաշարեալ ամենայն զօրքն Հոռոմց եւ զելս իրացն ոչ կարէին գտանել: Եւ յայնժամ զօրք այլազգեացն տեսին զբարկութեան կատարածն ի վերայ քրիստոնէիցն եւ գիտացեալ զի Աստուած պատերազմի ընդ նոսա եւ առ հասարակ բախեցան զօրքն այլազգեաց ի վերայ քրիստոնէից զօրացն եւ յանխնայ սրախողխող կոտորեցին զնոսա անողորմ.

Եւ էին արք իբրեւ յիսուն հազար, եւ սակաւք էին որ կարացան փախչել յերեսաց սրոյն. եւ մեծ մասն զօրացն կոտորեցան: Եւ զզօրավարն զԴեմեսլիկոսն եւ զայլ մեծամեծ իշխանսն Հոռոմց ձերբակալ արարին եւ ածին ի քաղաքն Ամիթ, քառասուն իշխանք մեծամեծք եւ անուանիք ընդ նմա: Եւ յորժամ տեսին իշխանք այլազգեացն զկորուստ զօրացն Հոռոմց, զարհուրեալ երկեան յոյժ եւ ասացին՝ եթէ «Զայս ամենայն արիւնս, զոր հեղաք ի տանէն Հոռոմց, մեզ ոչ մնայ. զան Հոռոմայեցիքն եւ անցուցանեն զտունս Տաճկաց: Եկայք արասցուք սէրս եւ միաբանութիւնս ընդ զօրապետս եւ ընդ իշխանս Հոռոմց եւ առցուք երդումն ի նոցանէ եւ արձակեսցուք զնոսա խաղաղութեամբ յաշխարհն իւրեանց»:

After a few days, Divine Wrath came down from Heaven for, behold, a violent windstorm arose of such severity that the ground shook from the sound it made and—from the violence of the wind—the soil itself swirled into the air and dispersed upon the troops of the Christians. Thick dust covered man and beast and all their baggage, which ended up in the river. The dust darkened everything, blinding man and beast. It was from Divine Wrath that the dust clogged and darkened every eye, cutting off the light. All the Byzantine troops thus were besieged and were unable to extricate themselves. And then, when the troops of the foreigners saw the angry destruction so visited upon the Christians and realized that it was God who was warring against them, the foreigners one and all fell on the Christian troops and mercilessly put them to the sword.

They had been [an army] of some 50,000 men, but very few of them managed to escape the sword. The majority of those troops perished. Then the general, the domesticus, and forty other grandee and renowned princes of Byzantium were arrested and taken into the city of Amida. Now when the foreign princes saw the destruction of the Byzantine troops, they were exceedingly frightened and said: "All the blood which we shed from the House of the Byzantines will not benefit us. Rather, the Byzantines will come and enter the House of the Tachiks. Come, let us make friendship and unity with the Byzantine military commander and princes, secure an oath from them, and release them in peace to their own land."

Եւ ի խորհելն նոցա զայս՝ եհաս համբաւ սպանմանն Նիկիփոռայ թագաւորին Հոռոմց: Եւ յայնժամ իշխանք այլազգեացն յուղարկեցին զիշխանս քրիստոնէից զքառասունսն առ խալիփայն ի Բաղդատ քաղաք, եւ ամենեքեան անդ մեռան: Եւ գրեաց Դեմեսլիկոսն ի Կոստանդնուպօլիս թուղթ, եւ գրեաց ի նմա անէծս ցաւագինս եւ սաէր այսպէս, զի թէ «Մեք ոչ էաք արժանի ըստ օրինի քրիստոնէից մտանել ի յօրհնեալ հող գերեզմանի, այլ եղաք ժառանգորդս անիծեալ հողոյ եւ չարագործաց գերեզմանի. եւ ահա մեք զձեզ ոչ գիտեմք, որ նստաւ յաթոռ սուրբ թագաւորութեանն Հոռոմց. եւ զմահս մեր եւ զարիւն, զոր հեղաւ ի դուռն Ամիթ քաղաքին, եւ զօտար մահս մեր ի գլխոյ խնդրեսցէ Քրիստոս Աստուած մեր ի յաւուր դատաստանին, եթէ ոչ արասցես վրէժխնդրութիւն ի քաղաքէն Ամթայ»: Եւ իբրեւ հասանէր թուղթս այս առ թագաւոր Չմշկիկ ի Կոստանդնուպօլիս, եւ եղեւ յորժամ լուաւ զայս թագաւորն, շարժեալ լինէր մեծաւ բարկութեամբ եւ լի իսկ եղեալ ամենայն սրտմտութեամբ. եւ ի նոյն ամին զօրաժողով արար առ հասարակ զամենայն աշխարհն արեւմտից, գայր զօրացեալ, որպէս հուր բորբոքեալ լինէր, եւ յարձակեցաւ ի պատերազմ ի վերայ Տաճկաց եւ կամեցաւ զմուտն յաշխարհն Հայոց առնել:

6. Յայնժամ ամենայն թագաւորազունքն Հայոց՝ ազատքն եւ իշխանքն եւ ամենայն մեծամեծքն աշխարհաց տանն արեւելից ժողով արարին առ թագաւորն Հայոց Աշոտ Բագրատունի. թագաւորն Կապանին Փիլիպպէ եւ թագաւորն Աղուանից Գուրգէն, Աբաս Կարուց տէրն եւ Սենեքերիմ Վասպուրականիս տէրն եւ Գուրգէն Անձեւացեաց տէրն եւ բովանդակ ամենայն տունն Սասանու. եւ բանակ հարեալ ի Հարքայ գաւառին արք իբրեւ ութսուն հազար:

While they were so conferring, news came of the murder of the emperor of the Byzantines, Nicephorus. At that point, the princes of the foreigners sent the 40 Christian princes to the caliph[6] in Baghdad. All of them died there. [Prior to this] the domesticus had written a letter to Constantinople which contained hurtful curses in this vein: "We are unworthy to enter the blessed cemetery for believing Christians, rather, we shall be inheritors of a cemetery for criminals where the ground is accursed. Behold, we do not know you who sits on the throne of the blessed Byzantine empire. But if you do not wreak vengeance on the city of Amida, Christ our God on Judgment Day shall hold you accountable for our death and blood which was shed at the gates of the city of Amida, and our death in a foreign land." When this letter reached Emperor Tzimisces in Constantinople and when he heard its contents, he was transported into a furious rage. That same year he assembled troops from all the Western lands and, so armed, came like a blazing fire to attack the Tachiks, wanting to enter the land of the Armenians.

6. Then all the royal offspring of the Armenians, the azats, princes, and all the grandees of the lands of the House of the East assembled by the king of the Armenians, Ashot Bagratuni. [This included] the king of Kapan, P'ilippe', and the king of the Aghuans, Gurge'n; Abas, lord of Kars; Senek'erim, lord of Vaspurakan; Gurge'n, lord of Andzewats'ik', and everyone from the House of Sasan. In the district of Hark' they assembled an army of some 80,000 men.

---

6 *Caliph* al-Muti, 946-974.

Եւ եկեալ հրեշտակ թագաւորին Հոռոմց առ նոսա եւ տեսին պատրաստական զամենայն տունն Հայոց ժողովեալ ի մի վայր եւ երթեալ պատմեցին թագաւորին Չմշկանն. գնացին եւ յիշխանացն Հայոց զկնի հրեշտակացն Հոռոմց՝ իմաստասէրն Լեւոն եւ Ստատ իշխանն Թոռնեցին եւ այլ եպիսկոպոսք եւ վարդապետք եւ արարին սէր եւ խաղաղութիւն ընդ թագաւորին Հոռոմց եւ ընդ Աշոտայ արքային Հայոց: Եւ գայր խաղայր թագաւորն Չմշկիկ ահագին բազմութեամբ եւ հասանէր ի Տարօն գաւառ Հայոց եւ իջեալ ի Մուշ առաջի Այծեաց բերդին. եւ յառաջին գիշերն բազում նեղութիւն կրեաց զօրքն Հոռոմց ի հետեւակ զօրացն Սասանու եւ եկին իշխանքն եւ վարդապետքն Հայոց առ թագաւորն Հոռոմց եւ մատուցանէին առաջի նորա զթուղթն Վահանայ Հայոց կաթուղիկոսին:

Եւ թագաւորն առեալ ընկալաւ զնա եւ յոյժ մեծարեաց զթուղթն եւ զբերողն. եւ հաստատեաց ուխտ սիրոյ ընդ Հայք եւ խնդրեաց զօրս յԱշոտոյ գալ նմա յօգնականութիւն. եւ տուեալ Աշոտ զօրս ի տանէ Հայոց վառելոց եւ այր պատեբազմողս իբրեւ տասն հազար, խնդրեաց կերակուրս, ռոճիկս. եւ զամենայնն տուեալ նմա Աշոտ: Եւ զվարդապետն Հայոց զՂեւոնդ, զեպիսկոպոսն եւ զիշխանսն մեծաւ պարգեւօք յուղարկեաց առ Աշոտ թագաւորն Հայոց:

Then emissaries of the Byzantine emperor came to them and observed the preparedness of the entire House of the Armenians, assembled in one place. They went back and related this to Emperor Tzimisces. Following after the Byzantine envoys were [a group of] Armenian princes [including] the philosopher Lewon, Prince Stat Tor'net'si, as well as others, bishops and *vardapets*, and they established friendship and peace between the emperor of the Byzantines and Ashot, king of the Armenians. Then Emperor Tzimisces advanced with an awesome multitude and arrived in the Armenian district of Taron, descending on Muş in front of Aytseats' fortress. On the first night the Byzantine troops endured numerous harassments from the infantry troops of Sasan. Then Armenian princes and vardapets arrived by the Byzantine emperor and showed him a letter from Vahan[7], Catholicos of the Armenians.

The emperor took and read it and greatly exalted both the letter and its bearers. He confirmed an oath of friendship with the Armenians and requested from Ashot troops which would come to assist him. Ashot provided some 10,000 armed fighters, and [when the emperor] requested stipends for [their] food, Ashot gave that and everything else [requested]. Then [the emperor] sent the Armenian vardapet Ghewond, the bishops, and princes back to Ashot, king of the Armenians, with grand gifts.

7 *Vahan I*, Siwnets'i, 968-969.

Յայնժամ Չմշկիկ՝ որ ասէին Կիւռժան, դարձաւ ի պատերազմ ի վերայ Տաճկաց եւ մեծաւ յաղթութեամբ եւ սրտմտութեամբ, կոտորածով եւ արեամբ ելից զամենայն երկիրն. եւ զբազում քաղաքս եւ զամուր բերդս ի հիմանց քարայատակս արար՝ երեք հարիւր մինչեւ ի սահմանս Բաղդատ քաղաքին: Բայց զՈւռհա ոչ արար աւեր յաղագս կրօնաւորացն, որ բնակեալ էին ի լերինն եւ ամենայն սահմանս նորա՝ իբրեւ երկոտասան հազար. եւ գայր հասանէր ի վերայ Ամթայ քաղաքին բազում սրտմտութեամբ: Իսկ տէրն Ամթայ քաղաքին կին էր, որ էր քոյր Համտնոյ ամիրային Տաճկաց: Եւ յառաջ ժամանակաց թագաւորն խառնակեալ էր ընդ նմա մեղօք եւ վասն այնորիկ չարաչար հնարս առնելոյ զքաղաքն Ամիթ: Եւ ելեալ կնոջն ի վերայ պարսպի քաղաքին, ասէ ցթագաւորն. «Ի վերայ կնոջ գաս ի պատերազմ եւ չհամարի՞ս զայս քեզ նախատինք»: Եւ ասէր թագաւորն. «Երդում ունիմ առ իս քակել զպարիսպ քաղաքիդ, եւ ազատեսցին մարդիկդ»: Ասէր տիկինն քաղաքին. «Էջ քակեա զկանդարայն՝ որ կայ ի վերայ Տգլաթ գետոյ, եւ այնու կատարեսցես զերդումն քո»:

Եւ արար թագաւորն այսպէս. եւ առեալ բազում գանձս ոսկւոյ եւ արծաթոյ, եւ թողեալ զԱմիթ վասն կնոջն իւրոյ եւ վասն զի Չմշկիկն էր ի գաւառէն Խոզնայ, ի տեղւոյն, որ այժմ կոչի Չմշկածակք, եւ կինն ի նմին սահմանացն էր. զի յայնմ ժամանակին Տաճկունքն էին տիրեալ բազում տեղեաց: Եւ ահա թագաւորն Յունաց խաղայր գնայր ընդ աշխարհին Տաճկաց արեանհեղութեամբ մինչեւ ի սահմանս Բաղդատ քաղաքին. եւ շրջան առեալ զներքին կողմն աշխարհին՝ գնայր յԵրուսաղէմ քաղաքն.

Tzimisces, whom they called Kiwr'zhan,[8] then turned to warfare against the Tachiks with great triumph and in anger, filling up the entire country with killings, and blood. He demolished to their foundations many cities and secure fortresses—some 300 of them—as far as the borders of Baghdad. But he did not destroy Edessa, because of some 12,000 clerics who dwelt on the mountain there and throughout all the [city's] borders. [Tsimisces] arrived at the city of Amida in great anger. However, the lord of the city of Amida was a woman, who was the sister of Hamdan, emir of the Tachiks. Now in previous times the emperor sinfully had commingled with her and, therefore, he did not make a stratagem to capture the city of Amida. The woman went up onto the city wall and said to the emperor: "Do you come in battle against a woman and not consider it an insult?" The emperor replied: "I have sworn to demolish the walls of your city, to free the people." The woman of the city responded: "Descend and pull down the bridge which spans the Tigris River, and thereby you will fulfill your oath."

And that is what the emperor did. Thus, after taking much gold and silver treasure, he left Amida because of its woman and also because Tzimisces was from the district of Khozan, from the place now called Ch'mshkatsak and the woman was from the same area. For in that period the Tachiks ruled over many places. Behold, the emperor of the Byzantines went through the land of the Tachiks shedding blood as far as the borders of the city of Baghdad. Then he turned through the interior of the land and went to the city of Jerusalem.

8 *Kiwr'zhan:* Kyr John.

7. Եւ գրեաց թագաւորն Չմշկիկ թուղթ առ Աշոտ թագաւորն Հայոց այսպէս.

«Աշոտ շահնշահ Հայոց մեծաց, եւ իմ հոգեկան զաւակ, լուր եւ իմացիր թէ ո՛րչափ ինչ սքանչելիս արար Աստուած առ մեզ եւ զարմանալի յաղթութիւնս, որ եւ իմանալն անկարելի է զԱստուծոյ քաղցրութիւնն եւ զհաւոր մարդասիրութիւնն՝ զոր արար տէր ընդ ժառանգութիւնս իւր: Ի յայսմ տարւոջս ի ձեռն թագաւորութեանս մերում կամեցաք եւ քո փառաւորութեանդ ծանուցանել, ո՞վ Աշոտ Բագրատունի եւ զաւակ իմ. իմացուցանեմ քեզ, որ եւ դու, որպէս եւ քրիստոնեայդ ես եւ հաւատարիմ սիրելի թագաւորութեանս մերում, ուրախանաս եւ փառաւորես զհաւոր զմեծութիւնն Քրիստոսի Աստուծոյ մերոյ եւ գիտասցես թէ ո՛րչափ օգնեացէ Աստուած քրիստոնէից յամենայն ժամանակի քանզի յետ հարկատու առնելոյ թագաւորութեանս մերոյ զամենայն արեւելս Պարսից. եւ կամ թէ ո՛րպէս հանաք զնշխարս սրբոյ հայրապետին Յակոբայ՝ Մծբնայ ի քաղաքէն Տաճկաց եւ առաք ի Տաճկաց զհարկն մեր, եւ զգերութիւնն հանաք ի նոցանէն եւ ելեալ գնացաք: Եւ վասն ամբարտաւանութեան եւ հպարտութեան Ամիր-ըլ-մումնոյ իշխանին Ափրիկեցւոց, զորս Մախըր Արապիկ կոչեն, որ եւ բազում զօրօք եկեալ ի վերայ մեր եւ առ ժամ մի ի վըտանգի արկին զօրսն մեր, եւ ապա յաղթեցաք նոցա մեծաւ զօրութեամբ եւ օգնականութեամբն Աստուծոյ, եւ ամօթալից դարձան որպէս զայլ թշնամիսն:

7. Emperor Tzimisces wrote a letter to Ashot, king of the Armenians, with this content:

"To Ashot, *shahnshah* of Greater Armenia, and my spiritual son. Hear and learn just what kinds of marvels and amazing victories God has given us. Knowing about them it is impossible to comprehend the sweetness of God and His great love for humanity and the astounding benevolence in making friendship among His inheritance. We should like to inform you about what we were able to accomplish during this year, O glorious Ashot Bagratuni, my son. I shall make you aware of it as you are a Christian and faithful to our beloved empire, to make you happy and so that you glorify the awesome greatness of Christ our God and realize the extent to which God always helps the Christians. For He made tributary to our empire the entire Persian East. [You shall learn also] how we removed the relics of the blessed patriarch James of Nisibis from a Tachik city and extracted our tribute from the Tachiks; how we took from them our captives and arose and departed. Now it happened that [the caliph, or Commander of the Faithful, the] Amir al-Muminin[9]—prince of the [Fatimid] Africans, whom the Arabs call Maghrebis—in his arrogance and pride arose and came against us with many troops. And for a while he put our troops in danger, but then we conquered them with the great strength and assistance of God. As our other enemies [had done], they also turned back in disgrace.

9 *Amir al-Mumin:* al-Mu'izz (A.D. 953-975).

«Եւ յայնժամ առաք զներքին կողմն աշխարհին նոցա եւ ի սուր սուսերի մաշեցաք զզաւառս բազումս եւ փութապէս դարձաք ի դուրս եւ արարաք ձմերոց եւ զամենայն հեծելազօրսն մեր հողեցաք. Յապրիլի ամսեանն ի մուտն դիմեալ խաղացաք ի յաշխարհն Փինիկեցւոց եւ Պաղեստինացւոց եւ քննայոյզ առնէաք զպիղծ Ափրիկեցիսն, որք եկեալ էին ի գաւառն Շամայ: Եւ ելեալ ամենայն զօրօք մերովք դիմեալ խաղալով գնացաք ի յԱնտիոքայ եւ անցաք ընդ ամենայն զաւառսն մերոյ թագաւորութեանս եւ ի հնազանդութիւն արարաք մեծաւ հարկատրութեամբ եւ անհամար գերութեամբ եւ հասաք մինչեւ ի Հէմս քաղաք. եւ ելեալ ընդունեցին զմեզ բարւոք՝ որք մեր հարկատուքն էին գաւառականքն. եւ հասանէաք մինչեւ ի Կատոլվէքն, որ անուանեալ կոչի Իլուպօլիս, որ է Արեգ քաղաք, երեւելի եւ ահաւոր պարսպեալ մեծ յոյժ եւ հարուստ: Եւ ելին պատերազմաւ ընդ առաջ մեր, եւ բազմութիւնք զօրաց մերոց հալածական արարին զնոսա եւ ի բերան սրոյ կոտորեցին: Եւ յետ սակաւ աւուրց պաշարեցաք զԱրեգ քաղաք. բազում գերութիւնս, մանկունս եւ աղջկունս առին զօրքն մեր եւ զգանձս ոսկւոյ եւ արծաթոյ անասունս բազումս առին.

«Եւ ահա անտի ելեալ յառաջացաք ի մեծ քաղաքն Դամասկոս, կամեցաք եւ զայն պաշարել: Իսկ քաղաքապետն ալեւոր էր եւ այր իմաստուն, առաքեաց առ թագաւորութիւնս մեր եւ բազում ընծայիւք աղաչեաց զմեզ չանկանիլ ի գերութիւն եւ ոչ գնալ ի ծառայութիւն, որպէս զԿատոլվէքայ զբնակիչսն, եւ ոչ զգաւառսն աւերել որպէս զնոցայն:

"After this, we took the interior portion of their land, putting many districts to the sword. Then we quickly turned and exited. We made our winter quarters and paid stipends to all our cavalry. At the beginning of the month of April, we applied ourselves to the land of the Phoenicians and Palestinians and avenged ourselves on the impious Africans, who had come to the district of Syria. Then, arriving with all our troops, we went on to Antioch, subduing and adding all these districts to our empire. Taking great tribute and countless captives, we went as far as the city of Homs. Those who were of the districts tributary to us, arose and received us well. Then we reached Baalbek, which is called Heliopolis, which is Areg ["Sun"] City. This had noteworthy and daunting fortifications and was very large and rich. They arose before us in battle. But the multitude of our troops put them to flight and put them to the edge of the sword. After a few days, we besieged Sun City. Our forces took many captives, boys and girls, and treasures of gold and silver as well as many animals.

"After this we arose and advanced to the large city of Damascus. We also wanted to besiege it. However, the head of the city was an old and wise man. He sent many gifts to our majesty and beseeched us not to enslave them or lead them into servitude as had happened to the residents of Baalbek, and not to ruin their districts as [we did] with the others.

«Եւ բերին բազում տուրս պատուականս եւ յոլով ձիս եւ ջորիս երեւելիս եւ գեղեցիկ սարք յոսկւոյ եւ արծաթոյ եւ հարկս յԱրաբացեաց ոսկւոյն քառասուն հազար դահեկանս. առին եւ ի մէնջ զօրավարս եւ տուին մեզ գիրս, զի յաւիտեան ծառայք կայցեն թագաւորութեանս մերում՝ ազգ զհետ ազգի եւ ցեղ զհետ ցեղի: Եւ կարգեցաք անդ զօրավար զայր ոմն, որ կոչէր Թուրք, այր փառաւոր Բաղդատեցի, որ եկն առ մեզ ի ծառայութիւն հինգ հարիւր ձիաւորով եւ հաւատաց ի Քրիստոս. որ եւ յառաջն ծառայեալ էր թագաւորութեանս մերում: Եւ Դամասկացիքն արարին դաշինս երդման, զի տացեն անխափան զհարկն, եւ ասացին գով թագաւորութեանս մերում, եւ ընդ մեր թշնամիսն մարտնչել. եւ յաղագս այսորիկ անպաշարելի թողաք զնոսա:

8. «Եւ անտի յարուցեալ գնացաք ի Տիբերական ծովն, ուր Տէր մեր Յիսուս Քրիստոս հարիւր յիսուն եւ երեք ձըկամբն զսքանչելիս արար. կամեցաք եւ զայն քաղաքն պաշարել, իսկ նոքա եկին ի հնազանդութիւն մերոյ թագաւորութեանս եւ բերին մեզ ընծայս բազումս, որպէս Դամասկացիքն, եւ հարկս երեսուն հազար դահեկանս առանց այլ տրոց եւ խնդրեցին զօրավարս ի մէնջ եւ գիր ծառայութեան տուեալ մեզ հաստատուն որպէս զԴամասկացիքն՝ հնազանդ լինել մեզ յաւիտեան եւ տալ անխափան զհարկն մեր: Յայնժամ թողաք զնոսա ազատ ի գերութենէ եւ ոչ աւերեցաք զքաղաքն եւ ոչ զգաւառսն՝ եւ ոչ արարաք զնոսա յաւարս, վասն զի հայրենի տուն էր սրբոց առաքելոցն: Նա աւանիկ եւ զՆազարէթ, ուր զաւետիսն իսկ ի հրեշտակէն լուաւ Աստուածածին սուրբ կոյսն Մարիամ. նոյնպէս գնացաք եւ ի Թափօրական լեառն եւ ելաք յայն տեղւոջն, ուր այլակերպեցաւ Քրիստոս Աստուած մեր:

"They brought many valuable gifts and numerous excellent horses and mules and beautifully wrought creations of gold and silver and taxes from the Arabs amounting to 40,000 dahekans. They received generals from us and gave a document [confirming] that they would eternally be subject to our realm from generation to generation. We set up there as general a certain glorious man from Baghdad, who was named T'urk'. He came to us in service with 500 cavalry, and believed in Christ. Formerly, he had served our empire. The Damascenes wrote an oath that they would pay taxes unimpeded and also praised our realm and [vowed that they] would fight against our enemies. Then we left them without a siege.

8. "From there we arose and went to the Sea of Tiberias, where our Lord Jesus Christ had performed a miracle with 153 fish. Now we also wanted to besiege that city. However, they came out in submission to our realm and brought us many gifts, as the Damascenes had done, and 30,000 dahekans in taxes along with other gifts. They requested military commanders from us and gave us a document expressing submission, as had the Damascenes, [confirming] that they would remain obedient to us forever and pay our tax without hindrance. Thus, we left them without taking captives, did not destroy the city or the district, or plunder them. For this place was a patrimonial home of holy Apostles. [We had respect] here and also for Nazareth, where the Mother of God, the blessed Virgin Mary, heard glad tidings from the angels. Then we went to Mt. Tabor and ascended to the place where Christ our God was transfigured.

«Եւ մինչդեռ յայն տեղւոջն կայաք, եկին առ մեզ ի Ռամլէէ եւ յԵրուսաղեմէ աղաչել զթագաւորութիւնս մեր՝ ողորմութիւն գտանել ի մէնջ. խնդրեցին զօրավար եւ եղեն հարկատուք եւ ուխտեցին լինել մեզ ի ծառայութիւն, զոր արարաք իսկ: Կամեցաք եւ զսուրբ գերեզմանն Քրիստոսի Աստուծոյ մերոյ ազատել ի գերութենէն Տաճկաց: Կարգեցաք զօրավարս յամենայն թէմս, որք հնազանդեցան եւ եղեն հարկատուք թագաւորութեանս մերում, որ է Պենհաղա, որ կոչի Դեկապօլիս, եւ Գենեսարէթ եւ յԱրկեա, որ կոչի Պտողմիա եւ գրով յանձին կալան ամ յամէ անխափան տալ զհարկն եւ լինել ընդ ծառայութեամբ մեր: Գնացաք մինչեւ ի Կեսարիա, որ է եզր մեծի ծովուն Ովկիանոսի, հնազանդեցան եւ եկին ընդ մերով իշխանութեամբս: Եւ եթէ ոչ էին փախուցեալ ծովերաց բերդերն, որք էին բնակեալ պիղծ Ափրիկեցիքն, զարհուրեալք ի մէնջ, օգնականութեամբն Աստուծոյ ի սուրբ քաղաքն յԵրուսաղէմ էաք գնացեալ եւ ի սուրբ տեղիսն Աստուծոյ էաք յաղօթս կացեալ: Եւ իբրեւ լուաք եթէ փախեան ծովեզերաց բնակիչքն, յայնժամ զվերին կողմն աշխարհին հնազանդեցուցաք եւ ընդ Հոռոմց իշխանութեամբ արարաք եւ կարգեցաք անդ զօրավար եւ ի մեր կոյս արարաք եւ զոչ հնազանդեալսն պատերազմաւ պաշարեցաք եւ առեալ գնացաք ընդ ծովեզերին պողոտայն, որ դէմ յանդիման երթայր ի Վռիտոն քաղաքն յերեւելին եւ յանուանին պարսպեալ յոյժ, որ այժմ ասի Պէրութ, պատերազմեալ եւ սաստիկ կռուով առեալ զնա եւ հազար Ափրիկեցի ձերբակալս արարաք, նոյնպէս եւ զՆուսերի զԱմիր-ըլ-մումնոյ եւ զայլ լաւագոյն իշխանսն. եւ յայն քաղաքն զօրավար եդաք եւ անտի կամեցաք ի Սիդովն անցանել:

"While we were there, [people] came to us from Ramla and Jerusalem to beseech our majesty and to find mercy from us. They also requested a general, became tributary, and pledged to remain our subjects—all of which we granted. We also wanted to free from Tachik captivity the Sepulcher of Christ our God. We designated generals in all the themes which submitted and became tributary to our empire: Beisan, also called Decapolis, Genesareth, and Acre, also called Ptolemais. In writing, they agreed to pay taxes yearly and without impediment, and to be in service to us. We advanced as far as Caesarea, located on the shore of the Ocean Sea [Mediterranean]. They submitted and came under our rule. Furthermore, if the loathsome Africans had not fled to the coastal fortresses and holed up there out of fear of us, with the aid of God we would have gone on to the holy city of Jerusalem to pray in the holy places of God. When we heard that the coastal population had fled, we brought into obedience the upper part of the land, placing them under Byzantine sovereignty. We established a general there and also brought over to our side by siege and warfare those who had not submitted. After taking them, we went via the coastal route, which leads directly to the prominent, renowned, and very well-walled city of Vr'iton, which is now called Beirut. Engaging in fierce battle, we also took that [city] and arrested a thousand Africans, including Nasir [the general] of the Amir al-Mu'min and others of the best princes. We put a general in that city and wished to go thence to Sidon.

«Իսկ յորժամ լուան Սիդովնացիքն, առաքեցին առ մեզ զծերսն քաղաքին իւրեանց. եկին եւ աղաչեցին զթագաւորութիւնս մեր եւ խնդրեցին, զի հարկատուք լինիցին մեզ մեծաւ ահիւ եւ կալ մնալ մեզ ի ծառայութիւն. զոր լուաք իսկ աղաչանաց նոցա եւ կատարեցաք զկամս նոցա եւ առաք ի նոցանէ զհարկն եւ տուաք նոցա զօրավարս: Եւ անտի յարուցեալ գնացաք ի Բիբղոն հին եւ ամուր բերդն եւ զայն եւս պատերազմեալ առաք եւ զբնակիչս նորա ի գերութիւն մատնեցաք. եւ մեծաւ աւարաւ եւ գերութեամբ անցաք ընդ ամենայն ծովեզերաց քաղաքանին ընդ դըժուար եւ ընդ նեղ ճանապարհին ընդ որ այլք զօրք հեծելոց ոչ երբէք էր անցեալ նեղ եւ նուրբ եւ չար ճանապարհ. եւ անդ գտանէաք շէն եւ վայելուչ քաղաքանի եւ ամուր բերդեր, յորում կային Տաճիկ պահապանք, զամենայն պաշարեցաք եւ քարայատակ կործանեցաք, եւ զբընակիչսն ի գերութիւն վարեցաք: Եւ յառաջ քան զհասանիլն մեր ի Տրապօլիս հեծելազօրս առաքեցաք զԹիմացիսն եւ զՏաշխամատացիսն ի կապանն, որ կոչի Քարերես, ասն զի լուեալ էր մեր, եթէ պիղծ Ափրիկեցիքն անդ նստէին ի կապանին. եւ հրամայեցաք քինս դնել եւ դարանս մահու գործեցաք նոցա. եւ որպէս պատուիրեցաքն՝ նոյնպէս եւ արարին. եւ երկու հազարք յայտնի ելեալ ի նոցանէ ի վերայ զօրաց մերոց՝ զորս զբազումս ի նոցանէ սպանին եւ յոլովս ի նոցանէ արարին կալանականս, եւ ածին առաջի մերոյ թագաւորութեանս. նոյնպէս եւ ուր հանդիպէին՝ փախստականս առնէին զնոսա: Եւ իսպառ ջնջեցաք զամենայն աշխարհն Տրապօլսոյ, զայգիսն եւ զձիթենիսն եւ զբուրաստանս նոցա առհասարակ կոտորեցաք եւ յաւեր դարձուցաք եւ արմատախիլ արարաք զամենայն գաւառսն. եւ Ափրիկեցիքն, որ էին անդ՝ համարձակեցան եւ ելին ի պատերազմ ընդդէմ մեր: Յայնժամ յարձակեցաք ի վերայ նոցա եւ կոտորեցաք զամենեսեան առ հասարակ:

"When the people of Sidon heard about this, they sent their city elders to us. [The elders] came and beseeched our majesty and, in great fear, asked to become tributary to us and to be and remain in our service. When we heard their requests, we assented to them, taking taxes from them and giving them generals. Then we arose from there and went to the old fortress of Byblos, which we also seized in battle, taking its residents into captivity. With a great amount of booty and captives, we went through all the coastal cities via a difficult and narrow road, by which route other cavalry had never passed due to its narrowness and difficulty. We found there flourishing and lovely cities and fortified strongholds. In them were Tachik guards. We besieged all of them, destroyed them to their foundations, and led their inhabitants into captivity. Before we reached Tripoli, we sent both thematic and garrison cavalry to the pass called K'areres,[10] since we had learned that the loathsome Africans were occupying that pass. We ordered that an ambuscade be set there, creating a deadly trap for them. What we ordered was implemented. Two thousand of their [fighters] arose from their concealment and fell upon our troops. Many of [the enemy] were killed, while many others were taken captive and brought before our imperial majesty. Moreover, wherever others of them were encountered, they were put to flight. We completely destroyed the entire land of Tripoli, cutting down their vineyards, olive groves, and gardens, and generally wrecking and ruining all districts, and pulling them up by the roots. The Africans who were there dared to arise against us in battle. Then did we attack and generally destroy all of them.

10 *K'areres:* "Stone Face".

9. «Եւ ապա առաք զմեծ քաղաքն զՃուէլն, որ Գաբաւոնն կոչէին, եւ զՎաղանեացն եւ զՍիհունն, եւ զինքն իսկ զհոչակաւորն Զուրզաւ, եւ ոչ մնաց մինչեւ զՌամլէ եւ զԿեսարիա՝ ոչ ծով եւ ոչ ցամաք, որք ոչ հնազանդեցան թագաւորութեանս մերում, զօրութեամբն Անեղին Աստուծոյ, զի մինչեւ զԲաբելոն հնազանդ արարաք թագաւորութեանս մերում եւ արարաք ծառայս զնոսա մեզ: Վասն զի ամիսս եւթն շրջեցաւ թագաւորութիւնս մեր յայնմ աշխարհին հանդերձ զօրօք բազմօք. եւ սպառեցաք զքաղաքս եւ զգաւառս եւ ոչ իշխեաց ելանել Ամիր-ըլ-մումնի ի Բաբելոնէ ընդդէմ մեր եւ կամ հեծեալս արձակել յիւր զօրացն յօգնութիւն: Եւ եթէ չէր լեալ խստագոյն խորշակ եւ անջրդի ճանապարհ ի յայն տեղիսն, որ մերձ է ի Բաբելոն, որպէս եւ քո փառաւորութիւնդ իսկ գիտենալ ունի, թագաւորութիւնս մեր մինչեւ ի Բաբելոն երթեալ էր. որ եւ զինքն իսկ յերկիրն Եգիպտացւոց հալածեցաք եւ ի սպառ յաղթահարեալ շնորհօքն Աստուծոյ, որ թագաւորեցոյցն զիս:

«Ազատեցան այժմ ամենայն Փիւնիկէ եւ Պաղեստին եւ Ասորիք ի ծառայութենէ Տաճկաց եւ Հաւանեցան ընդ Հոռոմց իշխանութեամբ: Այլ եւ Լիբանանու մեծ լեառն հընազանդեցաւ ընդ մերով իշխանութեամբս. եւ զամենայն Տաճկունք, որ անդ կային, ահագին բազմութեամբ, գերութեամբ առաք եւ բաշխեցաք հեծելոց մերոց. եւ զԱսորեստան քաղցրապէս եւ մարդասիրապէս հովուեցաք. հոգիք իբրեւ քսան հազար հանաք, եւ ի Գաբաւօն բնակեցուցաք: Ահա գիտացես, զի այսպիսի յաղթութիւնս ետ Աստուած քրիստոնէից, որ ոչ եղեւ երբէք:

9. "Next we took the great city called Chue'l, which is called Jabala, and also Valania, and Saone, and even the renowned Burzuya. And thus there remained no place of either sea or land between Ramla and Caesarea which had not submitted to our majesty, by the power of the Increate God. Indeed, we made obedient to our empire [territory] as far as Babylon and made them our servants. For it was seven months that our imperial majesty circulated around with many troops in that land. We emptied cities and districts, while [the Commander of the Faithful], the Amir al-Muminin did not dare to issue forth from Baghdad against us nor to send his cavalry to aid his own troops. Moreover, had it not been for the great heat and the waterless route from there to the environs of Babylon—as your highness himself knows—our royal majesty then would have gone on to Babylon. Indeed, through the grace of God Who enthroned us, we would have chased him to the country of the Egyptians and completely conquered him.

"We now have freed from servitude to the Tachiks all of Phoenicia, Palestine, and Syria, and convinced them to enter under Byzantine rule. Furthermore, we subjected to our rule the great Mount Lebanon and all the Tachiks who were there. We took a great number of captives and divided them among our cavalry. Mildly and humanely, we shepherded Asorestan, removing therefrom some 20,000 souls and settling them in Jabala. Behold, and realize that God gave to the Christians such a victory as had never occurred before.

Եւ գտաք յայնմ քաղաքին ի Գաբաւոնն զսուրբ հողաթափն Քրիստոսի Աստուծոյ մերոյ, որով եւ շրջեցաւ իսկ ի վերայ աշխարհի. նոյնպէս եւ զպատկերն Փրկչին մերոյ, զորս Հրէայքն յետ ժամանակի խոցեալ էին, ուստի վաղվաղակի ել արիւն եւ ջուր, եւ զխոց տիգին. գտաք եւ յայնմ քաղաքին զպատուական հերս գլխոյ Կարապետին եւ Մկրտչին Յովհաննու եւ առեալ տանիմք ի պահպանութիւն աստուածապահ քաղաքին մերոյ: Եւ արդ ի սեպտեմբեր ամսոյն հաճութեամբն Աստուծոյ զմեր աստուածակեցոյց զօրքս ի յԱնտիոք հանաք եւ վասն այսորիկ քո փառաւորութեանդ գիտացուցաք, վասն զի ի ձեռն մեր հրամանացս զարմանաս եւ դու ինքն իսկ փառաւորես զԱստուծոյ մեծ մարդասիրութիւնն եւ գիտասցես թէ ո՛րչափ բարի գործեցան այժմիկ եւ կամ քանի՛ յաւելան եւ լայն եւ ընդարձակ եղեւ իշխանութիւն սրբոյ Խաչին Քրիստոսի եւ մինչեւ ցայս տեղիք անունն Աստուծոյ գովի եւ փառաւորի. եւ ճոխանայ թագաւորութիւնս մեր անուամբ մեծութեամբ եւ զօրութիւնն Աստուծոյ բարեբանեալ գովի ի բերանոյ մերմէ. զորս ընդ ձեռամբ մերով հնազանդեցոյց Աստուած, ընդ որում հանապազօր օրհնեալ տէր Աստուած Իսրայէլի:

«Եւ յանափոռտէն պռտօսպաթրին Դերջնայ, Լեւոնի եւ Տարօնոյ զօրավարին ողջոյն եւ ի տէր խնդալ:

10. «Արդ գրեցաք որ զԱյծեաց բերդն որպէս յանձին կալար՝ չես տուեալ. եւ այժմ գրեցաք առ զօրավարդ մեր, որ ոչ բերդն առնու եւ ոչ զցորեանն զոր պոմանեցեր, զի այժմ չեղեւ առ մեզ պէտք. բայց զքառասուն հազար սոփօլօնն, զոր յուղարկեցաք, տուր տանել առ զօրավարն մեր, որ առաքէ առ թագաւորութիւնս մեր. եւ զվաստակոցդ քոց եւ զարմտեացդ գտանես զփոխարէնն ըստ սերմանեացն զամենայն բարի մի ըստ միոջէ»:

Beyond this, we discovered in that city of Jabala the blessed sandals of Christ our God which He wore as he walked the earth, and an image of our Savior which subsequently the Jews had pierced and [from which hole] immediately flowed blood and water. The hole made [in the picture] from the lance also [was visible]. In the same city we also found venerable hairs from the head of John, [known as] the Precursor and the Baptist. We took them for safety to our God-preserved city. Then, with the assent of God, in the month of September, we returned our God-supported troops to Antioch. We inform your majesty about what was accomplished at our direction, so that you admire these achievements and also glorify God's great love for humanity, and how much goodness was accomplished here and how enlarged and extended the realm of the holy Cross of Christ has become, and how far the name of God is praised and glorified. Our kingdom has grown rich with renown, and praise for the glory of benevolent God is on our lips. It was God Who subdued those who were brought under our control. Blessed be the Lord, God of Israel, forever.

"From a report of Lewon, *protospatharius* of Derjan and military commander of Taron, we have received salutations and joy in the Lord.

10. "[Moreover, in that report] we have learned that you have not given up Aytseats' fortress, which you took for your own. Now we have written to our generals not to take that fortress nor to take the grain you provisioned there, since at present we have no need of it. But as regards the 40,000 *sovo'lo'ns* we sent [to you], have them taken to our general for him to send to our kingdom. For your crops and cereals you shall receive equal value, good for good."

Դարձեալ գրեաց եւ առ վարդապետն Հայոց ի Ղեւոնդն այսպէս.

«Մեր հաճելի եւ սուրբ թագաւորութեանս սիրեցեալ մեծ իմաստասէր Պանդալեւոն, ողջոյն: Ահա հրամայեցաք մեք որ ի դարձին մեր ի Տաճկաց՝ գտանեմք զձեզ ի սուրբ քաղաքս եւ կամ ի Սլեսինն, յորժամ եկիր առ մեզ ի յԱշոտոյ շահնշահէ եւ հոգիական զաւակէ մերմէ եւ դարձուցեր զամենայն սրտմտութիւնս ի նմանէ եւ տարար զԲագրատ ի Պապն Յանձաւացին. դու եւ ես Սատ Թոռնեցին պըռտօսպաթարն: Եւ արդ ջանացիր, որ գտանեմ զքեզ յաստուածապահ քաղաքին մեր եւ անդ արասցուք տօն մեծ հողաթափացն Քրիստոսի Աստուծոյ մերոյ եւ սուրբ հերացն Մկրտչին Յովհաննու: Եւ արդ ահա հաճեալ ունիմ եւ զայս ինչ ի քէն, վասն զի խօսեցիս ընդ մեր իմաստասէրսն եւ ընդ փիլիսոփայիցն մերոց, եւ ուրախասցուք մեք ի ձեզ. եւ Աստուած ի մեզ եւ ի ձեզ. եւ տէր Յիսուս եղիցի ընդ իւրում ծառայիցդ»:

Իսկ յորժամ լուաւ զայս վարդապետն Հայոց Ղեւոնդ, յարուցեալ գնաց ի Կոստանդնուպօլիս, եւ արարին տօնս հրաշափառս հողաթափացն Աստուծոյ եւ հերաց սրբոյ Կարապետին: Եւ եղեւ յայնմ աւուր մեծ ուրախութիւն ի Կոստանդնուպօլիս, եւ խօսեցաւ վարդապետն Հայոց առաջի թագաւորին ընդ ամենայն իմաստասիրացն Հոռոմոց եւ անպարտելի երեւեցաւ ի մէջ վարդապետացն տանն Յունաց. վասն զի յամենայն հարցմունսն հաճելի երեւեցաւ: Եւ բազում գովութեամբ բարեբանեցին զնա եւ զուսուցիչսն նորա, եւ մեծաւ պարգեւօք ի թագաւորէն երեւելիք եւ պատուականք շնորհեցաւ նմա. եւ գնաց մեծաւ ուրախութեամբ յաշխարհին Հայոց ի մեծ տունն Շիրակայ:

[Tzimisces] also wrote to the Armenian vardapet Ghewond, as follows:

"Greetings to you, Pandaleon, great philosopher, dear and beloved to our blessed and agreeable kingdom. We command that when we have returned from the Tachiks, we find you [present] in our blessed city, or at Slesin. [Be there] when you have come from [seeing] Shahnshah Ashot, our spiritual son, and have deflected all his anger [against us], and after you have taken Bagrat to Pap Andzewats'i, as well as Smbat T'or'nets'i, the protospatharius. Endeavor that I find you in our God-protected city and there we shall celebrate a great festival for the [discovery of the] sandals of Christ our God, and for the blessed hair of John the Baptist. Moreover, it would please us if you confer with our sages and philosophers, so that we may rejoice in you and so that God [may rejoice] in us and in you, and so that Lord Jesus [may rejoice] in his servants."

Now when the Armenian vardapet Ghewond heard this, he arose and went to Constantinople. They held a marvelous celebration in honor of the sandals of [Christ] God and the hair of the blessed Precursor. That was a day of great rejoicing in Constantinople. And the vardapet of the Armenians spoke in the emperor's presence with all the Byzantine philosophers, and revealed himself as invincible among the vardapets of the House of the Byzantines, since all his responses to their questions were agreeable. They lauded him and his teacher with much praise and the emperor bestowed on him great, noteworthy, and valuable gifts. Then [vardapet Ghewond] returned with great joy to the great House of Shirak in the land of the Armenians.

Արդ ի յետ բազում պատերազմացն եւ յաղթութեանցն, զոր վանեաց կայսրն Չմշկիկ, անկանէր ի վերայ նորա մահու երկիւղն եւ ահն սոսկալի դատաստանին Աստուծոյ եւ զմտաւ ածեալ յիշեալ զանիրաւ մահն արդարոյն Նիկիփոռայ եւ զանպարտ արիւն նորա, կոծ առեալ լայր եւ յոգւոց հանէր: Եւ յայնժամ խորհեցաւ վարս առաքինութեան ստանալ, զի թերեւս ապաշխարութեամբ մաքրել զարիւնն, զոր հեղաւ ի տարապարտուց. եւ հինգ ամ միայն կալեալ զաթոռ թագաւորութեանն Յունաց: Եւ մինչդեռ զայս ամենայն զմտաւ ածէր, խորհեցաւ բարի խորհուրդս, որ ըստ կամացն Աստուծոյ էր, եւ յուղարկեալ ի Վասակաւանն ի գաւառն Յանձթայ եւ բերել տայր զՎասիլ եւ զԿոստանդին զորդիսն Ռոմանոսի թագաւորին, զորս փախոյց առ Սպրամիկն ի յահէ անօրէն թագուհոյն, վասն զի չարաբարոյ էր յոյժ: Իսկ յորժամ եբեր զՎասիլն ի Կոստանդնուպօլիս, ժողով արարեալ զամենայն իշխանս մեծամեծս տանն Յունաց. եւ եղեւ ահաւոր հանդէս ի պաղատ թագաւորին: Եւ յայնժամ թագաւորն Չմշկիկ առեալ զթագն ձեռօք իւրովք ի գլխոյ իւրմէ եւ եդեալ ի գլուխն Վասլի եւ նստեցուցանէր զնա յաթոռ թագաւորութեանն իւրոյ եւ երկիրպագանէր ի վերայ երեսաց իւրոց Վասլին. եւ զամենայն թագաւորութիւն տանն Յունաց նմա յանձն արարեալ: Եւ տուեալ ի Վասիլն զիւր հայրենական աթոռ, եւ ինքն դիմեալ յանապատ, եւ յանձն իւր առեալ զկարգս կրօնաւորութեան՝ ի վանս ընթացեալ բնակէր: Ահա որ յերեկեան աւուրն թագաւոր եւ այսօր ընդ աղքատս նստեալ դաղարէր կամաւոր աղքատութեամբ, վասն զի ժառանգեսցէ զերանութիւն սուրբ Աւետարանին եւ վճարեսցէ զպարտ անմեղ անձինն Նիկիփոռայ:

Now after many battles and victories which Emperor Tzimisces had pursued, there fell upon him the fear of death and dire dread of God's judgment, and he recalled the unjust death of Emperor Nicephorus and his innocent blood. He lamented, sighing and weeping. He thought to lead a virtuous life so that perhaps, through repentance, he might wipe away the blood which had been wrongfully shed. He occupied the throne of the empire of the Byzantines for only five years. While he was pondering all these things, he came up with a good plan which was in accordance with God's will: he sent to Vasakawan in the district of Andzit' and had retrieved Basil and Kostandin, sons of Emperor Romanus. He had caused them to flee to [the woman] Spram, out of fear of the impious empress who was extremely malicious. As soon as Basil had been brought to Constantinople, an assembly was convened of all the grandee princes of the House of the Byzantines, and an imposing ceremony took place in the imperial palace. Then, with his own hands, Emperor Tzimisces removed the crown from his head, and placed it on the head of Basil, and seated him on the throne of his kingdom. Then [Tzimisces] prostrated himself before Basil and entrusted to him the entire kingdom of the House of the Byzantines. He gave to Basil his own patrimonial throne, while he himself went to a retreat. [Tzimisces] became a cleric and went and resided in a monastery. Behold the man who was king on the previous evening and who, today, sits among the poor in voluntary poverty. [This was done] so that he might inherit the joy of the blessed Gospel and pay off [his] debt for the innocent blood of Nicephorus [which he had shed].

11. Դարձեալ ի բարձրանալ թուականութեանս Հայոց ազգիս յամի ՆԻԴ թագաւորեաց Վասիլ հայրն ամենեցուն՝ որդին Ռոմանոսի ծերոյ, որդւոյ Կոստանդեայ կայսերն Հոռոմոց բարի ազգաւ ի մէջ Յունաց: Եւ կարի յոյժ երեւելի երեւեալ այրս այս Վասիլ եղբայրն Կոստանդէ: Սա տիրեաց թագաւորական աթոռոյն Յունաց եւ զբազում ապստամբսն արար հնազանդս եւ անուն բարի ստացաւ ի վերայ արարածոցս՝ ողորմած ի վերայ այրեաց եւ գերեաց եւ իրաւարար զրկելոց:

Յայսմ աւուրքս եղեւ կոտորած զօրացն Հայոց յԱնձաւացեաց գաւառին, ի բանակն կոչեցեալ անուն նենգութեամբ առն քաջին Ապլղարիպայ: Վասն զի թագաւորն Անձաւացեաց, որում անուն Դերենիկն ասէին, եհան զԱպլղարիպն ի սպարապետութենէ զօրաց իւրոց, զայր հզօր եւ զքաջ, եւեդեալ ի տեղի իւր զՍարգիս զոմն ազատ: Եւ կարի յոյժ վիրաւորեալ լինէր հզօրն Ապլղարիպ. եւ յայնժամ բանատու լինէր առ հզօրսն այլազգեաց, եւ զամենայն պատճառս ծանուցանէր նոցա եւ ասաց, թէ՝ «Ես ոչ ելից ի պատերազմ ընդ ձեզ. եւ արդ՝ ի գիշերի յարուցեալ եկայք ի վերայ բանակիս մեր. եւ ահա այս նշան ձեզ իմոյ վրանին, յորդան կարմիր է, եւ ի վերայ բլրին հարեալ կայ, եւ զօրք իմ ընդ իս»: Իսկ զօրք այլազգեացն եկին ի վերայ նոցա յանկասկած ժամու. եւ էր թագաւորն եւ զօրքն իւր ի մեծ ուրախութեան, եւ ի գիշերի անկան ի վերայ զօրացն Հայոց զօրք այլազգեացն եւ արարին կոտորած մեծ. եւ մեռան բազում պատերազմողք եւ երեւելի քաջք: Բայց ապաշաւելի այս իսկ էր, վասն զի չէր պատերազմ ի պատեհ ժամու. եւ արարին ձերբակալ զԴերենիկ զթագաւորն. եւ ընդ Ապլղարիպայ վրանովն ոչ իշխեաց անցանել ոք, վասն զի կայր ընդ վրանին զօրօք իւրովք պատրաստական: Եւ յայնժամ տարան զԴերենիկ ի Հեր քաղաքի:

11. At the beginning of the year 424 of the Armenian Era [A.D. 975/976], Basil[11] reigned as the father of all. He was the son of the old Romanus, son of Constantine, emperor of the Romans, of a good lineage among the Byzantines. This Basil, the brother of Kostand, was a very noteworthy man. He ruled over the royal throne of the Byzantines, subduing many rebels, and acquiring a goodly reputation among all creation, [being] merciful to widows and captives and just toward the dispossessed.

In this period there took place a destruction of Armenian troops in the district of Andzewats'ik'. [This occurred] from the army of the brave [commander] Aplgharip [who acquired] the name of a traitor. The king of Andzewats'ik', whose name was Derenik, had removed the mighty and valiant Aplgharip from the [position of] commander-in-chief of his forces. In his place [Derenik] put a certain nobleman named Sargis. The mighty Aplgharip was greatly wounded by this. He began acting as a spy for the powerful foreigners, informing them about everything, and saying: "I shall not come out in battle against you. Now arise and come against our army in the nighttime. Let my tent be a sign for you [to avoid]: it is red and pitched on a hill, and my troops will be with me." The troops of the foreigners thus came against [Derenik's troops] at an unexpected hour, while the king and his soldiers were making merry. The foreigners' troops fell upon the Armenian troops in the night and wrought a great slaughter. Many noteworthy and brave combatants died. It was regrettable that the battle had occurred at an unsuitable hour. King Derenik was arrested, while no one dared to come near Aplgharip's tent, since his troops were there and were prepared. Derenik was taken to the city of Her.

11 *Basil* II Bulgaroctonus, 960-963; 963-976; 976-1025.

Յայնմ աւուր Վարազ եւ ամենայն վանորայք անէծս ցաւագինս եւ սաստիկս կարդացին Ապլղարիպայ, միայնակեացք եւ միաբանակեացք դղրդեալ ի վերայ նորա լուծին զնա ի հաւատոց եւ հանին ի արտաքս ի յեկեղեցւոյն Աստուծոյ: Իսկ Ապլղարիպայ եկեալ ի միտս իւր՝ լայր, վասն զի էր այր հաւատարիմ եւ երկիւղած յԱստուծոյ, եւ կարի յոյժ ապաշաւէր զհեղումն արեան քաջ արանցն զօրացն Հայոց: Եւ յայնժամ հարցուկ լինէր վասն թագաւորին, եթէ յորում բերդի կայ արգելած ի Հեր քաղաքի. եւ ծանուցին նմա եթէ ամիրայն Ապլհաճա ի կապանացն արձակեաց զԴերենիկն, եւ յամենայն ժամ հանէ զնա ի խաղ գնդին ի մայտանն՝ արտաքոյ քաղաքին Հերայ: Եւ լուեալ զայս Ապլղարիպ ուրախ լինէր յոյժ եւ յուղարկեալ գաղտաբար առ թագաւորն Դերենիկն եւ ասէր ցնա այսպէս. «Ահա ես յայս ինչ ժամու յայնմ տեղւոջ լինիմ. ամենայն կարողութեամբ պատրաստ արա զքեզ, յընտիր եւ ի սուր ձիոջ հեծիր, եւ հանց ջանա որ ի յիս անկանիս»:

12. Եւ յաւուր միում Ապլհաճա ելեալ խաղայր ի գունդն բազում ազատօք իւրովք, եւ արք հազարք եւ զինուք շուրջ զնոքօք, եւ Ապլղարիպն կայր ի քմին յիսուն արամբք. եւ Դերենիկն ի բուն պարոնաց աւագէն խնդրեալ իւր սուր ձի եւ տուեալ ինչս իւր. եւ յայնժամ Դերենիկն եհար զգունդն եւ վարէր ի դիհն, ուր Ապլղարիպ թագուցեալ կայր ի մէջ անտառախիտ դրախտացն Հերայ, եւ քահեալ զերիվարն ուժգին՝ ի բաց թողեալ զգունդն եւ ելս արարեալ:

On that day [the monastery of] Varag and all the monks invoked painful and severe curses on Aplgharip. Monks and cenobites were so roused against him that they excommunicated him from the faith and expelled him from the Church of God. As for Aplgharip—when he came to his senses—he wept, since he was a man of faith and fearful of God. He greatly regretted the shedding of the blood of the braves from the Armenian forces. And then he made inquiries about the king, [asking] in what fortress he was being kept at Her. Furthermore, they told him that Emir Aplhach had released Derenik from fetters and was always taking him outside the city of Her to a *maytan* for playing ball. When Aplgharip heard this, he was overjoyed and secretly sent to King Derenik, saying: "Behold, I will be at that spot at such and such a time. Ready yourself and be completely prepared. Mount a choice and swift steed and try to encounter me."

12. Now as it happened, on a certain day Aplhach went out to play ball, accompanied by many of his azats. There were a thousand armed men around him. Meanwhile, Aplgharip was hiding in an ambuscade with fifty men. Derenik asked one of the senior barons to give him his swift horse, and [the man] gave it to him, all equipped. Then Derenik struck the ball and raced in pursuit of it to the very place where Aplgharip was concealed in the densely forested gardens of Her. Then Derenik forcefully spurred his horse, leaving the group behind, and escaping.

Եւ տեսեալ ամիրային Ապլհաճէի եւ զօրացն, զհետ յարձակեցան մեծաւ ցասմամբ. եւ թագաւորն յԱստուած յուսացեալ գնայր քաջապէս եւ անկանէր առ Ապլղարիպն: Իսկ ի զօրացն այլազգեաց ոմն խափշիկ, այր հզօր եւ քաջ, ընթացեալ զհետ եւ հասանէր ի վերայ Ապլղարիպայ. եւ որպէս զառիւծ գոչեաց Ապլղարիպն, հասեալ ի վերայ նորա, եւ գազանաբար հարկանէր զնա, եւ յերկուս բաժանեաց եւ պատառեաց զնա ի վերուստ մինչեւ ցերանսն: Եւ տեսեալ զայն այլազգեացն՝ ի փախուստ դարձան. եւ Ապլղարիպ ձայն տուեալ քաջ արանց իւրոց, զհետ յարձակեալ եւ հասանէր ամիրային Ապլհաճէի. եւ կամեցաւ զնա ի ձիոյ առնուլ եւ մինչեւ ի դուռն քաղաքին վարեաց զնա. եւ ամիրայն որպէս զփայլակն մտանէր ընդ դուռն քաղաքին Հերայ: Յայնժամ Ապլղարիպն պողովատ ճկռովն հարկանէր զերկաթի դուռն քաղաքին եւ պատառեալ զերկաթն եւ յայն դեհն անցուցանէր, որ եւ անել մնաց ճկռուն մինչեւ ցայսօր ժամանակի. եւ ի տեղն պնդեցին որպէս զբեւեռն: Եւ այսպիսի օրինակաւ ի ծառայութենէ եհան զթագաւորն զԴերենիկ քաջն Ապլղարիպն: Այս ինչ եղեւ ի Ճուաշ գաւառին Հայոց աշխարհին, ի գեւղն՝ որ կոչի Բակ, սահմանակից Վասպուրականայ: Իսկ ի շարժել յաւելմամբ թուականս Հայկազունեաց ազգիս ի յամս ՆԻԵ եղեւ կոչումն յԱստուծոյ սրբոյ հայրապետին Հայոց Անանիայի. եւ ձեռնադրեցին հանդերձ բազմութեամբ յաթոռ կաթուղիկոսութեան Հայոց զլաւն ի բնաւիցս զերանելին զՎահան. որ էր գլուխ ժողովոյն կաթուղիկոսն Աղուանից տէր Յովհաննէս: Արդ՝ ի յայսմ ամի նստաւ յաթոռ հայրապետութեան տանն Հայոց տէր Վահան ի մեծն Արգինա հրամանաւ Անանիայի, Յովհաննիսի եւ Աշոտոյ Հայոց թագաւորացն:

When Emir Aplhach and his troops saw this, they pursued in great wrath. The king, trusting in God, bravely advanced to Aplgharip. Now among the forces of the foreigners was a certain *xap'shik* [black], a strong and brave man who charged forward, coming against Aplgharip. Aplgharip roared like a lion, rode against him, and struck him savagely, splitting the man in half, from his head to his waist. When the foreigners saw this they turned in flight. Aplgharip shouted to his brave men and pursued them, reaching Emir Aplhach, whom he wanted to unhorse. [Aplgharip] continued, chasing after him as far as the city gates. But the emir, like a streak of lightning, passed through the gates of Her city. Then Aplgharip struck the iron gates of the city with his steel ax, piercing through the iron to the other side. This ax has remained there to this day, firmly held in, like a bolt. In this fashion did brave Aplgharip remove King Derenik from captivity. This occurred in the Chuash district of the land of the Armenians, bordering on Vaspurakan, at the village called Bak. At the beginning of the year 425 of the Armenian Era [A.D. 976], the call came from God to the blessed patriarch of the Armenians, Anania [I Mokats'i, 946-968]. With a great throng, [clerics] ordained to the throne of the Catholicosate of the Armenians the venerable and goodly Vahan.[12] At the head of the assembly was Lord Yovhanne's, Catholicos of the Aghuans. And so it came about that in this year, by order of Anania, and the Armenian kings Yovhanne's and Ashot, Lord Vahan was seated on the throne of the patriarchate of the House of the Armenians, in [the city of] great Argina.

12 *Vahan* I Siwnets'i, 968-969.

Յայսմ ժամանակի ապստամբեցաւ ոմն իշխան անօրէն ի վերայ Վասլի Հոռոմց թագաւորին, որում ասէին Սկելառոս, զօրաժողով արարեալ բազմութեամբ անիրաւաց եւ անօրինաց եւ սրով անցուցանէր զաշխարհն Հոռոմց. եւ բազում զօրօք գայր հասանէր եւ մտանէր յաշխարհն Հայոց, եւ արար անթիւ կոտորած օտարացեալն յԱստուծոյ: Եւ յայնժամ զօրքն Հայոց հասանէին ի վերայ նորա եւ յաղթահարեցին անօրէն իշխանին այն մեծաւ յաղթութեամբ, եւ կոտորածով փախստական արարին զնա: Իսկ նա ոչ համարձակեցաւ դառնալ յերկիրն Հոռոմց, արար զյոյս իւր ի յազգն Տաճկաց, եւ գնաց անօրէնն եմուտ ի Բաղդատ քաղաք. եւ զկնի երեք ամի ելեալ անտի եւ գայր մեռանէր յերկիրն Հոռոմց յազգն իւր:

13. Դարձեալ ի թուականութեանս Հայոց ՆԼԲ մեռանէր սուրբ հայրապետն Հայոց Վահան, կացեալ զամս հինգ ի յաթոռ սրբոյն Գրիգորի. եւ ձեռնադրեցին յաթոռ կաթուղիկոսութեան Հայոց զտէր Ստեփանոս՝ զայր աստուածազգեաց, զարդարեալ ամենայն բարի առաքինութեամբ որ ի Քրիստոս Յիսուս. նստուցանեն զնա հայրապետ Հայոց հրամանաւ եւ օրհնութեամբ տեառն Վահանայ. որ էր իսկ գլուխ ժողովոյն Աղուանից տէր Յովհաննէս, ընդ ժամանակս Վասլին Յունաց թագաւորին, եւ Յովհաննիսի եւ Աշոտոյ Հայոց արքայից, եւ Սենեքերիմայ որդւոյ Ապուսահլի. որդւոյ Աշոտոյ որդւոյ Դերենկանն, որդւոյ Գագկայ Արծրունեաց յազգէն Սարասարայ:

In this period a certain impious prince who was called Scelerus rebelled against the Byzantine emperor Basil. Scelerus mustered troops in a multitude of unjust and impious men and put the land of the Byzantines to the sword. With many troops [Scelerus, this man] alienated from God, came and entered the land of the Armenians. Then the troops of the Armenians went against him and defeated that impious prince with great triumph, and made him flee because of his casualties. [Scelerus], not daring to return to the country of the Byzantines, placed his hopes on the *Tachik* nation. That impious man went and entered the city of Baghdad. After three years he emerged and came to his own folk on Byzantine territory, where he died.

13. In 432 of the Armenian Era [A.D. 983] Vahan, the blessed patriarch of the Armenians, died having occupied the throne of Saint Gregory for five years. They ordained to the throne of the Catholicosate of the Armenians Lord Step'annos,[13] a man clothed in divinity, adorned with all goodly virtues in Jesus Christ. They seated him as patriarch of the Armenians by order of, and with the blessings of, Lord Vahan. The head of the assembly was Lord Yovhanne's of the Aghuans. This took place during the time of Basil, emperor of the Byzantines, and of Yovhanne's and Ashot, kings of the Armenians, and of Senek'erim, son of Apusahl, son of Ashot, son of Derenik, son of Gagik Artsrunik', of the line of Sanasar.

---

13 *Step'annos* III Sewants'i, 969-972.

Արդ ի սոցա աւուրս զօրաժողով արարեալ անօրէն եւ պիղծ բռնակալն Պարսից Մամլան, ամիրապետն անօրինաց եւ ժանդաբարոյ գազանութեամբն իւրով իբրեւ զարինարբու վիշապ յարձակեալ գայր ի վերայ հաւատացելոցն Քրիստոսի եւ խորհեցաւ կոտորած մեծ ածել ի վերայ աշխարհին Հայոց: Եւ գայր խաղայր ահագին եւ անհամար բազմութեամբ եւ ելից զլերինս եւ զդաշտս զօրօք իւրովք. եւ յահէ անօրինին սասանեալ դողայր ամենայն երկիր, եւ սրով եւ հրով գերեաց զբազում տեղիս. եւ զեկեղեցիս հրկէզ արարեալ խափանեաց յօրհնութեանցն եւ բազում բանս հայհոյութեանց ի վեր ի բարձունս խօսեցաւ առ Բարձրեալն: Եւ անդ էր տեսանել զմեծ եւ զահեղ կատարածն քրիստոնէից ի յահէ չար գազանին այն, զի զբարկութիւն չար թիւնիցն իւր որպէս զմաղձ դառնաշունչ եհեղ ի վերայ հաւատացելոցն. եւ գայր հասանէր այսքան բազմութեամբն յԱպահունեաց գաւառին, յերկիրն Դաւթի կուրապաղատին՝ Վրաց իշխանին: Եւ գրեաց թուղթ առ աստուածասէր եւ սուրբ այրն Աստուծոյ Դաւիթ կուրապաղատն եթէ չարաչար բանիւք սպառնացեալ նմա եւ խօսէր զայս ինչ.

«Մի՛ խաբեսցէ ոք զքեզ, ո՛վ այր դու Դաւիթ, ամենազարշ եւ ժանդ եւ նենգեալ ալեօրդ, զի ահա՝ թէ ոչ վաղվաղակի առաքեսցես ինձ զհարկս տասն տարւոյ եւ ի պատանդ զորդիս ազատաց քոց եւ գիր ծառայութեան ինձ՝ այժմ հասեալ գամ ի վերայ քո մեծաւ զօրութեամբս իմով եւ ո՞վ իցէ այն, որ փրկեսցէ զքեզ ի ձեռաց իմոց, զի ահա չարաչար եւ դառն նեղութիւն ածից ի վերայ քո, պիղծ եւ դառն ալեւոր»:

In these days Mamlan, the impious and loathsome tyrant of the Persians, mustered troops. [Mamlan] was the chief emir of the impious ones, a venomous beast who resembled a bloodthirsty dragon. He came forth attacking the believers in Christ, and planned a great destruction against the land of the Armenians. He came with an enormous, countless multitude, filling up the mountains and the plains with his troops, while the entire country trembled with fear from this impious man. With sword and with fire he enslaved many places. He set fire to churches, obstructing their blessings and hurling many insults to the heavens, to Him On High. One could see there the great and frightful destruction of Christians wrought by that wicked beast, for the wrath of his wicked poison was spewed forth over the faithful like venomous bile. With such an enormous mob he advanced to the district of Apahunik', to the country of Dawit' the *curopalate*, prince of the Georgians. And he wrote a letter with this content to that God-loving and blessed man of God, Dawit' the curopalate, threatening him with very wicked words:

"Don't let anyone fool you, O Dawit', you who are filthy, stinking, and rotting in your old age. For behold, if you don't quickly send me ten years' worth of taxes, as well as the sons of your *azat*s as hostages, and a document [indicating] your submission to me, I shall come against you with my great forces. And then who will save you from my clutches? For I shall subject you to very wicked and bitter suffering, O you loathsome and bitter old man."

Եւ այսպիսի բազում սպառնալեօք որոտայր ի վերայ նորա: Իսկ յորժամ ընթերցաւ Դաւիթ զթուղթն անօրէն իշխանին Մամլանայ, ի դառնութենէ թղթոյն՝ զթուղթն արտաքս ձգեաց եւ ինքն լալով առ Աստուած աղաչանս արձակէր եւ ասէր. «Զարթո՛ զզօրութիւնս քո Տէր եւ յիշեա Տէր իմ, զոր արարեր ընդ Ռափսակ եւ ընդ Սենեքարիմ անօրէն թագաւորն Ասորեստանեայց. եւ զայս բանքս անօրէնութեան եւ նա խօսեցաւ, Տէր իմ Յիսուս Քրիստոս, մի՛ անտես առնէր զհաւատացեալքս սուրբ անուն քո»:

Յայնժամ հրամայեաց ժողով լինել զօրաց իւրոց զաստս եւ զամենայն հեծելազօրս իւր, զՎաչէ եւ զՏեւղատ եւ զՓերոն եւ զայլ զօրսն Հայոց աշխարհին. հետեւակս աղեղնաւորս երեք հազար, եւ ձիաւորս երկու հազար եւ հինգ հարիւր: Եւ անօրէնն Մամլանն կայր բանակեալ յԱպահունիս ի գեւղն, որ Խօսօնս կոչէին, երկու հարիւր հազարով: Եւ Դաւիթ յարուցեալ գնայր ընդդէմ չար գազանին Մամլանայ եւ զամենայն աշխարհն յաղօթս եւ ի պաղատանս եւ յաղաչանս մեծաւ պաղատանօք ի խնդրուածս Աստուծոյ կացուցանէր: Եւ գնաց իջաւ Դաւիթ ի սահմանս Ապահունեաց եւ զԿարմրակէլն զայր քաջ՝ եօթն հարիւր ձիաւորով պահապան գիշերոյն կացուցանէր. եւ ինքն Դաւիթ զամենայն գիշերն յաղօթսն Աստուծոյ անցուցանէր: Եւ յառաւօտու պահուն գայր ոմն ի զօրաց այլազգեացն հազար ձիաւորով, որ էր եւ նա պահապան զօրաց նորա:

With many such threats did [Mamlan] thunder against [Dawit']. Now when Dawit' read this letter from the impious Prince Mamlan, he threw it out because of its very bitterness and then he began to weep, beseeching God and saying: "Arouse your strength, Lord, and recall what you did to Rabshakeh and to Sennacherib, the impious king of the Assyrians, who also spoke similar words of impiety. My Lord Jesus Christ, do not ignore those who believe in Your blessed name."

Then [Dawit'] ordered a muster of his troops, the azats and all his cavalry, Vach'e' and Tewdat and P'eron and other troops from the land of the Armenians. [Included were] 3,000 infantry bowmen and 2,500 horsemen. Meanwhile, the impious Mamlan had encamped in Apahunik' at the village called Xo'so'ns with 200,000 men. Dawit' arose and went against that wicked beast Mamlan, while he also exhorted the entire land to greatly beseech God with prayers, entreaties, and supplications. Dawit' advanced, descending to the borders of Apahunik'. He designated that valiant man, Karmrake'l [Gamrakel], as a night watchman with 700 horsemen. Dawit' himself passed the entire night praying to God. In the morning there approached a certain man from the infidels' forces with a thousand horsemen. This man was a guard of [Mamlan's] forces.

14. Եւ ի գիշերին յայնմիկ ընդ միմեանս հարան. եւ էր լոյս լուսնին սաստիկ, եւ յայնժամ երեւեցաւ սակաւ ինչ անձրեւ ի վերայ լերանց, եւ ամենայն լերինքն փայլատակէին իբրեւ զբոց հրոյ. եւ տեսին զայն զօրքն այլազգեաց, կարծեցին թէ այն ամենայն բազմութիւն զօրաց քրիստոնէիցն իցեն եւ յայնժամ առ հասարակ ի փախուստ դարձան: Եւ Կարմրակէյն տեսեալ զի դարձան ի փախուստ՝ սըրով ի վերայ յարձակեցաւ եւ իբրեւ զանտառ մայրի կոտորէր զնոսա յանխնայ. կալաւ զկինն Մամլանայ եւ զիւր պատերազմի ձին եւ վաղվաղակի յուղարկեաց առ Դաւիթ, եւ ձայն աւետեաց մատուցանէին նմա՝ եթէ հարաք զՄամլան: Եւ նա դեռ յաղօթս կայր առ Աստուած. եւ լուեալ զայս Դաւիթ՝ հիանայր: Եւ յայնժամ զհետ մտեալ ամենայն զօրօքն՝ արարին զզօրսն անօրինացն փախստական սաստիկ կոտորածով, առին անթիւ եւ անհամար գերութիւն եւ աւար ոսկւոյ եւ արծաթոյ: Եւ անօրէնն Մամլան գընաց ամօթով յաշխարհին իւր եւ ամբարտաւանեալ յոյժ ընդ Աստուած՝ եւ յերկինս ոչ հայեցաւ բնաւ եւ զիւր անարժան աղօթսն ոչ մատուցանէր Աստուծոյ:

Իսկ յետ ամաց ինչ խորհեցան չար խորհուրդս վասն սուրբ եւ արդար իշխանին Դաւթայ սպանանել զնա. եւ չար իշխանաց իւրոց նմանեալ լինէին Կայենի եւ այլոց սպանողացն: Եւ յարուցին ի չար խորհուրդս իւրեանց զարհի եպիսկոպոսն Վրաց աշխարհին զԻլարիոն. եւ այս Իլարիոնս զԱստուած կրկնակի ի խաչ եհան, վասն զի ի կենդանարար մարմին եւ յարիւնն Քրիստոսի դեղ մահու խառնեաց եւ արար զապրեցուցիչն՝ մահացուցիչ. եւ զկնի սպանող պատարագին իւրոյ դնէր ի բերան սուրբ իշխանին զմասն խորհրդոյն խառնեցեալ մահաբեր դեղօք յանդիման Աստուծոյ ի մէջ եկեղեցւոյն:

14. That night [the two armies] clashed with each other. Now the moonlight was intense and some rain had fallen on the mountains, making them glisten like the flames of a fire. When the troops of the foreigners saw this; they thought that there was a huge multitude of Christian troops present, and they turned to flee, one and all. When Karmrake'l saw that they had turned to flight, he attacked them—wielding his sword as though it were a pine tree cut from a forest—and mercilessly killed them. He captured Mamlan's wife and his war horse, sending [them] quickly to Dawit' along with the glad tidings that "we have defeated Mamlan." [Dawit'] was still praying to God. When he heard [the news], he marveled. Meanwhile, all the troops pursued and made a great slaughter of the fleeing impious troops. They also took an innumerable number of captives as well as an inestimable amount of gold and silver booty. The impious Mamlan went to his land in disgrace. [This man], who had been so arrogant toward God, never looked to Heaven, and never offered his worthless prayers to God.

Now it happened that after some years, [some conspirators] hatched a wicked plan to slay the blessed and righteous Prince Dawit'. [These were] his princes, who resembled Cain and other murderers. Joining their plot was the archbishop of the land of the Georgians [Iberians], Ilarion. This Ilarion crucified God a second time, for he mixed a deadly poison into the life-giving body and blood of Christ [into the communion chalice], thus turning the bringer of life into a bringer of death. Following his murderous liturgy, [Ilarion] placed a piece of the sacrament mixed with deadly poison into the mouth of the blessed prince, right there in the church, in the presence of God.

Եւ գիտացեալ աստուածասէր իշխանին Դաւթի, ոչ ինչ խօսեցաւ բնաւ, այլ առեալ դեղ բժշկութեան շիջուցանել զցաւսն ի մարմնոյ իւրոյ: Իսկ անօրէն եպիսկոպոսն Իլարիոն դարձեալ բորբոքեցաւ ի չար խորհուրդսն իւր եւ մտեալ ի սենեակն՝ մինչ ննջէր բարեպաշտն Դաւիթ եւ խաղաղիկ ի քուն կայր, եւ առեալ նորա զբարձն ի սնարիցն դնէր ի վերայ բերանոյն Դաւթին եւ անկեալ սաստկապէս ուժգին ի վերայ նորա եւ չարչարանօք խեղդէր զաստուածասէր կուրապաղատն զԴաւիթ. զորս յետ սակաւ ամաց թագաւորն Վասիլ ըմբռնեալ զանօրէն եպիսկոպոսն Իլարիոն, քար մեծ կապեաց ի պարանոցն նորա, ընկէց զնա յովկիանոս եւ զայլ միաբանեալսն յազատացն, եւ անդ սատակեցան անիծից վաստակաւորքն, վասն զի հայր անուն էր Դաւիթ կուրապաղատն թագաւորին Վասլին, եւ վասն այնորիկ կորոյս զնոսա:

15. Եւ ի լինել թուականութեանս Հայոց ՆԼԴ մեռանէր Հայոց հայրապետն տէր Ստափանոս, եւ ձեռնադրեաց յաթոռն իւր զերանելին զտէր Խաչիկ, վասն զի էր այր փառաւոր եւ տեղեակ աստուածային կտակարանացն: Առ սա եկեալ թուղթ ի Հոռոմոց պատրիարգէն ի Թէոդորոսէն, որ նստէր ի մայրաքաղաքն Մելտենի, վասն զի էր այր կորովի եւ հմուտ գրոց պատուիրանաց. եւ վարդապետն Հայոց Սամուէլ գրեաց ընդդէմ նորա զպատասխանիսն վայելուչ եւ ցանկալի բանիւք, որ եղեւ իսկ հաճելի թուղթն այն ամենայն լսողացն, եւս առաւել մեծարեալ եղեւ առաջի Թէոդորոսի պատրիարգին Հոռոմոց եւ առաջի Խաչիկ կաթուղիկոսին Հայոց:

Now the God-loving Prince Dawit' was aware of this, but uttered not a word. Rather, he took medicine to reduce the pain in his body. However, the impious bishop Ilarion, further inflamed by his evil plan, entered the chamber where the pious Dawit' was sleeping peacefully. Then [Ilarion] took the pillow by his head, put it over Dawit's mouth, forcefully hurled himself on [Dawit'] and wickedly smothered the pious curopalate Dawit'. After a few years, Emperor Basil seized that wicked bishop Ilarion, tied a large rock to his neck and threw him into the ocean, along with the other azats who were involved. So perished these accursed men, for Dawit' the curopalate had been called "father" by Emperor Basil, and thus he killed them.

15. In 434 of the Armenian Era [A.D. 985] the patriarch of the Armenians, Lord Step'annos.[14] They ordained to his position the venerable Lord Xach'ik,[15] a glorious man well versed in Divine Scripture. A letter came to him from the Byzantine patriarch, T'e'odoros, who resided at the metropolis of Melitene, since [Xach'ik] was a man competent and knowledgeable in sacred writings. The Armenian vardapet Samue'l wrote a refutation of it, [skillfully] replying in appealing and appropriate words, to the point that the letter was pleasing to everyone hearing it. [Samue'l] was even more honored by T'e'odoros, patriarch of the Byzantines, and by Xach'ik, Catholicos of the Armenians.

14 *Step'annos* III Sewants'i, 969-972.
15 *Xach'ik* I Arsharunets'i, 973-992.

Իսկ յաւուրս ժամանակաց տօմարիս Հայոց ի յամի ՆԼԵ ապստամբեաց ոմն իշխան ի վերայ թագաւորին Վասլի, իշխանն Հոռոմոց Մօրավարդ, եւ արար աւերակս զմեծ մասն Հոռոմոց աշխարհին. եւ շրջեալ երթայր ընդ երկիր սրով եւ գերութեամբ: Եւ ժողովեալ զօրքն Հոռոմոց ի վերայ նորա, հալածական արարին զնա յաշխարհն Տաճկաց, զոր յետ ամի միոյ եկեալ մեռանէր ի թագաւորէն Վասլէ:

Դարձեալ ի թուականութեանս Հայոց ՆԼԷ ամի եղեւ սաստիկ շարժ ընդ ամենայն արարածս, եւ փլաւ սուրբն Սոփի ի Կոստանդնուպօլիս: Եւ յայսմ ամի կամեցաւ թագաւորն Վասիլ զաշխարհն Բուլղարաց ածել ի հնազանդութիւն իւրոյ թագաւորութեանն. եւ առաքեաց առ Ալի Օսմանն թագաւորն Բուլղարաց եւ առ ամենայն իշխանսն աշխարհաց գալ յերկրպագութիւն իւրոյ թագաւորութեանն. իսկ նոքա ոչ եկին զհետ հրամանաց թագաւորին Վասլի: Յայնժամ թագաւորն Վասիլ ժողով արար զամենայն աշխարհն իւրոյ թագաւորութեանն եւ մեծաւ սրտմտութեամբ յարձակեցաւ ի վերայ աշխարհին Բուլղարաց եւ սրով եւ գերութեամբ ապականէր զերկիր: Իսկ թագաւորն Բուլղարաց Ալի Օսմանն ժողով արարեալ եւ գայր բազում զօրօք ի վերայ Վասլին, եւ արարին սաստիկ պատերազմ ընդ միմեանս: Եւ թագաւորն Բուլղարաց յաղթեաց Վասլին եւ դարձոյց զամենայն զօրսն ի փախուստ մինչեւ ցԿոստանդնուպօլիս. եւ առին բազում աւար եւ գերութիւն ի զօրաց Վասլին. եւ Վասիլն լի ամօթով մտանէր ի Կոստանդնուպօլիս: Եւ յետ երկու ամի դարձեալ ժողով արարեալ թագաւորն Վասիլ եւ գնաց ի վերայ թագաւորին Բուլղարաց առ ի խնդրել զվրէժս իւր. եւ հանդիպեալ զօրացն Բուլղարաց, դարձոյց ի փախուստ զնոսա եւ վարէր առաջի իւր: Եւ նեղեաց Վասիլն զաշխարհն Բուլղարաց սովով, սրով եւ գերութեամբ եւ դարձաւ եմուտ ի Կոստանդնուպօլիս մեծաւ ուրախութեամբ:

Now in the year 435 of the Armenian Era [A.D. 986], a certain prince rebelled against Emperor Basil. [The rebel was] the Byzantine prince M'oravard[16] and he ruined a large part of the Byzantine land, circulating through the country with the sword and taking captives. Byzantine troops assembled against him, chasing him to the land of the Tachiks. He returned a year later and was killed by Emperor Basil.

In the year 437 of the Armenian Era [A.D. 988] a severe earthquake occurred throughout all creation and the blessed [church of Hagia] Sophia collapsed in Constantinople. In this same year Emperor Basil sought to make the land of the Bulghars subject to his realm. [Basil] sent to Ali O'sman, king of the Bulghars, and to all the princes of the land to come and prostrate themselves before his imperial majesty. However, they did not come as Emperor Basil had ordered. Then Emperor Basil mustered troops from all the lands in his realm and, in great anger, attacked the land of the Bulghars, polluting the country with the sword and with captive-taking. Now the king of the Bulghars, Ali O'sman, mustered his forces and came against Basil with many troops.Fierce fighting took place between them. The king of the Bulghars defeated Basil and put all his troops to flight as far as Constantinople. [The Bulghars] took a great amount of booty and captives from Basil's troops, while Basil, full of shame, entered Constantinople. Two years later Emperor Basil again assembled troops and went against the king of the Bulghars, seeking vengeance. Encountering the Bulghar forces, [Basil]put them to flight before him. He harassed the land of the Bulghars with the sword, famine, and captive-taking. Then he turned back and entered Constantinople in great joy.

---

16 *M'oravard:* "Black Rose," Bardas Phocas.

Կաթողիկոսն Տէր Խաչիկ, որ կացեալ յաթոռ հայրապետութեան Հայոց ամս վեց եւ ձեռնադրեաց յաթոռ իւր զտէր Սարգիս, որ էր այր կորովի գիտութեամբ պատուիրանացն Աստուծոյ. եւ էր սա հաճոյ Աստուծոյ եւ մարդկան, եւ էր կիրթ վարուց առաքինութեանց, եւ լուսաւոր վարդապետութեամբն իւրով զարդարեաց զեկեղեցին Աստուծոյ: Յայսմ ամի զօրքն Եգիպտոսի, որ Մախր Արապիկք կոչին, մըտին յաշխարհն Անտիոքայ քաղաքին եւ բազում աւերմամբ լցին զամենայն գաւառն. եւ ժողովեցան զօրք Հոռոմց ընդդէմ նոցա ի պատերազմ. եւ ի հանդիպիլ միմեանց արարին փախստական զզօրսն Հոռոմց եւ զմեծամեծ իշխանս գերի առին եւ տարան յԵգիպտոս: Իսկ յետ երկու ամի ելանէր մեծ տունն Հոռոմց եւ գայր բազում զօրօք ի վերայ աշխարհին Հայոց. եւ սրով եւ գերութեամբ անողորմ յարձակեցան ի վերայ հաւատացելոց Քրիստոսի. եւ գազանաբար սպանմամբ ընթանայր իբրեւ զօձ թունաւոր, որ եւ ելից իսկ զտեղի անհաւատ ազգացն: Եւ եղեւ ի մտանելն նորա յաշխարհի Հայոց, ժողովեցան ընդ յառաջ նորա զօրքն Հայոց ազատացն, եւ ի դիպելն ընդ միմեանս բախեցին գազանաբար, եւ քաջ ընդ քաջս ելանէին եւ անպարտելի հանդիսանային յերկու կողմանց: Եւ անդ էր տեսանել զաստիկ կոտորած յերկուց կողմանցն. եւ յայնժամ ի սաստկանալն մեծի պատերազմի, եղեն պարտեալ զօրքն Հոռոմց առաջի զօրացն Հայոց եւ դարձան ի փախուստ դիմօք յաշխարհն իւրեանց ամօթ երեսօք մազապուրծ փախմամբ:

Յայսմ ամի ելեալ գայր ամիրայն Տաճկաց, որոյ անունն երկայնաձեռն կոչէին, եւ բազում զօրօք ի յաւեր եւ ի գերութիւն մատնեաց զԵդեսացւոց աշխարհին, եւ վիշտս մեծամեծս ի վերայ Ուռհայոյ եւ անցանէր ընդ մեծ գետն Եփրատ, եւ գերեաց զայն կոյս զսահմանսն Հայոց աշխարհին եւ դարձաւ մեծաւ յաղթութեամբ յաշխարհն Ափրիկեցւոցն:

At the start of 440 of the Armenian Era [A.D. 991/992] there died the Catholicos of the Armenians, Lord Xach'ik, who had occupied the patriarchate of the Armenians for six years. He ordained Lord Sargis[17] to his position. [Sargis was] a man skilled in the knowledge of divine precepts, pleasing to God and to man, schooled in virtuous conduct, who adorned the Church of God with his radiant doctrine. In this year the forces of Egypt, called Maghrib Arabs [Fatimids], entered the territory of the city of Antioch and filled the entire district with extensive destruction. The forces of the Byzantines massed against them in battle. When they encountered one another, the Byzantine troops were put to flight and their grandee princes were captured and taken to Egypt. Two years later, the great House of the Byzantines arose and came with many troops against the land of the Armenians. With sword and captive-taking they mercilessly attacked the believers in Christ. With bestial killings they advanced, like a poisonous snake, appearing no different from unbelieving peoples. When they entered the land of the Armenians, troops of the Armenian azats massed against them. They clashed savagely, with brave after brave from both sides fighting undefeated. One could see there great destruction on both sides. When the great battle grew even fiercer, the forces of the Byzantines were defeated before the forces of the Armenians. They turned to flight shamefacedly, back to their own land, escaping by a hairsbreadth.

In the same year the emir of the Tachiks, who was styled "Long Hand" arose and came with many troops subjecting the land of the Edessans to destruction and captive-taking and occasioning the greatest sorrow for Edessa. [Long Hand] crossed the great Euphrates River and enslaved that side of the borders of the land of the Armenians before turning back in great triumph to the land of the Africans.

17 *Sargis* I Sewants'i, 992-1019.

Եւ եղեւ ի փոխել թուականութեանս Հայոց ամի ՆԽԶ ելանէր յերկինս աստղ մի գիսաւոր եւ երեւեալ սոսկալի եւ ահաւոր տեսլեամբ լուսատեսիլ եւ զարմանալի:

Իսկ յամի ՆԽԹ թուականութեանս Հայոց եղեւ սէր եւ միաբանութիւն մեծ ընդ թագաւորն Վասիլ եւ ընդ Սենեքարիմ արքայն Հայոց: Եւ յայսմ ամի եղեւ վախճան Սահակայ մարզպանին Վարաժնունեաց Տեառն:

16. Յորժամ լինէր թուականն Հայոց ՆԾԵ. զօրաժողով արար թագաւորն Վասիլ զամենայն աշխարհս տէրութեան իւրոյ եւ խաղայր գնայր ի վերայ աշխարհին Բուլղարաց. եւ բազում ժամանակս արարեալ յաշխարհին այն մեծաւ պատերազմաւ: Եւ յայնմ աւուրսն մեծ խռովութիւն եղեւ ի քաղաքն ի Կոստանդնուպօլիս եւ յամենայն աշխարհն Յունաց, վասն զի յաւուր մեծի զատկին մոլորեալ եղեն ի կատարելոյ զսուրբ Յարութեան օրն Զատկին. եւ ամենայն վարդապետք տանն Յունաց ընդ ստութեամբ փակեցին զուղղորդ պատուիրանս Աստուածաշունչ գրոց եւ զսուտ եւ զխաբեբայ տումարն հակառակամարտին Իրինոի ընկալան, եւ զճըշմարտագիր տումարն մեծին Անդրիասայ ոչ ընկալան, այլ ածիննորքա զլրումն Զատկին ի կիրակիէն ի շաբաթն եւ զկնի աւուր միոյ Զատիկ արարին, զոր պարտ էր զկնի ութ աւուրն կատարել. եւ ամենայն տանն Յունաց մոլորեալ ի սուրբ Զատկէն, եւ եղեւ սուգ մեծ ի վերայ սուրբ եկեղեցւոյն Կոստանդնուպօլսի, եւս առաւել ի սուրբ եւ յաստուածակերտ քաղաքն յԵրուսաղէմ, զի հպարտութեամբ բարձրավզեալ ածին զԶատիկն ի յաւուր Ծառզարդարին, եւ եղեն հակառակողք ամենայն ազգաց տունն Յունաց, եւս առաւել Քրիստոսի, վասն զի պատերազմեցան ընդ Հոգւոյն Սրբոյ տունն փիլիսոփայից:

At the beginning of the year 446 of the Armenian Era [A.D. 997-998] a comet arose in the heavens and was visible with a dreadful, awesome, astounding illumination.

In the year 449 of the Armenian Era [A.D. 1000] friendship and great unity developed between Emperor Basil and Senek'erim, [a] king of the Armenians. In the same year there died Sahak, *marzpan* and lord of the Varazhnunik'.

16. In 455 of the Armenian Era [A.D. 1006] Emperor Basil mustered troops from all the lands of his realm and advanced against the land of the Bulghars. [He] spent a great deal of time in that land engaged in extensive warfare. In this period a great disturbance erupted in the city of Constantinople and in the entire land of the Byzantines. This was because [the Chalcedonians] had deviated from [the correct observance of] the day of the great feast of the Resurrection, Easter. All the [Chalcedonian] Byzantine doctors of the Church had wrongly ignored the true precepts of Scripture and had adopted the false and fraudulent calendar of the contrarian Irion. The accurate calendar of the great Andreas they did not accept. Instead, they moved the day of the full moon of Easter from Sunday to Saturday and celebrated Easter on the next day, despite the fact that it should have been celebrated eight days later. The entire House of the Byzantines deviated from Holy Easter, and great sorrow descended upon the blessed Church of Constantinople and more so on the holy and God-built city of Jerusalem, since with their stiff-necked arrogance, [the Byzantines] celebrated Easter on Palm Sunday. Thus [the Byzantine reformers] went contrary to all peoples in the House of the Byzantines and more so against Christ, for this home of philosophers warred against the Holy Spirit.

Եւ յայնմ Զատկի ոչ վառեցաւ լոյս կանթեղացն ի սուրբ գերեզմանն աստուածընկալ ի քաղաքն յԵրուսաղէմ, վասն զի սուտ էին, անօրէնութեամբ արարին Զատիկն իւրեանց: Իսկ յայնմ աւուր ազգն անօրինաց, որ կային ի քաղաքն Երուսաղէմ, իբրեւ տեսին զԶատիկն քրիստոնէիցն ի մէջ սուրբ Յարութեանն, կոտորեցին սրով զամենայն քրիստոնեայսն՝ ոգիք իբրեւ տասն հազար, եւ լցաւ սուրբ Գերեզմանն Քրիստոսի արեամբ աղօթաւորացն. եւ դեռ մինչեւ ցայսօր կան ոսկերք նոցա լցեալ ի յայրի անդ յարեւմտից կուսէ քաղաքին Երուսաղէմի, զոր այժմ Մանկանց նշխարք կոչեն զնոսա: Արդ զայս այսպէս արարին հանճարեղ իմաստունքն Յունաց:

Իսկ թագաւորն Վասիլ իբրեւ յաղթեաց եւ էառ զթագաւորութիւնն Բուլղարաց, դարձաւ ի Կոստանդնուպօլիս մեծաւ ուրախութեամբ: Եւ յորժամ լուաւ զայս ամենայն կոտորածս, որ եղեւ սուրբ Զատկին, կոչեաց զամենայն իմաստունսն Յունաց եւ հարցանէր զպատճառն. եւ նոքա ըստ կամաց իւրեանց սկսան բազմադիմի մոլորեցուցանել զթագաւորն օտարոտի պատասխանատրութեամբն: Եւ ծանեաւ թագաւորն զայլակերպ պատասխանիս նոցա, իմացաւ՝ որ սուտ էին եւ մոլորեալք: Իսկ յառաջագոյն լըւեալ էր թագաւորն վասն Հայոց վարդապետացն՝ եթէ յաղթողք եւ կորովիք են գրոց պատուիրանաց, եւ յանուանէ գիտէր վասն Յովսեփայ Ընծայոյց հօրն եւ յաղագս Յովհաննիսի, որ հոմանուն ասէին Կոզեռն. եւ յայնժամ գըրեաց առ Յովհաննէս արքայն Հայոց, զի առաքեսցէ զնոսա առ ինքն ի Կոստանդնուպօլիս, զի ի նոցանէ գիտասցէ զճշմարիտ պատճառն եւ զուղղորդ Զատիկն:

On that [erroneous] Easter, the light of the lamps did not [self-]ignite in the holy Sepulcher, which contained God, in the city of Jerusalem. [This was because] they were wrong, impiously celebrating their Easter. On that day, once the nation of the impious [Muslims] who were in the city of Jerusalem, saw Easter being celebrated by Christians [on the wrong day] in the holy [church of the] Resurrection, they put all the Christians to the sword, some 10,000 people. Thus the holy Sepulcher of Christ was filled with the blood of the worshipers. To this day their bones may be seen there in a cave on the western side of the city of Jerusalem. They are presently called Relics of the Children. This was what was brought about by those genius philosophers of the Greeks.

Now once Emperor Basil had defeated and taken the realm of the Bulghars, he returned to Constantinople in great joy. When he heard about all the destruction which had occurred over holy Easter, he summoned all the savants of the Byzantines and asked the reason. Willfully they began giving numerous irrelevant explanations to mislead the emperor. But the emperor recognized their distorted replies and that they were false and devious. Now previously, the emperor had heard about the Armenian vardapets who were triumphant and competent in [explaining] the precepts of Scripture. By name he was familiar with Yovsep', the abbot of E"ntsayuts' [Monastery] and with Yovhanne's, who was nicknamed Kozer'n. Then he wrote to Yovhanne's, king of the Armenians, so that [the two vardapets] would be sent to him in Constantinople, so that he would learn from them the true cause [of the problem] and the correct [day for celebrating] Easter.

Իսկ նոքա ոչ առին յանձն գնալ, այլ թղթօք գեղեցկաշար բանիւք հասկացուցին զթագաւորն ամենայն խորին քննութեամբ: Եւ յայնժամ հակառակեալ կղերիկոսք եւ ոչ հաւանեցան թղթոյն, մինչեւ դարձեալ թագաւորն Վասիլ յուղարկեալ ի Հայք առ Յովհաննէս շահնշահն եւ առ Տէր Սարգիս կաթուղիկոսն Հայոց եւ մեծաւ խնդրուածօք ետ բերել առ ինքն զՀայոց վարդապետն զՍամուէլ, այր կրովի եւ յաղթող եւ կացուցանէր զնա յատենի խօսել ընդ վարդապետացն Յունաց: Իսկ իմաստունքն Յունաց շարժեցին ի վերայ Սամուէլի զամենայն գրեանս տանն Յունաց, եւ ոչ կարացին շարժել զնա ի ճշմարտութեանց անտի: Եւ սկիզբն արար Սամուէլ ի յառաջին աւուրն արարչութենէն եւ գայր հասանէր մինչեւ ցվերջին պատկեր աւուրն եւ զամենայն պատճառ պատճէնից սուրբ արանց յառաջին իմաստնոցն հաստատուն կացուցանէր: Եւ հաճոյ լինէր թագաւորին ամենայն բանք նորա. եւ ասէին իմաստունքն Յունաց ընդ թագաւորն. «Ով տէր արքայ, հրամայեա եւ ած այսր զմեծ վարդապետն Եբրայեցւոց, որ բնակեալ է ի կղզւոջն Կիպրացւոց, այր կորովի եւ հմուտ տումարի եւ ամենայն արուեստից ի մանկութենէ իւրմէ»: Եւ յուղարկեալ թագաւորն ի Կիպրոս եւ ածէր զՄուսի վարդապետն Եբրայեցւոց: Եւ նա կացեալ յատենի առաջի թագաւորին Վասլի, այր ճարտարաբան եւ հզօր, եւ սկսանէր խօսել զարուեստս տումարին եւ յամօթ եւ սուտ արար զամենայն իմաստունս տանն Յունաց եւ գովէր զբանսն Սամուէլի Հայոց վարդապետին: Իսկ թագաւորն յոյժ տրտմեալ ի վերայ վարդապետացն Յունաց եւ զբազումս եհան ի պատուոյ եկեղեցւոյն եւ ընկէց ի փառաց եւ զվարդապետն Հայոց յուղարկեալ մեծաւ պարգեւօք յաշխարհն Հայոց:

Now [the vardapets] did not consent to go. Rather, in beautifully composed letters they informed the emperor [about these issues] with a thorough investigation. However, the contrarian [Byzantine] clergy did not accept the [veracity of the contents of the] letter until once more Emperor Basil sent to the Armenians, to Yovhanne's shahnshah and to Lord Sargis, Catholicos of the Armenians, greatly requesting that they send to him the Armenian vardapet Samue'l. [Samue'l] was a skilled and triumphant [scholar] who could be seated at a session to speak with the Greek doctors of the Church. The Byzantine savants mustered against Samue'l all the writings of the House of the Byzantines, but they were unable to move [Samue'l] from the truth. Samue'l began [his discourse] with the first day of Creation and progressed to recent times, adducing as evidence and support all the reliable blessed savants of earlier times. The emperor was pleased with all his words. Then the Byzantine philosophers said to the king: "O Lord Emperor, command that the great doctor of the Hebrews be brought here. He lives on the island of Cyprus and is a man skilled and learned in the calendar and all the sciences, from his childhood." The emperor sent to Cyprus and had Muse, vardapet of the Hebrews brought to him. [The latter] came to the tribunal in the presence of the emperor Basil. [Muse] was an eloquent and powerful man. He commenced discoursing about calendrical science and put to shame all the savants in the House of the Greeks, proving them wrong, while praising the words of Samue'l, the Armenian vardapet. The emperor was very angry with the Byzantine vardapets and removed many of them from their ecclesiastical honors, deposing them from their glory. As for the Armenian vardapet, [Basil] sent him back to the land of the Armenians with great gifts.

17. Դարձեալ ի յաւուրս Վասլի Յունաց թագաւորին եւ ի Հայոց թուականութեանն ՆԾԲ ելանէր աստղ մի ի տեսիլ հրոյ երեւեալ ի յերկինս, նշան բարկութեան արարածոց եւ կատարածի աշխարհի: Եւ եղեւ շարժ սաստիկ ընդ ամենայն երկիր, մինչեւ կարծեալ բազմաց՝ թէ եհաս օրն վերջին եւ կատարածի աշխարհի, եւ որպէս առ ջրհեղեղաւն՝ եբերեալ դողաց ամենայն արարածք. եւ յահէ բարբառոյ բարկութեանն բազումք անկեալ մեռանէին եւ զկնի այնր բարկութեան անկանէր ցաւ յերկիր, որ անուանեալ կոչի Խովիկ, եւ անցոյց գաւառս եւ երթեալ հասանէր մինչեւ ի Սեբաստիա. եւ ցաւն այն երեւէր յայտնապէս ի մարմինն եւ ի դառնութենէն ոչ ժամանէին խոստովանութեան եւ հաղորդութեան: Եւ մարդ եւ անասուն պակասեցան յերկրէ, եւ մնացեալ չորքոտանիք՝ անմարդ շրջէին յերկրի:

Իսկ ի թուականին Հայոց ՆԿ զօրաժողով արար թագաւորն Վասիլ եւ գնայր ի վերայ աշխարհին Բուլղարաց եւ յաղթեաց թագաւորութեան նոցա եւ մաշեաց ի սուր սուսերի զբազում գաւառս մեծաւ բարկութեամբ. եւ յաւեր եւ ի գերութիւն մատնեաց զամենայն արեւմուտք եւ բնաջինջ եբարձ զամենայն թագաւորութիւնս Բուլղարաց եւ դեղ մահու արբուցանէր Ալիօսխանին առն քաջի՝ Բուլղարաց թագաւորին. եւ այսպիսի օրինակաւ հանէր զնա ի կենաց, առեալ զկնի նորա եւ զորդիս արկանէր ի Կոստանդնուպօլիս:

17. Also in the days of Basil, emperor of the Byzantines, in the year 452 of the Armenian Era [A.D. 1003-1004], a fiery star appeared in the sky, a sign of [divine] anger toward created beings as well as a sign of the end of the world. There was also a severe earthquake throughout all the countries, to the point that many believed that the Last Days, the end of the world, had arrived. As had happened at the time of the Flood, all creatures were shaking and many, from fear of such wrath, fell down and died. Moreover, an ailment descended upon the country. It was called xovik and spread through many districts, reaching as far as Sebastia. The disease clearly manifested itself on the body, and from its intensity, [the afflicted] had no time for confession or communion. People and animals diminished in the country, while the surviving quadrupeds wandered around the country without masters.

Now in 460 of the Armenian Era [A.D. 1011], Emperor Basil mustered troops and went against the land of the Bulghars. He conquered their kingdom and, in great wrath, put many districts to the sword. He subjected the entire western [areas] to the sword and to captive-taking, and obliterated the entire realm of the Bulghars. He also forced that brave man, Ali O'sman, king of the Bulghars, to drink poison, thereby removing him from life. Then [Basil] took [Ali O'sman's] wife and sons and brought them to Constantinople.

Յորժամ թուականութիւնն Հայոց հասանէր ի յամս ՆԿԵ, զարթեաւ աստուածասաստ բարկութիւնն ի վերայ ամենայն քրիստոսական ժողովրդեանն եւ երկրպագողաց սուրբ Խաչին, զի զարթեաւ վիշապն մահաշունչ հանդերձ մահաբեր հրով, եհար զհաւատացեալս Սրբոյ Երրորդութեանն: Յայսմ ի թուականիս սասանեցաւ հիմունք առաքելականացն եւ մարգարէականացն, վասն զի օձք թեւաւորք հասին եւ կամին ցոլանալ ընդ ամենայն աշխարհս հաւատացելոցս Քրիստոսի. այս է առաջին ելն արեանարբու գազանացն: Ընդ աւուրսն ընդ այնոսիկ զօրաժողով լինէին խուժադուժ ազգն անօրինացն, որք անուանեալ կոչին Թուրք, եւ հասեալ մտանէին յաշխարհն Հայոց ի Վասպուրական գաւառին եւ անողորմ ի բերան սրոյ կոտորէին զհաւատացեալքս Քրիստոսի:

18. Յայնժամ հասանէր համբաւ կատարածիս այս առ թագաւորն Սենեքարիմ. յայնժամ աւագ որդւոյ նորա Դաւթի ժողովեալ զզօրս ազատացն հասանէր ի վերայ Թուրք բանակին. եւ հարան սաստկապէս ընդ միմեանս ահաւոր պատերազմաւ: Իսկ մինչեւ յայնմ ժամանակին չէին բնաւ տեսեալ Թուրք զօրք հեծելոց. եւ ի հանդիպիլն նոցա՝ տեսին այլակերպ զնոսա. աղեղնաւորս եւ հերարձակս իբրեւ զկանայս. եւ յայնժամ զօրքն Հայոց չէին սովոր պատրաստ լինիլ ընդդէմ նետիցն. եւ քաջաբար ի վերայ այլազգեացն յարձակեցան եւ առ հասարակ մերկացուցին զսուսերն իւրեանց ի պատենիցն եւ արիաբար ի պատերազմ ընթանային արիական գունդն Հայոց եւ զբազումս յայլազգեացն սատակէին: Իսկ այլազգիքն նետաձգութեամբ զբազումս ի զօրացն Հայոց վիրաւորէին խոցելով:

When 465 of the Armenian Era arrived [A.D. 1018-1019], divine anger was unleashed against all Christian peoples and worshipers of the Holy Cross. For there awoke a dragon with death-bringing breath and fire, which struck at believers in the Holy Trinity. In this year the foundations of the apostles and the prophets were shaken, for winged snakes arrived and wanted to penetrate all the lands of the believers in Christ. This was the first emergence of these bloodthirsty beasts. During those days, the barbarous infidel people called Turks massed troops and reached as far as Vaspurakan district in the land of the Armenians, which they entered, and put to the sword the believers in Christ.

18. News of what had occurred reached King Senek'erim. His senior son, Dawit', mustered troops from the azats and went against the Turks' army. They violently clashed with each other in a frightful battle. Until then, [the Armenians] had never seen the Turkish cavalry, which now appeared to them as a strange [phenomenon]: archers with [long] hair, like women. The Armenian troops were not then accustomed to or prepared for arrows and, unsheathing their swords, attacked the foreigners valiantly, killing many of them. However, the foreigners struck and wounded with their arrows many Armenian troops.

Եւ տեսեալ զայն ամենայն Շապուհ՝ ասէր ցԴաւիթ. «Դարձիր, թագաւոր, յերեսաց թշնամեացս, վասն զի ի նետիցս վիրաւորեալ եղեն մեծ մասն զօրացս, գնասցուք եւ ընդդէմ այսմ զինուցս, զոր տեսանեմք առ այլազգիսդ, ա՛յլ զգեստ պատրաստեսցուք ընդդէմ նետիցդ»: Իսկ Դաւիթ առ մեծութիւն իւր հայելով, հպարտացեալ մեծաւ ամբարտաւանութեամբ, ոչ լսէր Շապհոյ, դառնալ ի պատերազմէն: Յայնժամ Շապուհ բարկութեամբ դիմեաց ի վերայ Դաւթի եւ բռնցի հարեալ զթիկունսն ուժգնակի մղէր զնա դառնալ. վասն զի Շապուհ էր այր քաջ եւ պատերազմող հզօր եւ էր մանկակալ եւ սնուցիչ Դաւթի, վասն այնորիկ անահ էր ի նմանէ. եւ այսպիսի օրինակաւ դարձուցանէր զԴաւիթ հանդերձ զօրօքն: Եւ գնացին յՌստան քաղաքն եւ պատմեցին թագաւորին Սենեքարիմայ եւ ասացին զորպիսութիւն այլազգեացն կերպարանաց: Եւ լուեալ Սենեքարիմայ յոյժ վիրաւորեալ լինէր. ոչ եկեր եւ ոչ էարբ, այլ կայր մտախոհի, լի տրտմութեամբ եւ զգիշերն ամենայն անքուն անցուցանէր եւ նստեալ քննէր զժամանակագրութիւնս եւ զասացուածս աստուածախօս տեսանողացն, զսրբոց վարդապետացն, եւ գտանէր գրեալ ի գիրսն զժամանակն ելանելոյ Թուրքաց զօրաց եւ զօրականաց. եւ ծանեաւ զկորուստ եւ զկատարած ամենայն երկրի. եւ գտանէր ի գիրսն գրեալ այսպէս, եթէ

«Ի ժամանակին յայնմիկ փախիցեն յարեւելից յարեւմուտս, ի հիւսիսոյ ի հարաւ, եւ հանգիստ ոչ գտանեն ի վերայ երկրի, վասն զի արեամբք ծածկին դաշտք եւ լերինք. եւ այս էր զոր ասաց Եսայի եթէ «Սմբակք երիվարաց նոցա հաստատուն»:

Seeing this, Shapuh said to Dawit': "King, turn back from the enemy, because most of our troops have been wounded by arrows. Let us go and prepare [armored] garments to resist the arrows which we see them fighting with." However, Dawit', mindful of his greatness, pridefully, and with great indignation, did not heed Shapuh's [advice] to withdraw from the battle. Then Shapuh angrily applied himself to Dawit', and, hitting him on the side with his fist, forcibly compelled him to turn. Shapuh was a brave, martial man who had nourished and raised Dawit' and for that reason had no fear of him. Thus, he got Dawit' and his troops to turn back. They went to the city of Ostan and related to King Senek'erim what had transpired and about the appearance of the foreigners. When Senek'erim heard this, he was deeply disturbed, and neither ate nor drank. Rather, he was plunged into deep thought full of sorrow and passed the entire night sleepless, seated and examining the chronicles and sayings of divinely-inspired prophets, the holy vardapets. He found in those writings mention of the time of the emergence of Turkish troops and forces. He recognized the ruin and destruction of the entire country, which he found described as follows:

"In that time, [people] will flee from East to West, from North to South, and will find no rest upon the earth, for the plains and the mountains will be covered with blood, just as Isaiah said, 'The hooves of their horses do not falter.'"[18]

18 Isaiah 5:28.

Յայնժամ խորհեցաւ տալ զաշխարհ հայրենեաց իւրոց յարքայն Յունաց Վասիլ եւ առնուլ զՍեբաստիա եւ գրէր վաղվաղակի առ թագաւորն. զոր իբրեւ լուաւ թագաւորն Վասիլ՝ ուրախ եղեւ եւ ետ նմա զՍեբաստիա. եւ տայր Սենեքերիմ զաշխարհն Վասպուրականի. թեմաբերդս ՀԲ եւ գեւղս ՏՆ եւ զվանորայսն ոչ ետ, այլ պահեաց իւր աղօթարարս. ՃԺԵ վանք եւ ետ զայս ամենայն գրով ի Վասիլն: Եւ առաքեաց թագաւորն Վասիլ առ Սենեքերիմ առաքել առ նա զԴաւիթ թագաւորական ճոխութեամբ եւ առաքեաց զորդին իւր, ընդ նմին եւ որդիս ազատաց եւ զեպիսկոպոսն Տէր Եղիշէ եւ բեռնակիր ջորիս Յ, բարձեալ գանձիւք եւ պէսպէս կազմութեամբ, եւ տաճիկ ձիս Ռ. եւ այսպիսի փառաւորութեամբ եմուտ Դաւիթ ի Կոստանդնուպօլիս՝ եւ դըղրդեցաւ քաղաքն եւ ելին ամենեքեան ընդ առաջ նորա եւ զարդարեցին զփողոցս եւ զապարանս եւ գանձս բազումս ցանէին ի վերայ նորա: Եւ յոյժ ուրախացաւ թագաւորն Վասիլ ընդ տեսիլն Դաւթի եւ տարաւ զնա ի սուրբն Սոփի եւ արար զնա իւր որդեգիր եւ պատուէին զնա որպէս զորդի թագաւորի: Եւ ետ նմա թագաւորն բազում պարգեւս եւ դարձոյց զնա առ հայրն իւր եւ ետ նմա զՍեբաստիա բազում գաւառօք. եւ ելեալ Սենեքերիմ ամենայն ընտանեօք իւրովք եւ ռամկօք եկն ի Սեբաստիա եւ անտերացաւ աշխարհն Հայոց ի թագաւորաց եւ յիշխանաց:

It was then that [King Senek'erim] thought to give his patrimonial land to the Byzantine emperor Basil, and to receive [in exchange] Sebastia. He immediately wrote to the emperor. As soon as Emperor Basil heard about this, he was delighted and gave Sebastia to him. Senek'erim handed over the land of Vaspurakan [including] 72 regional fortresses, and 4,400 villages. However, he did not give 115 monasteries, which he kept so that they would offer prayers for him. He gave all this to Basil in writing. Emperor Basil sent to Senek'erim for him [also] to send Dawit', in royal splendor. And so, [Senek'erim] sent his son [along] with him, the sons of azats and bishop Lord Eghishe', 300 pack mules laden with treasure and various goods, as well as 1,000 Arabian horses. With such glory did Dawit' enter Constantinople. The city reverberated and everyone came out before him; the streets and mansions were decorated and [the residents] showered much money on him. Emperor Basil greatly rejoiced at the sight of Dawit', taking him to Saint Sophia, adopting him, and honoring him as a monarch's son. The emperor gave him many gifts and then sent him back to his father, giving him Sebastia with many districts. Senek'erim arose with his entire family and troops and came to Sebastia. And thus did the land of the Armenians become masterless, without kings or princes.

19. Ի թուականութեանս Հայոց ՆՀ ելանէր Վասիլն յարեւելս անթիւ զօրօք եւ խնդրեաց ի թագաւորէն Հայոց զԱնի եւ զԿարս: Եւ Յովհաննէս որդին Գագկայ խորհեցաւ տալ վասն թուլութեան սրտին իւրոյ. իսկ Վասիլն դարձաւ յաշխարհն իւր եւ գրեաց առ Գորգի թագաւորն Վրաց գալ նմա ի հնազանդութիւն. զոր ոչ ընկալաւ եւ ոչ յանձն էառ: Յայնժամ գայ Վասիլն պատերազմաւ ի վերայ նորա. եւ զօրքն Վրաց գնացին ընդդէմ նորա եւ Ռատն եւ Ջոյատն՝ արք քաջք՝ եղբարք Լիպարտին, ուժգին բախեցին զզօրսն Վասլին՝ մինչեւ սպանաւ Ռատն, զի ձին նորա խրեցաւ ի տեղի մի տիղմ եւ անդ սպանաւ. եւ ապա դարձան ի փախուստ զօրքն Վրացեաց. եւ զօրք Վասլին զկնի կոտորէին. եւ կացեալ Վասիլն անդ ամիսս Գ մինչեւ հաւանեցոյց զնոսա եւ ի Տրապիզոն ձմերեաց: Եւ գնայր առ թագաւորն Վասիլ Տէր Պետրոս կաթողիկոսն Հայոց եւ սուրբ վարդապետն Յովհաննէս Կոզեռն բազում սպասուք. եւ թագաւորն ընկալաւ զնոսա մեծաւ պատուով. եւ ի հասանելն մեծի աւուր մկրտութեան Տեառն մերոյ մեծարեաց թագաւորն զՏէր Պետրոսն եւ զվարդապետսն Հայոց եւ ի վեր եւտ կացուցանել քան զառաջնորդսն Յունաց եւ յառաջ Տէր Պետրոսի հրամայեաց օրհնել զջուրն. զոր իբրեւ արկանէր զմիւռոն սուրբ ձիթոյն ի ջուրն եւ հարկանէր սուրբ Նշանաւն զջուրն, հուր սաստկապէս ցոլացեալ երեւէր ի վերայ ջրոյն եւ կապեցաւ գետն առ վայր մի եւ ոչ շարժէր. եւ տեսեալ թագաւորին եւ զօրացն զարհուրեցան եւ խոնարհեալ թագաւորն՝ արկանէր զօրհնեալ ջուրն ի վերայ գլխոյն աջովն Տէր Պետրոսի: Եւ դարձաւ Տէր Պետրոսն մեծաւ պարգեւօք յաշխարհն Հայոց:

19. In 470 of the Armenian Era [A.D. 1021-1022], Basil arose and went to the East with countless troops. He demanded Ani and Kars from the Armenian king. [King] Yovhanne's, son of Gagik, thought to give them [to Basil] because of the weakness of his own heart. Meanwhile, Basil returned to his own land and wrote to Giorgi,[19] king of the Georgians, to come forth to him in submission. [Giorgi] neither accepted this, nor undertook to comply with it. Then Basil came against him militarily. The troops of the Georgians [which] went against him [included] the brave men R'at and Zoyat, who were brothers of Liparit. Basil forcefully struck the troops of the Georgians until R'at was slain. For his horse had become stuck in a muddy spot and he was killed there. At that, the troops of the Georgians turned in flight, with Basil's forces pursuing and killing them. Basil remained there for three months, until he had subdued them. Then he wintered in Trebizond. Lord Petros, Catholicos of the Armenians, and the blessed Armenian vardapet, Yovhanne's Kozer'n, went to Emperor Basil with many [church] vessels and the emperor received them with great honor. When the day for [celebrating] the great [feast-]day of the baptism of our Lord arrived, the emperor honored Lord Petros and the Armenian vardapet by having them placed above the Byzantine prelates, and he ordered Lord Petros to bless the waters first. When [Petros] had cast the chrism of holy oil on the water and then struck the water with the blessed cross, an intense fire appeared blazing over the water and the river froze up for a moment, motionless. When the emperor and the troops saw this, they were terrified. The emperor, bowing down, had Lord Petros sprinkle the holy water on his head. Then Lord Petros returned to the land of the Armenians with great gifts.

19 *Giorgi* I, 1014-1027.

Իսկ Վասիլն յետ ժամանակաց գայ յԱնտիոք ի ծածուկ Գ արամբք հաւատարմօք եւ եկեալ ի Սեաւ լեառն ի տեղին, որ կոչի Պաղակձիակ, եւ ի հօրէ եւ յառաջնորդէ տեղւոյն առնու զքրիստոսական կնիքն եւ յայնմ հետէ եղեւ որպէս զհայր աշխարհիս Հայոց [...]:

Ի թուականութեանս Հայոց ՆՀԱ մեռաւ Տէր Սարգիս կաթողիկոսն Հայոց եւ հաստատեաց յաթոռ իւր հայրապետ զՏէր Պետրոս: Ի սոյն ամի իշխան ոմն յաղթանդամ ի տանէն Յունաց Նիկիփոռ անուն ծռվիզ յարեաւ ի վերայ Վասլին եւ կոչեաց ի միաբանութիւն իւր զթագաւորն Վրաց Գորգի եւ զորդիսն Գագկայ. գնաց յահէ նորա Դաւիթ առ նա զօրօքն Հայոց, եւ ահ մեծ եղեւ ի վերայ Վասլին: Եւ յղեաց Վասլին առ Դաւիթ աղաչանս, զի հնարեսցէ զկորուստ նորա: Եւ ծռվիզն յոյժ սիրէր զԴաւիթ եւ խոստանայր նստուցանել զնա յաթոռ թագաւորութեան Հայոց, բայց Դաւիթ ոչ կամեցաւ լուծանել զդաշինս Վասլին: Եւ յաւուր միում գնայր Դաւիթ ի տուն իւր խռովութեան աղագաւ եւ յարուցեալ Նիկիփոռն միայն եւ գրկեաց զնա եւ աղաչէր դառնալ. իսկ Դաւիթ ակնարկեալ արանցն, եւ նոյնժամայն սպանին զծռվիզն, եւ զօրքն նորա ցրուեալ եղեն փախստական. եւ լուեալ զայն Վասլին՝ ուրախ եղեւ յոյժ եւ տայր պարգեւս Դաւթի զԿեսարիա եւ զԾամնդաւ եւ Խաւատանէքն հանդերձ սահմանօքն: Եւ Վասիլն մեծաւ զայրացմամբ գայր ի վերայ Գորգէի Վրաց թագաւորին բազում զօրօք. եւ արարին Չիօնից բերդին առաջի մեծ պատերազմ. եւ Գորգի փախստական լեալ անկանէր յամուր բերդս եւ գրէր զանձն իւր ծառայ Վասլին եւ տայր պատանդ զորդին իւր:

After some time, Basil went to Antioch secretly with three trusted men, where he visited Black Mountain at a place named Paghakdziak. And there he received a Christian baptism from the abbot and director. Thereafter [Basil] became like a father to the land of the Armenians [...].[20]

In the year 471 of the Armenian Era [A.D. 1022], Lord Sargis,[21] Catholicos of the Armenians, died, and the patriarch Lord Petros[22] was established on his throne. In the same year a certain powerful prince from the House of the Byzantines, Nicephorus, named Tsr'viz,[23] arose against Basil and summoned Giorgi, king of the Georgians, and his son Gagik to join him. Out of fear of him, Dawit' went to him with Armenian troops. And great fear engulfed Basil. Basil sent to Dawit', beseeching him to find some way of ruining [Nicephorus]. Meanwhile, Tsr'viz [Nicephorus] liked Dawit' a lot and promised to install him on the throne of the kingdom of the Armenians. However, Dawit' did not want to dissolve [his] alliance with Basil. One day Dawit' went to his home because of some disturbance. Nicephorus, alone, arose and embraced him, begging him to return. But Dawit' signaled to his men and they immediately killed Tsr'viz, while his forces split asunder and fled. When Basil learned about this, he was overjoyed and gave to Dawit' as gifts Caesarea, Tsamndaw, and Xawatane'k', with their borders. Basil, in a great rage, went against Giorgi, king of the Georgians, with many troops. They had a great battle before Dzio'nk' fortress. Dawit' [was defeated and] fled into this secure fortress, enrolling himself as a vassal of Basil and giving his son as a hostage.

20 There is a lacuna in the original text here.

21 *Sargis* I Sewants'i, 992-1019.

22 *Petros* I Getadardz, 1019-1058.

23 *Tsr'viz:* "Crooked Neck".

Եւ յետ այնորիկ գնայր Վասիլն յաշխարհն Պարսից եւ բնակէր ի դուռն քաղաքին Հերայ. եւ էր ժամանակն ամառնային. եւ յաւուր միում եկն ձիւն սաստիկ ի վերայ բանակին եւ ոչ գիտէին զինչ արասցեն. եւ դարձան փախստական ի մեծ տագնապէն. եւ ծովացաւ երկիրն ի բազմութենէ ջըրոյն. եւ եկեալ ի տեղի մի ոչ կարէին անցանել ի տղմոյն եւ գումարեալ ոչ գիտէին թէ զինչ արասցեն: Ապա հըրամայեաց թագաւորն կոտորել ի հետեւակէն եւ կոտորեցին ԺԳՌ այր եւ լցին ի տեղին յայն եւ զօրքն անցին ի վերայ եւ եկեալ ձմերեաց ի Մելտենի:

20. Ի թուականութեան Հայոց ՆՀԱ յամս կայսերն Յունաց Վասլի յերկինս ահաւոր նշան եւ սոսկալի եւ բարկութիւն ի վերայ ամենայն արարածոց. ի Հոկտեմբեր ամսոյ Գ յերրորդ ժամու աւուրն պատառեցաւ վերին հաստատութիւնն երկնից յարեւելից կուսէ մինչեւ յարեւմուտսն՝ ընդ երկուս հերձաւ կապուտ երկինդ եւ լոյս պայծառ յերկիր թափեցաւ ի հիւսիսային կողմանէ. եւ մեծաւ շարժմամբ դողաց ամենայն երկիր. եւ նախ քան զնուազիլ լուսոյն եղեւ դոջիւն եւ թնդիւն ահաւոր ի վերայ ամենայն արարածոց. խաւարեցաւ արեգակն եւ աստեղք երեւեցան որպէս ի մէջ գիշերի, եւ սուգ զգեցան ամենայն երկիր. եւ դառն արտասուօք աղաղակէին ամենայն աղինք առ Աստուած: Եւ ապա յետ երեք աւուր ժողովեցան ամենայն իշխանք եւ ազատքն հրամանաւ թագաւորին Հայոց Յովհաննիսի եւ եկեալ առաջի սուրբ վարդապետին Յովհաննու Կոզեռանն, որ էր այր աստուածազգեաց եւ հրեշտակակրօն եւ լի իսկ առաքելական եւ մարգարէական գրոց գիտութեամբ:

After this, Basil went on to the land of the Persians and encamped at the gates of the city of Her. It was summertime, but one day a violent snowstorm fell upon the camp and they did not know what to do. They turned and fled in great panic. The ground became flooded like a sea from the volume of water. They were trapped at one place and unable to cross, because of the mud. Gathered there, they did not know what to do. Then the emperor ordered that some men from the infantry should be killed—they killed some 13,000 of them—and filled [their bodies] into that place. And then the troops crossed over them and came and wintered in Melitene.

20. In the year 471 of the Armenian Era [A.D. 1022-1023], during the reign of Basil, emperor of the Byzantines, an awesome and terrifying sign appeared in the heavens and [divine] wrath fell upon all created beings. On the third day of the month of October, at the third hour of the day, the upper firmament of the heavens was rent asunder from east to west, and the blue sky was torn in two. A bright light fell upon the earth from the northern part [of the sky], and the entire country was convulsed with a great earthquake. Before the light was reduced, a frightful roaring and exploding [sound was heard] by all living creatures. The sun became dark, and the stars appeared as though in the middle of night. The entire country dressed in mourning and, with bitter tears, all peoples beseeched God. After three days, all the princes and *azats* assembled at the command of Yovhanne's, king of the Armenians, and went before the blessed *vardapet* Yovhanne's Kozer'n. [He was] a man clothed in divinity, with an angelic faith, full of the knowledge of apostolic and prophetic literature.

Եւ յորժամ եկին իշխանքն Հայոց հարցանել զնա եւ իմանալ վասն հրաշալի տեսլեանն եւ նշանին՝ եւ տեսին զսուրբ վարդապետն Յովհաննէս անկեալ ի վերայ երեսաց իւրոց տրտմութեամբ եւ լայր դառնապէս: Եւ ի հարցանելն նոցա, նա դառն ոգով եւ աղիողորմ հառաչանօք ետ պատասխանի եւ ասաց. «Ո՛վ որդիք, լուարուք ինձ. վայ եւ եղուկ է ամենայն մարդկան, զի ահա այսօր հազար ամ է կապանացն սատանայի, զոր կապեաց Տէրն մեր Յիսուս Քրիստոս խաչիւն իւրով սրբով, մանաւանդ իւր սուրբ մկրտութեամբն ի Յորդանան գետն. եւ արդ արձակեցաւ Սատանայ ի կապանաց իւրոց ըստ վկայութեան տեսլեանն Յովհաննու աւետարանչին, որպէս ասաց նմա հրեշտակն Աստուծոյ՝ թէ Ռ ամ կապեսցի սատանայ եւ դարձեալ արձակեսցի ի կապանաց իւրոց: Եւ ահա այսօր արձակեցաւ սատանայ ի հազար ամէ կապանաց իւրոց, որ Հայոց թըւականն եւ ՆՀԸ ամ է եւ կալ զառաջինն ՇԾԲ, որ լինի ՌԼ ամ. զերեսուն ամն տուր յառաջ քան զմկրտութիւնն եւ կալ զհազարն մինչեւ ցայսօր: Եւ արդ վասն այսորիկ եղեւ պատառումն երկնից: Եւ ահա յայսմհետէ ոչ ոք կարասցէ կալ հաստատուն ի հաւատս Քրիստոսի եւ ի պատուիրանսն Աստուծոյ՝ ո՛չ հայրապետ եւ ո՛չ վարդապետ, ո՛չ եպիսկոպոս եւ ո՛չ քահանայ, ո՛չ աբեղայ եւ ո՛չ կրօնաւոր, ո՛չ իշխան եւ ո՛չ ժողովուրդ.

When the Armenian princes came to ask him and learn about the amazing appearance and sign, they found the blessed vardapet Yovhanne's down on his knees with sorrow, and weeping bitterly. At their inquiries, he replied with bitter grief and piteous sighs, saying: "O my sons, hear me. Woe and disaster has come to all mankind. For behold, today marks the 1,000th year of Satan's bondage. Our Lord Jesus Christ bound him through His crucifixion and especially by His blessed baptism in the Jordan River. Now Satan has been freed from his bonds according to the testimony in the Revelation of the Evangelist John, just as the angel of God told him that Satan will be bound for 1,000 years and then released from those bonds.[24] Now behold, today Satan has been freed from the thousand years of his bondage. This is the year 478 of the Armenian Era [A.D. 1029-1030]. Add to that the first 552 years, for [a sum of] 1,030 years. When you subtract 30 years for the period prior to Christ's baptism, you arrive at 1000 years for the present [date]. The rending of the heavens was due to this. Hereafter no one will be able to remain firm in the faith of Christ and [faithful] to God's commands—neither patriarch nor vardapet, neither bishop nor priest, neither abbot nor cleric, neither prince nor commoner.

24 *cf.* Revelation 20:1.

«Իշխանք յարենան ի գողս եւ յաւազակս եւ յափշտակողս, դատաւորք ի կաշառս եւ յանիրաւ դատաստանս. կրօնաւորք թողուն զանապատս եւ զմենաստանս եւ յաշխարհի զբազմունս դեգերին եւ շրջին ընդ փողոցս եւ ի մէջ կանանց, ատեն զաղօթս եւ թողուն զկարգս կրօնաւորութեան իւրեանց, սիրեն զվարս աշխարհի եւ զհետ երթան գովեստից մարդկան, որոճալով որոճեն զդիւական երգս եւ փքացեալ ի վերայ ընկերացն ասելով թէ՝ Ես կրցորդ եւ մեղեդի գիտեմ եւ դու ոչ. եւ այսու պատճառաւ պղտորեն զկարգ ժամատեղացն. լինին եւ բազումք ուսումնատեացք, ծոյլք եւ դատարկաբանք, տրտնջողք եւ ամբաստանողք՝ եւ ուր ուրեք երեւի ճշմարտութիւն ի մարդիկ, զի լինին կամապաշտք, անձնասէրք եւ ընկերատեացք, շոգմոգք, քսուք, ստախօսք, հպարտք, փառասէրք, անձնահաճք, ինքնահաւանք, որկորամոլք, գինեսէրք եւ ցանկասէրք: Որդեա՛կք իմ, ահա յայսմհետէ խափանեսցի փառաբանութիւնն Աստուծոյ ի մարդկանէ եւ ոչ երեւի ճշմարտութիւն առ մարդիկք: Այլ եւ իշխանք պիղծ եւ մեծախտիւ յանդգնեալ եւ մոլորեալ. թողուն զհոգս շինութեան տանց եւ զյաջողուածս գործոց եւ միշտ եւ հանապազ ի գինարբուսն դեգերին վասն սիրոյ եւ ցանկութեան չար եւ պիղծ ախտին. հայրապետք եւ եպիսկոպոսունք եւ քահանայք եւ կրօնաւորք արծաթասէրք առաւել քան աստուածասէրք:

"Princes will join with thieves, robbers, and plunderers. Judges will take bribes and produce unjust verdicts. Clerics will leave their retreats and places of solitude and, engaging in worldly pursuits, will wander about the streets among women. They will hate praying and abandon their priestly orders They will love the ways of the world and pursue the praises of men. They will delight in diabolical songs and will boast to their comrades, saying: "I am the one who knows about harmony and melody, not you." And thus will they pollute the order of the churches. Many will hate scholarship, be lazy, idle, grumblers and accusers. Nowhere will the truth show itself among men, for they will be stubborn, selfish, haters of friends, slanderers, informers, liars, prideful, seekers of glory, boastful, vainglorious, greedy, drunkards and lechers. My sons, hereafter the glorification of God by mankind will be obstructed and truth will not manifest itself among mankind. Moreover, loathsome and diseased priests will be emboldened and will stray [from the truth]. They will abandon their concern for building homes and the success of their works, and will turn to constant, endless drunkenness for the love of that foul desire and disease. Patriarchs, bishops, priests, and clerics will love silver more than God.

«Որդեա՛կք իմ, ահա յայսմհետէ սատանայի կամքն առաւել կատարեսցի յորդիս մարդկան քան զԱստուծոյն եւ ի ձեռն անարժան պատարագողացն, որ յայսմ հետէ լինելոց է, բարկանայ Աստուած ի վերայ արարածոցս, եւս առաւել ի վերայ մատուցողին զնա, զի յանարժանիցն պատարագելոց է Քրիստոս եւ յանարժանսն բաշխի. եւ առաւել վիրաւորելոց է Տէր մեր Յիսուս Քրիստոս ի յանարժան քահանայիցն քան զչարչարիլն եւ զխաչիլն ի Հրէից, զի արձակեցաւ սատանայ ի հազար ամէ կապանաց իւրոց, զոր կապեաց Քրիստոս: Եւ զայս, որդեա՛կք իմ, պատուիրեմ ձեզ հառաչանօք սրտիւ լալով եւ ողբալով, վասն զի քակտին բազումք ի հաւատոց եւ պարծանօք ուրանան զՔրիստոս, եւ վասն այսորիկ խաւար կալաւ զամենայն արարածս»:

21. Զայս այսպէս ասաց սուրբ վարդապետն Հայոց վասն կատարածի բարկութեան նշանին եւ այլ բազում ինչ ճառեաց, որ կատարելոց էր ի վերայ հաւատացելոցս, զոր ահա ամենայն ինչ կատարեցաւ մի առ մի ի ձեռն ելից կատաղի եւ շուն ազգին թուրքաց, անօրէն եւ պիղծ որդւոցն Քամայ:

"My sons, behold, henceforth the will of Satan will be fulfilled by the sons of man, more so than the will of God. The unworthy celebrants who shall come forth from now on will draw God's wrath upon creation and even more so upon those who offer mass to Him. For the unworthy shall offer mass to Christ and shall distribute [communion] to the unworthy. Our Lord Jesus Christ will be more wounded by such worthless priests than by the torments and crucifixion of the Jews. For after a thousand years, Satan has been set free from the bonds with which Christ bound him. My sons, I tell you this with a heart that sighs, weeps, and mourns, for many will be pulled away from the faith and will boast of denying Christ. Because of this, darkness has covered all creation."

21. Thus did the blessed vardapet of the Armenians speak concerning the sign of wrath which had occurred. He also said many other things about what would befall the faithful. And indeed all of them were brought about one by one by the crazed, dog-like nation of Turks, the impious and filthy sons of Ham.

Յայսմ ամի ի թուականութեանս եւ ահաւոր նշանիս մեռանէր սուրբ թագաւորն Հոռոմց Վասիլ, կացեալ յաթոռ թագաւորութեան Հոռոմց ամս յիսուն եւ ութ. եւ կոչեցեալ զեղբայր իւր զԿոստանդին, եւ մինչդեռ կենդանի էր դնէր զթագն ի գլուխ եղբօրն իւրում եւ նստուցանէր զնա յաթոռ թագաւորութեանն իւրոյ եւ երկրպագանէր ի վերայ երեսաց իւրոց. եւ զամենայն թագաւորութիւնն իւր նմա յանձն արարեալ եւ անդարձ արարեալ նմա վասն աշխարհին Հայոց, զի հայրաբար սիրով խնամեսցէ զազգն զայն: Դարձեալ զորդիսն Սենեքարիմայ նմա յանձն արար՝ զԴաւիթ եւ զԱտոմ եւ զԱպուսահլ եւ զԿոստանդին՝ եւ զամենայն իշխանս տանն Հայոց եւ պատուիրեաց բարի մտօք կալ հանապազ ի վերայ հաւատացելոցն Քրիստոսի: Վասիլն զամս յիսուն եւ ութ թագաւորեաց ի վերայ Հոռոմց, սրբութեամբ եւ կուսութեամբ վարեաց զայս կեանս, եւ բարի խոստովանութեամբ ննջեաց ի Քրիստոս Յիսուս, եւ թաղեցին զնա ընդ սուրբ թագաւորսն բարի յիշատակաւ:

Յայսմ ամի մեռաւ եւ Սենեքարիմ թագաւորն Հայոց, եւ տարան զնա ի գերեզմանատունն հարց իւրոց, ուր առաջին թագաւորքն Հայոց թաղեալ կան ի Վարագայ, վանքն սրբոյ Նշանին եւ անդ թաղեցին զՍենեքարիմ ընդ հարսն իւր. եւ հաստատեալ լինէր թագաւորական իշխանութիւնն տանն Հայոց յաւագ որդին իւր ի Դաւիթ, վասն զի էր այր փառաւոր եւ պատուական եւ ահարկու ի վերայ երկրի: Յայսմ ամի մեռաւ եւ Գուրգի թագաւորն Վրաց, եւ նստուցին յաթոռ նորա զորդի նորա զԲագրատ, թագաւորեալ ի վերայ ամենայն աշխարհին Վրաց:

In the same year as the frightening [astronomical] sign [A.D. 1022-1023], the blessed emperor of the Byzantines, Basil,[25] died after reigning for 58 years. Before he died, he summoned his brother, Constantine, to him, placed the crown on his brother's head, seated him on the throne of his kingdom, and prostrated himself before him. [Basil] entrusted his entire realm to him and got him to remain constant regarding the land of the Armenians, such that he would protect that people with a father's love. [Basil] also entrusted to him the sons of Senek'erim, Dawit', Atom, Abusahl, and Constantine, and all the princes of the House of the Armenians, enjoining him always to be well-disposed toward the Christian faithful. Basil, who ruled over the Byzantines for 58 years, led a holy and chaste life and reposed in Jesus Christ with a goodly confession. They buried him along with the other blessed emperors of good memory.

In the same year, Senek'erim,[26] king of the Armenians, died. They took him to the mausoleum of his fathers in Varag, at the monastery of the Holy Cross, where the first kings of the Armenians were buried. And they buried Senek'erim there among his fathers. The royal authority of the House of the Armenians was confirmed on his senior son, Dawit', as he was a glorious, honorable, and awesome man in the country. In this year Giorgi,[27] king of the Georgians, died and they seated on his throne his son, Bagrat,[28] to rule over the entire land of the Georgians.

25 *Basil* II Bulgaroctonus, 976-1025.
26 *Senek'erim*-Hovhannes 1003-1021, d. 1027.
27 *Giorgi:* George I, 1014-1027.
28 *Bagrat* IV, 1027-1072.

Արդ ի յայսմ ամի թագաւորեաց Կոստանդին եղբայր Վասլին ի վերայ ամենայն աշխարհին Հոռոմոց: Եւ եղեւ Կոստանդ այր բարի եւ աստուածասէր, ողորմած այրեաց եւ գերեաց, անյիշաչար ի վերայ ամենայն յանցաւորաց, վասն զի սա արձակեաց զամենայն բանտարկեալսն ի կապանաց եւ զկորստական տունն, զոր արարեալ էր Վասիլն, հրամայեաց այրել հրով, զոր Վասիլ լի իսկ արարեալ էր իշխանօքն Յունաց, վասն ահի թագաւորութեանն զաղտ ի ծածուկ խեղդամահ արարեալ զփառաւորսն Յունաց. եւ կախեալ կային զգեստօքն ընդ փողիցն ի ճանկս երկաթիս. զոր տեսեալ Կոստանդին՝ լայր զնոսա եւ հրամայեաց զնոսա թաղել եւ զտունն հրով ասաց այրել. եւ մեղադիր լինէր եղբօրն իւրոյ եթէ «Երբ մահն առաջի կայ, այս է՞ր է չարաչար մահս վասն մարմնաւոր եւ անցաւոր կենաց»: Եւ ինքն Կոստանդին խաղաղութեամբ կացեալ յաթոռ թագաւորութեան Հոռոմոց՝ քաղցրութեամբ հովուեաց զամենայն հաւատացեալս Աստուծոյ եւ կացեալ յաթոռ թագաւորութեանն զամս չորս, եւ մեռանէր բարի խոստովանութեամբ ի Քրիստոս Յիսուս եւ բարի յիշատակաւ գնաց առ հարս իւր. եւ սուգ մեծ լինէր աշխարհին՝ զրկեալ յայնպիսի թագաւորէն: Եւ մինչդեռ կենդանի էր Կոստանդին, սա զդուստր իւր զԿուրազոյնի կին ետ Ռոմանոսի մեծի իշխանին, վասն զի որդի ոչ գոյր նորա: Եւ Ռոմանոսն նստեալ յաթոռ թագաւորութեանն Հոռոմոց, եւ ամենայն երկիրն եկին նմա ի հնազանդութիւն:

Now in this year Basil's brother, Constantine, ruled over the entire land of the Byzantines. Constantine[29] was a good, pious man, merciful toward widows and captives, and lenient to all transgressors. For he released from fetters all those imprisoned, and he commanded that a prison which Basil had built should be burned down. Basil had filled this place with Byzantine princes. It was out of fear for his rule that [Basil] secretly had the Byzantine magnates strangled and their bodies, still clothed, were there hanging by the necks from iron hooks. Now when Constantine saw this, he wept and ordered that they should be buried, and he said that the prison should be burned down. He blamed his brother, saying: "When one faces death, why must it be such a cruel death to a life which [itself] is physical and transitory?" As for Constantine himself, he peacefully occupied the throne of the Byzantine kingdom, benevolently shepherding all believers in God. He occupied the throne of the realm for four years, dying with a good confession in Jesus Christ and, leaving behind a good memory, he went among his fathers. There was great mourning in the land, deprived as it was of such a king. Now while Constantine was still living he had given his daughter, Kurazoyn [Zoe] as a wife to the great prince Romanus, since they had no son. Then Romanus[30] sat on the throne of the Byzantines and the entire country came to him in submission.

---

29 *Constantine* VIII, 1025-1028.

30 *Romanus* III Argyrus, 1028-1034.

22. Իսկ ի թուականութեանս Հայոց յամի ՆՀԹ զօրաժողով արար թագաւորն Հոռոմոց Ռոմանոսն զամենայն զօրսն Յունաց աշխարհին եւ խաղայր հասանէր բազմութեամբ ի վերայ աշխարհին Տաճկաց եւ եկեալ բանակեալ ի վերայ ամուր բերդին, որ կոչի Ազազ, մերձ ի Հալպ քաղաք. եւ ժողովեցան զօրքն Տաճկաց անթիւ բազմութեամբ եւ եկին ի վերայ թագաւորին Ռոմանոսի։ Եւ թագաւորն զարհուրեալ լինէր եւ ոչ համարձակէր ելանել ի պատերազմ ընդ զօրսն Տաճկաց, վասն որոյ եւ զանգիտեալ երկեաւ, զի թուլամորթ էր եւ տկար եւ յոյժ չարաբարոյ եւ կարի հայհոյիչ ուղղափառ հաւատոյ. եւ յաղագս այսորիկ զօրքն ոչ էին ընդ նմա միաբան եւ խորհէին զի ի ժամ պատերազմին թողցեն զնա ի մէջ զօրացն Տաճկաց եւ ինքեանքն զերեսս դարձուցանիցեն ի պատերազմէն, զի սատակեսցի անօրէն թագաւորն։ Յայնժամ մի ոմն իշխան ի զօրաց իւրոց, որ կոչէր Ապուքապայն, որ յառաջն վրանապահ էր լեալ Դաւթի կիւրապաղատին Վրաց, սորա ազդ արարեալ թագաւորին զնենգութիւն զօրացն. եւ զայս լուեալ թագաւորն եւ երկեաւ յոյժ եւ յարուցեալ լինէր փախստական ի գիշերի հանդերձ մեծամեծօք իւրովք։ Եւ լուեալ զայս զօրքն Տաճկաց յարձակեցան զհետ զօրացն Հոռոմոց եւ արարին սաստիկ կոտորածս իբրեւ քան հազարաց. եւ ցրրուեցան զօրքն Հոռոմոց մի առ մի ընդ երեսս դաշտի։

22. In the year 479 of the Armenian Era [A.D. 1030] Romanus, emperor of the Romans, massed all the troops of the land of the Greeks and advanced with this multitude against the land of the Tachiks. [The Byzantines] came and encamped near the secure fortress called Azaz, close to the city of Aleppo. The troops of the Tachiks assembled in a countless multitude and came against Emperor Romanus. The emperor was terrified and did not dare to fight with the Tachiks. He was frightened since he was a coward, weak, and very malicious, and one who greatly cursed the Orthodox [i.e., Miaphysite] faith. For these reasons, the troops were not at one with him and planned to abandon him in the midst of the Tachik troops during battle, while they themselves would turn from the fight, and thereby the impious emperor would be killed. Now it happened that one of the princes of his troops, who was called Apuk'ap, and who previously had been the guard of the tent of Curopalate Dawit' of Georgia, notified the emperor about the treachery in his army. When the emperor heard about this, he was greatly frightened. Arising, he fled at night with his grandees. When the troops of the Tachiks learned of this, they went after the Byzantine troops, attacking them and causing severe destruction, killing some 20,000 men. Thus the Byzantine troops divided and scattered throughout the land.

Եւ զկնի չորեքտասան աւուր շինական մի ի քաղաքէն Կուրիսոյ գտանէր զթագաւորն Ռոմանոս անկեալ ի մէջ ծառոցն եւ կայր ընդարմացեալ իբրեւ զմեռեալ ի ցրտոյն. եւ թողեալ զգործս իւր տարաւ զնա ի տուն իւր եւ դարման-եալ զնա էած ի կենդանութիւն եւ ոչ գիտէր թէ ով ոք իցէ. եւ յետ աւուրց եհան արձակեաց զնա զհետ արանց: Եւ հասեալ ի Մարաշ քաղաք, ժողովեցան առ նա մնացեալ զօրքն եւ տարան զնա ի Կոստանդնուպօլիս: Իսկ զկնի աւուրց ինչ անցելոյ կոչեաց Ռոմանոս զայրն զայն եւ արար զնա տէր ամենայն գաւառացն Կուրիսոյ, մեծաւ պարգեւօք յուղարկեաց զնա ի տուն իւր մեծաւ գոհութեամբ:

Դարձեալ ի վերանալ Հայոց թուականութեանս ամին ՆՉ մեռանէր ամիրայն Ուրհայոյ քաղաքին, որում անուն աւէին Շէպլ: Յայնմ ժամանակին նստէր յՈւրհայ երկու ամիրայ, Շէպլն եւ Ուտայրն. եւ կայր ի քաղաքն Ուրհայոյ երեք կլայ, երկու կլայն եւ երկու բաժին քաղաքին՝ Շէպլա-յին էր, եւ մէկ կլայն եւ մէկ բաժին քաղաքին՝ Ուտայրին էր: Եւ երկոքեանն ունէին խորհուրդ զմիմեանս կորուսանել: Եւ յաւուր միում Ուտայրն զՇէպլն ի ճաշ հրաւիրեաց. եւ հան-եալ զնա արտաքոյ քաղաքին, որ կոչի Արճիճի վանք, ուր քարէ սիւն կայ հանդէպ կլային, եւ գրեալ էին երկոքեանն իւրաքանչիւր զօրս ի քմին գաղտ իւրոց սպանանել զՈւ-տայրն, հասին վաղվաղակի զօրքն Ուտայրայ եւ սպանին զՇէպլն: Եւ արար Ուտայր ժողով ի վերայ աւագ կլային Շէպլայ եւ կամեցաւ պատերազմաւ առնուլ զնա:

Fourteen days later, a certain *shinakan* from the city of Cyrrhus discovered Emperor Romanus fallen among some trees and numb from the cold, as though dead. [The peasant] left off his work and took him to his own home where he cured him and brought him back to life, not knowing who he was. After some days, [the peasant] released [Romanus] and sent him off accompanied by some men. [Romanus] reached the city of Marash where the remainder of his troops assembled by him and took him to Constantinople. After some days had passed, Romanus summoned that man [who had saved him] and made him lord of all the districts around Cyrrhus. Then [Romanus] sent him to his home with grand gifts and great thanks.

At the beginning of the year 480 of the Armenian Era [A.D. 1031], the emir of the city of Edessa, who was called Shabal, died. In that period two emirs sat in Edessa, Shabal and Utayr. The city of Edessa had three fortresses, of which two fortresses and two sections of the city belongs to Shabal, while one fortress and one section of the city were Utayr's. Each [man] had the intention of ruining the other. Now one day Utrayr invited Shabal to dinner, taking him outside the city to the monastery called Archich, where there stood a stone pillar, opposite the fortress. Unbeknownst to the other, each man had placed his troops in an ambuscade. Now when Shabal signaled his troops to kill Utayr, suddenly Utayr's troops arrived and killed Shabal. Then Utayr assembled [his troops] against Shabal's senior fortress and wanted to take it through fighting.

Եւ էր Սալման ոմն բերդապահ վերին կլայն. եւ նեղեաց զՍալմանն Ուտայր սաստիկ պատերազմաւ. եւ անճարեալ Սալմանն եւ առաքեաց առ Նուրտօլ, որ էր մեծ ամիրայն Տաճկաց, որ նստէր ի Մուփարղին, եւ տայր զկլայն Ուրհայոյ ի նա. եւ Նուրտօլ առաքեաց ի կլայն Ուրհայոյ զՊայէլ ռայիսն հազար ձիաւորով եւ տարաւ զՍալման առ ինքն կնաւն եւ որդւովքն, եւ արար իւր մեծ պարգեւք: Իսկ Ուտայր ինչ ոչ կարաց առնել, այլ նենգութեամբ միաբանեցաւ ընդ Պայէլ ռայիսն եւ գաղտ խորհէր սպանանել զնա. զոր իմացեալ Պայէլն եւ, մինչ էին ի գինարբուսն արտաքոյ քաղաքին, սպանանէր զամիրայն Ուտայր եւ տիրեաց ամենայն քաղաքին Ուրհայոյ: Յայնժամ կինն Ուտայրայ յորժամ տեսաւ՝ թէ սպանաւ Ուտայր, քաջապէս յարեաւ ի վերայ Պայէլին եւ կապեաց սեաւ նշանակ եւ մտաւ ճիչկան յամենայն ազգն Արապկաց եւ ասէր՝ թէ «Թուրք ազգին եկին առին զհայրենի քաղաքն Արապկաց, եւ սպանին զայրն իմ՝ զամիրայն Ուտայր»: Եւ այսու արար ժողովս բազումս, եւ յարուցեալ գայր ի վերայ Պայէլին. զոր իմացեալ Նուրտօլ՝ գայ բազում զօրօք ընդդէմ Արապկաց. եւ գնաց կինն Ուտայրայ ընդդէմ Նուրտօլայ եւ սաստիկ պատերազմաւ դարձուցանէր զնա ի փախուստ, եւ ինքն գայր իջանէր ի վերայ Պայէլ ռայիսին եւ արար ի վերայ կլային ահագին պատերազմ: Եւ անճարեալ Պայէլն, ելս իրացն ոչ գտանէր, յուղարկեալ առ Նուրտօլ եւ ծանուցանէր զվտանգն իւր եւ ասէր, թէ «Ի նեղութիւն կամ ես եւ ամենայն Քրթաստան»: Ապա անճարեալ Նուրտօլ առաքեաց զՍալման ի կլայն Ուրհայոյ եւ տարաւ զՊայէլն ի քաղաքն իւր ի Մուփարղին.

It happened that a certain Salman was fortress-keeper at the upper citadel, and Utayr put him into dire straits with fierce warfare. Having no other recourse, Salman sent to Nasir ad-Daulah, the great emir of the Tachiks, who resided in Mayyafariqin, and gave the citadel of Edessa to him.Nasir ad-Daula sent the commander Baye'l with a thousand cavalry and he brought to him Salman with his wife and children, giving him great gifts. As for Utayr, he was unable to accomplish anything. Rather, he treacherously united with Baye'l—though planning to kill him secretly. When Baye'l learned about this, when they were drinking outside the city, he killed the emir Utayr and ruled over the entire city of Edessa. Now when Utayr's wife saw that Utayr had been killed, she boldly arose against Baye'l, raised the black flag, and appealed to all the Arab peoples, saying: "The nation of Turks [or, Kurds] have come and taken a patrimonial city of the Arabs and have killed my husband, Emir Utayr." In this manner she assembled many men, arose and went against Baye'l. When Nasir ad-Daulah heard about this, he came against the Arabs with many troops. Utrayr's wife went against Nasir and, through fierce fighting, put him to flight. She herself came and descended against commander Baye'l, making frightful warfare against the citadel. Baye'l could find no way out of the situation, and so he sent to Nasir, familiarizing him with his danger and saying: "I and all Kurdistan are in dire straits." Nasir, also without options, sent Salman to the citadel of Edessa and took Baye'l to his city, Mup'arghin.

23. Եւ կինն Ուտայրի ոչ դադարէր զամենայն աւուրս պատերազմել ընդ Սալման: Յայնժամ ձանձրացեալ ի նըմանէ Սալմանն եւ առաքեաց ի Սամուսաթ առ Մանիակ իշխանն Հոռոմց, որ անուանեալ կոչէին Գէորգ. գրեաց առ նա Սալման եւ ասէր. «Եթէ առցես ի Հոռոմց թագաւորէն ինձ իշխանութիւն եւ զաւառս, ես տաց զՈւրհա ի ձեռս քո»: Զոր լուեալ Մանիկայ յոյժ ուրախ լինէր եւ խոստացաւ նմա մեծաւ երդմամբ, զի ի թագաւորէն Հոռոմց կատարեսցէ իւր զամենայն, զոր ինչ խնդրեաց եւ տալ նմա հայրենիս եւ իշխանութիւնս եւ որդւոց իւրոց: Եւ յայնժամ կոչեաց Սալման զՄանիակ եւ երետ զկլայն Ուրհայոյ ի նա: Եւ գայ Մանիակն չորս հարիւր արամբք եւ ի գիշերի գաղտ գայր ի դուռն կլային. եւ ազդ արարին Սալմանին զգալն Մանիկայ. եւ Սալման առեալ ի ձեռս իւր զբանալիս կլային եւ ելանէր առ Մանիակ՝ երկիրպագանէր նմա եւ տայր զկլայն ի նա, եւ ինքն ի նոյն գիշերի առեալ զկինն եւ զորդիսն իւր անցանէր ի Սամուսաթ: Եւ իբրեւ լուան զգալն Մանիակայ ազգն Տաճկաց՝ բազում եւ ահագին պատերազմ յարուցին ի վերայ Մանիակայ եւ ժողովեցան ի վերայ Ուրհայոյ անթիւ ժողովս, բախեցին ազգն Տաճկաց եւ ելան ի քաղաքէն:

23. Meanwhile, Utayr's wife did not stop daily warfare against Salman. Growing weary of her, Salman sent to Samosata, to the Byzantine prince Maniakes, who was called Ge'org. Salman wrote to him, saying: "I will give Edessa to you if you can obtain from the Byzantine emperor [in exchange] authority and a district." When Maniakes heard this he was overjoyed and promised [Nasir] with a great vow that everything he requested would be granted by the Byzantine emperor, and that a patrimony and authority would be given to him and to his sons. Then Salman summoned Maniakes and gave the citadel of Edessa to him. Maniakes arrived with four hundred men and at night secretly came to the door of the citadel and notified Salman to come forth to Maniakes. Salman took the keys to the citadel, arose and went to Maniakes, prostrated himself before him, and gave the citadel to him. That same night [Salman] took his wife and children and went to Samosata. When the Tachik people heard about Maniakes' arrival, they stirred up many difficult battles against him and assembled against Edessa countless hosts. The Tachiks struck at Edessa, and [the Tachiks inside the city] arose and departed.

Իսկ Ասորիքն ամրացան ի մեծ եկեղեցին ի սուրբն Սոփի. եւ զի վասն կանանցն իւրեանց եւ բազում ոսկւոյն եւ արծաթոյն ոչ համարձակեցան մտանել ի կլայն, զի մի՛ յափշտակեսցին ի նոցանէն, զի յետ սակաւ մի աւուրց հրով այրեցան բազումք ի նոցանէ եւ ամենայն ստացուածք իւրեանց. եւ մնացեալքն փախստական անկան ի կլայն առ Մանիակն եւ ապրեցան: Վասն զի պատերազմ մեծ յարուցին Տաճկունքն ի վերայ եկեղեցւոյն սրբոյն Սոփիայ, վասն զի ի հիւսիսական կողմանէն մեքենայ եդին եւ ուժգին հարկանէին զեկեղեցին, մինչ ի հիմանց խախտեալ եղեւ. եւ ապա հուր ձգեալ ի ներս, այրեցին զբազումս. եւ անթիւ ստացուածք եւ մթերք ամենայն բազմութեան քաղաքին այրեալ լինէր:

Եւ զկնի այսորիկ դղրդեցաւ ամենայն տունն Տաճկաց եւ գային ի վերայ Մանիկայ. եւ Մանիակ չորս հարիւր արամբք կայր ի հանդէս մեծ նահատակութեան ի կլայն Ուռհայոյ. եւ մեծամեծք ամիրայքն յիւրաքանչիւր քաղաքացն հասանէին ի քաղաքն Ուռհա, Եգիպտոս եւ ամենայն աշխարհքն Բաբելացւոց: Եւ ահա գայր Շէպլն ի Խառանայ, այն որ զխոցն էառ ի ծառայէն Մանիակայ ի յՈւզառ առնէն, որ թղթաւորի պատճառանօք յանկասկածս գնաց, իբրեւ մօտեցաւ, հարաւ ի վերայ ամիրային եւ ճկռովն հարկանէր զուսովն եւ ինքն որպէս զարծուի ի քաղաքէն խանդակն հասեալ անկանէր, իսկ ձին ի սաստիկ խոցուածոյն սատակեալ լինէր:

As for the Assyrians, they fortified themselves into the great church of Saint Sophia. Because of their women and the large amount of gold and silver, they did not dare enter the citadel, so they would not be ravished by them. But after a few days, many of them were burned in fire and all their possessions [were lost]. The survivors fled to Maniakes in the citadel and were saved. For the Tachiks offered a great battle against the church of St. Sophia. On the northern side they placed a [battering] machine and forcefully struck at the church until it collapsed on its foundation. Then they threw fire inside and burned many. Countless belongings and goods of the entire multitude of the city were burned.

And then the entire House of the Tachiks was roused and came against Maniakes. Maniakes was there in the citadel of Edessa, with 400 men, anticipating great martyrdom, while the grandee emirs from all their cities arrived at Edessa—Egypt and all the lands of the Babylonians. Even Shabal of Harran came, the man who had been wounded by Uzar', one of Maniakes' servants. [Uzar'] had been able to approach [Shabal] without suspicion as an emissary, but when he got close he threw himself on the emir, striking the man's shoulder with an axe. Then, with the speed of an eagle, he flew to the city's moat, but his horse perished from its many wounds. [Among the arriving Muslim combatants were:]

Գայր եւ Սալեհ ամիրայն ի Պլպայ,

եւ Մեմուտն ի Դէմշկայ,

Մահմէտն ի Հէմսայ,

Ազիզն ի Մսրայ,

Ալին ի Մընպիճայ,

Ապոլայն ի Բաղդատայ,

Խուրէշն ի Մօսլայ,

Նսրտօլն ի Մուփարղինայ,

Ալին ի յԱմթայ,

Պշարայն ի Ճըզիրայոյ,

Ահմատն ի Խլաթայ,

Ջուրայն ի Բաղիշոյ,

Հուսէնն ի Հերայ,

Կուտանն ի Սաղամաստայ,

Ահին ի յԱրզունէն,

Ահվարն ի Տիզբոնէ,

Ահլուն ի Պասսարայոյ, Վրէայնն ի Կերկեսերոյն,

Շահվարն ի Նսեպոյն եւ այլ եւս քառասուն ամիրայք.

24. Որ ժողովեցան ի վերայ կլային Ուրհայոյ եւ զամենայն ժամանակն ամառնային նեղէին զկլայն մեծաւ պատերազմաւ:

Saleh, emir of Aleppo;

Memut, from Damascus;

Me'hme't, from Hems;

Aziz, from Egypt;

Ali, from Manbij;

Abola, from Baghdad;

Xure'sh, from Mosul;

Nsrtol, from Mup'arghin;

Ali, from Amida;

Pshara, from Jazira;

Ahmat, from Xlat';

Zura, from Balish;

Huse'n, from Her;

Kutan, from Salmast;

Ahi, from Arzan;

Ahvar, from Ctesiphon;

Ahlu, from Basra; Vre'ayn, from Kerkeser;

Shahvar, from Nisibis; and forty other emirs.

24. They massed against Edessa and, for the entire summer, harassed the citadel with great warfare.

Եւ յետ բազում աւուրց կամեցան Տաճկունքն հրով այրել զամենայն քաղաքն եւ գնալ. զոր բնակիչք քաղաքին մեծաւ աղաչանօք եւ կաշառօք թափեցին յայրելոյ զքաղաքն եւ ասացին՝ եթէ Հոռոմք ի մէջ Տաճկացն ոչ կարեն պահել իւրեանց քաղաք, առ սակաւ մի ժամանակ թողուն եւ փախչին, եւ դառնայ ամենայն մարդ ի տուն իւր: Եւ հաճոյ թուեցաւ բանս այս ի լսելիս ամենայն մեծամեծացն Տաճկաց: Եւ յետ բազում նեղութեանցն եւ պատերազմացն գնացին ամենայն զօրքն Տաճկաց ի գաւառս իւրեանց. եւ Մանիակն կայր անդադար ի պատերազմն ի կլայն Ուրհայոյ. եւ գաւառացիքն ոչ դադարէին զտիւ եւ զգիշեր պատերազմել ընդ Մանիակն: Իսկ Մանիակն եւ ամենայն արքն որ ընդ Մանիակովն՝ կային ի մեծ նեղութեան, վասն զի հատաւ կերակուրն ի կլայէն, տնամուտ լեալ ի քաղաքն եւ գտանէին իւրեանց կերակուրս:

Յայնժամ առաքեաց թագաւորն եւ տարաւ զՍալմանն եւ զորդիսն իւր եւ արար զնոսա փառաւոր իշխանս եւ տայր նոցա գաւառս, եւ եղեն քրիստոնեայք. եւ ամ յամէ թագաւորն զօրս առաքէ յՈւրհա եւ շինեաց յիւր անուն բերդ եւ անուանեաց զնա Ռոմանապօլիս: Իսկ գաւառաց Արապիկքն յոյժ նեղութիւն արկանէին զզօրսն Հոռոմց ի Սամուսաթայ ճանապարհին մինչեւ ի յՈւրհա. եւ ամ յամէ անթիւ կոտորած լինէր քրիստոնէիցն, որ ոչ բաւէ բերան պատմել, զի որպէս զքարակոյտս երեւէին ոսկերք անկելոցն. եւ Մանիակն կայր ի մեծ վտանգի:

After many days, the Tachiks wanted to burn the entire city with fire, and depart. But the residents of the city—with great entreaties and bribes—prevented its burning, saying that the Byzantines would be unable to hold their city, in the midst of the Muslims and that, in a short time, they would leave it and flee, and all would return to their own homes. This seemed agreeable to all the Tachik grandees who heard it. Thus, after much harassment and warfare, all the troops of the Tachiks returned to their districts. And then Maniakes was involved in ceaseless warfare in Edessa's citadel, while the people of the district did not stop fighting against Maniakes, day and night. Maniakes and all the men with him were in dire straits, since food supplies to the citadel had been cut off, and they had to enter houses in the city [proper] to find their meals.

Then the emperor sent and took Salman and his sons and made them glorious princes, giving districts to them. And they became Christians. Every year the emperor sent troops to Edessa and he also built a fortress in his name, called Romanopolis. However, the districts of the Arabs greatly harassed the Byzantine troops traveling from Samosata to Edessa, and every year an innumerable, unrelatable number of Christians were killed, to the point that the bones of the fallen were heaped up in piles, like rocks. Maniakes was in great danger.

Եւ զկնի այսորիկ թագաւորն Ռոմանոս խորհեցաւ շալկով հաց արկանել ի քաղաքն: Եւ գային ի գիշերի վաթսուն հազար Հոռոմ կոնդորածք, անցան ընդ Եփրատ գետն եւ գային ի յՈւրհա. իսկ այլ չէն ոչ գոյր ի գաւառն Ուրհայոյ, բայց միայն Լտարն. յորժամ հասին ի Պարսուր, հարաւ Շիպիպն ի վերայ նոցա եւ մինչեւ ի Դեսնաձորն կոտորեաց զվաթսուն հազար կոնդորատսն. եւ այսպիսի նեղութեամբ կայր Ուրհա, մինչեւ զօրացաւ քաղաքն եւ յաղթահարեաց զթշնամիսն. եւ արար ընդ նոսա սէր, եւ եղեւ խաղաղութիւն ի վերայ Ուրհայոյ, եւ դադարեալ եղեւ հալածանք քրիստոնէից: Այս ամենայն եղեւ ի թագաւորութեան Աշոտոյ Բագրատունւոյ եւ ի հայրապետութեանն Տէր Պետրոսի Հայոց կաթողիկոսի: Եւ յաւուրս Տուղրիլ Սուլթանին Պարսից տէրութեանն առաւ ի Տաճկաց քաղաքն Ուրհա: Իսկ յետ այս ամենայն անցիցս եւ նեղութեանցս եւ չարչարանացս, զոր կրեաց քաջն Մանիակ, փոխեաց զնա Ռոմանոս եւ տայ զՈւրհա Ապուքապայ վրանպահուն Դաւթի Կուրապաղատին:

25. Իսկ ի փոխել թուականութեանս Հայոց տումարի յամս ՆՁԱ եղեւ սով սաստիկ ընդ ամենայն երկիր, եւ բազումք ի մարդկանէ մեռանէին յերեսաց սովոյն, եւ բազումք վաճառէին զկանայս եւ զորդիս իւրեանց յաղագս կարօտութեանց հացի. եւ ի բարկութենէ նեղութեանցս ընդ խօսելն ելանէր հոգին ի մարդոյն: Եւ այսպիսի օրինակաւ մաշեցաւ երկիր ի սովոյն: Դարձեալ ի թուականութեանս մերում յամս ՆՁԴ մեռաւ Ռամանոս թագաւորն դաւով նենգութեամբ ի թագուհւոյն իւրմէ: Քանզի դեղ մահու արբուցանէր անօրէնն թագաւորին եւ լուծանէր ի կենաց. եւ նստեալ լինէր յաթոռ թագաւորութեան Յունաց Միխայէլն հրամանաւ թագուհւոյն իւրոյ՝ դստերն Կոստանդեայ:

Following this, Emperor Romanus decided to send bread to the city, on the backs of men. At night, 60,000 Byzantine provision-bearers crossed the Euphrates River and approached Edessa. There was no other habitation in the district of Edessa, besides Ltar. When [the Byzantines] reached Parsur, Shipip fell upon them and killed the 60,000 provision-bearers as far as Desnadzor. Edessa was in such straits until the city strengthened, conquered the enemies, and the emperor established friendship with them. Then the persecutions against Christians stopped. All this occurred during the reign of Ashot[31] Bagratuni and in the patriarchate of Lord Petros[32] Catholicos of the Armenians. Now in the days of Tughril, sultan of the Persian kingdom, the city of Edessa was taken by the Tachiks. After all these events, harassments, and torments which brave Maniakes bore, Romanus replaced him and gave [the rule of] Edessa to Apuk'ap, the tent-guard of Dawit' the curopalate.

25. At the beginning of 481 of the Armenian Era [A.D. 1032-1033] there was a severe famine throughout the entire country and many people starved to death. Many sold their women and children because of the need for bread. Because of the severity of these deprivations, people would give up the ghost, just [from the effort of] speaking. Thus was the country worn out from famine. Again, in the year 484 of our dating [A.D. 1035], Emperor Romanus died through a treacherous plot of his queen. This impious woman had the emperor drink poison and he died. Then Michael[33] sat on the throne of the Byzantine realm, by order of his queen,[34] who was the daughter of Constantine.[35]

31 *Ashot* IV Bagratuni, 1021-1039.

32 *Petros* I Getadardz, 1019-1058.

33 *Michael* IV, the Paphlagonian, 1034-1041.

34 *Queen:* Zoe.

35 *Constantine* VIII, 1025-1028.

Յայսմ ժամանակի մեռանէր արքայն Դաւիթ՝ որդին Սենեքարիմայ արքային Հայոց, եւ տայ զիշխանութիւնն հայրենեաց իւրոց ի յեղբայրն իւր յԱտոմ, որ էր Ատոմս լցեալ առաքինութեամբ եւ արդարութեամբ եւ սուրբ վարուք ի Քրիստոս Յիսուս, լցեալ հեզութեամբ եւ քաղցրութեամբ, ողորմած ի վերայ տառապելոց, դարմանիչ աղքատաց եւ յոյժ սիրելի կրօնաւորական դասուն, եւ շինող եկեղեցւոյ եւ բազմացուցիչ վանորէից:

Արդ ի յամս եւ ի թուականութեանս Հայոց ՆԶԴ խաղացեալ բազում զօրօք Տաճկաց եւ գային ի վերայ Ուռհայոյ. եւ անցան յայնկոյս մեծ գետոյն Եփրատայ, սրով եւ գերութեամբ աւար հարկանէին զամենայն երկիր. եւ բազում քրիստոնեայք վարեցան ի գերութիւն յաշխարհն Տաճկաց. կոտորեցին զԱլարն եւ զՍեւերակ եւ զամենայն աղբերակունսն եւ զջրագնացս նորա լցին արեամբ. եւ յայնքան սաստիկ կոտորածէն հոսեալ լինէր երկիրն յարենէ քրիստոնէիցն: Յայսմ ամի ժողովեցան զօրքն Հոռոմց եւ գային ի վերայ Տաճկաց. եւ էր զօրավար եղբայր Միխայլին՝ թագաւորին Յունաց. եւ հեծելոց բազմութեամբն հասանէր մինչեւ ի քաղաքն Մելտենի. եւ զարհուրեալ եղեւ եւ ոչ ելանէր ընդ զօրսն Տաճկաց ի պատերազմ: Եւ լուեալ զայս զօրացն Տաճկաց դարձան յաշխարհն իւրեանց: Այսպէս աւարին եւ զօրքն Հոռոմց եւ ոչ իշխեաց մտանել յաշխարհ Տաճկաց, այլ դարձան խաղաղութեամբ մտանել յաշխարհն իւրեանց, եւ ի դառնալն առաւել աւար արկանէին քրիստոնէից քան զզօրսն Տաճկաց:

In this period there died King Dawit', son of Senek'erim, king of the Armenians. He gave his patrimonial principality to his brother, Atom. Atom was full of virtue and righteousness and saintly conduct in Jesus Christ. He was also full of mildness and sweetness, merciful to the afflicted, a healer of the poor, beloved of clerics, a builder of churches and someone who increased the monasteries.

Now in 484 of the Armenian Era [A.D. 1035], the Tachiks advanced with many troops, coming against Edessa. They crossed to the other side of the great Euphrates River, subjecting the entire country to slave-taking and the sword. Many Christians were led into captivity to the land of the Tachiks. They destroyed Alar and Sewerak and filled all their fountains and irrigation channels with blood. The destruction was so severe that the country flowed with the blood of Christians. In this year the forces of the Byzantines assembled and came against the Tachiks. Their general was the brother of Michael, emperor of the Byzantines. With a multitude of cavalry he reached the city of Melitene. However, he became terrified and would not go forth in battle against the Tachik troops. When the Tachik troops heard about this, they returned to their own land. The Byzantine troops did likewise: they did not dare to enter the land of the Tachiks; rather, they returned in peace to their own land. During that return, they looted the Christians' [wealth] more than the troops of the Tachiks had done.

Յայսմ տումարիս եւ ի թուականութեանս Հայոց ՆՁԵ խաւարեցաւ արեգակն ահաւոր եւ սոսկալի տեսլեամբ: Վասն զի՝ զոր օրինակ եղեւ խաւարեալ ի խաչելութեանն Քրիստոսի, նոյն օրինակաւ ծածկեաց զլոյսն իւր եւ խաւար զգեցաւ. եւ լուսաւորքն աշխարհիս ի մութն եւ սեաւ դարձան, եւ ամենայն երկինք իբրեւ զկամար կամար կապեցաւ խաւարաւն. եւ եղեւ սեւացեալ արեգակն ի միջօրէի, եւ ամենայն աստեղքն առ հասարակ երեւէին որպէս ի մէջ գիշերի: Եւ սաստկացաւ խաւարն եւ մութն, եւ գոչեաց առ հասարակ ամենայն արարածք, եւ հնչեցին ամենայն լերինք եւ բլուրք, եւ դողաց սասանելով լերինք եւ ամենայն ապառաժք, եւ երերալով ծփայր համատարած մեծ ծովն Ովկիանոս եւ սուգ առեալ լայր զամենայն որդիս մարդկան: Եւ եղեւ ի տեսանել զայս ամենայն որդւոց մարդկան, ահաբեկեալ լինէին յերկիւղէն որպէս մեռեալ: Յայնժամ լայր որդի առ հայր իւր եւ լայր հայր ի վերայ որդւոց. տըղայք զարհուրեալք ի յահէն անկանէին ի գիրկս ծնողացն. մարքն աղետեալ սաստիկ վառմամբ իբրեւ հրով՝ լային զտղայս իւրեանց: Եւ այսպէս ահաբեկեալ կային ամենայն արարածք եւ յերկիւղէն պաշարեալ կային եւ ելս իրացն ոչ գտանէին, ընդ սոսկալի նշանն զարհուրեալ հիանային եւ ահաբեկեալ կային առ հասարակ:

In 485 of the Armenian Era [A.D. 1036-1037] the sun darkened, presenting an awesome, terrifying vision. For just as it had grown dark at Christ's crucifixion, similarly, the sun's light was hidden and it was covered in darkness. The [celestial] luminaries turned the land dark and black, and the whole arc of the heavens went black. The sun was black at midday, while all the stars appeared as though in the middle of night. The gloom and darkness increased and all creatures cried out, with all the mountains and hills resounding. The mountains and all the rocks trembled, while the great Ocean sea [the Mediterranean], billowed as it moved back and forth. All the children of man wept and mourned at this spectacle, and were seized with terror. Then did the son weep for his father, and the father, for his son. Terrified children fell into their parents' embrace. Mothers, consumed with dread as though by fire, wept over their children. Thus all creation was terrified and beset by fear and could find no way out. Horrified by this dreadful omen, everyone was amazed and frightened.

Յայնժամ Տէր Պետրոս հայրապետն Հայոց եւ թագաւորն Յովհաննէս յուղարկեալ արք փառաւորք առ սուրբ հայրապետն Հայոց Յովհաննէս, որ կոչէին Կոզեռն, զի ի նմանէ գիտասցեն զմեկնութիւն մեծ նշանին. զի էր այր սուրբ եւ սքանչելի ճգնութեամբ զարդարեալ, եւ մեկնիչ հին եւ նոր Կտակարանացն Աստուծոյ, լցեալ վարդապետական շնորհօք: Իսկ որք առաքեցան առ վարդապետն Հայոց, Գրիգոր Մագիստրոսն որդին Վասակայ եւ հայկազնին մեծն Սարգիս եւ այլք ոմանք յազատաց տանն Հայոց եւ այլք ի քահանայիցն, զի զերկրորդելն ահաւոր նշանին գիտասցեն:

26. Եւ եղեւ իբրեւ գնացին առ վարդապետն Հայոց, գտանէին զնա՝ զի դարձեալ կայր ի գետինն երեսք ի վայր ի խոր տրտմութեան, եւ թացեալ լինէր արտասուօք զգետինն. եւ ի սաստկութենէ լալոյն եւ ի դառն հառաչանաց, որ ելանէր ի բերանոյ նորին, ոչ ոք իշխէր ինչ հարցանել զնա. վասն զի տեսանէին զնա ի խորին սուգս եւ յահագին տրտմութիւնս, եւ անդադար հեղոյր զարտասուսն եւ կոծէր զկուրծսն իւր: Եւ յայնժամ նստան իշխանքն Հայոց մերձ առ վարդապետն Յովհաննէս եւ զվեց ժամու աւուրն ոչինչ համարձակեցան խօսել եւ հարցանել վասն ահաւոր նշանին, եւ լային առհասարակ ամենայն եկեալքն առ նա:

Then Lord Petros, patriarch of the Armenians, and King Yovhanne's sent some eminent men to the blessed vardapet of the Armenians, Yovhanne's who was called Kozer'n, so that they might receive from him an explanation of the great sign. For [Kozer'n] was a holy man, adorned with marvelous asceticism, an interpreter of God's Old and New Testaments, filled with vardapetal graces. Those who were sent to this vardapet of the Armenians—Grigor Magistros, son of Vasak, the great Sargis Hayzkazn and others from the azats of the House of the Armenians and others from the clergy—were sent to learn about this dreadful second occurrence.

26. And it happened that when they went to the vardapet of the Armenians they found him, again, on the floor on his face in deep sorrow, and the floor was wet with his tears. No words issued from his mouth due to the severity of his tears and his bitter sighs. [The visitors] did not dare to ask him anything because they could see the depth of his sorrow and frightful grief. [Kozer'n] was ceaselessly crying and beating his breast. Then the Armenian princes sat down near the vardapet Yovhanne's and until the sixth hour of the day they did not dare to speak or ask [him] anything about the dreadful sign. Rather, all those who had arrived wept with him.

Յայնժամ իբրեւ ետես վարդապետն Հայոց զողբումն ամենայն եկելոցն, բացեալ զբերանն իւր՝ սկսաւ խօսել հառաչանօք եւ բազում արտասուօք եւ սկսաւ լալ զամենայն ազգս հաւատացելոց. լայր եւ զկարգ քահանայական եւ զեղծումն սրբութեան սրբոյ խորհրդոյն, լայր եւ զեկեղեցի Աստուծոյ եւ զքակտումն պատուիրանին որ ի նմա ծածկեալ կան աստուածեղէնքն: Եւ սկսաւ այսպէս ասել ցիշխանսն Հայոց.

«Ով փառաւոր որդիք իմ, լուարուք զբանս զայս ի վիբաւոր եւ ի վշտագնեալ Յովհաննիսէ. զի ահա այսօր լցան հազար ամ չարչարանաց Քրիստոսի խաչելութեանն եւ արձակմանն Բելիարայ, զոր կապեալ էր զնա Փրկիչն ի Յորդանան գետ, զոր յառաջին նշանէն ցուցաւ մեզ յառաջ քան չորեքտասան ամն զոր ասացաք, եւ յայնժամ դարձեալ երկրորդեաց, զի նախ երկինք պատառեցաւ եւ երկիրս մթացաւ: Եւ ահա յայսմ ամի լուսաւորքդ խաւարեցան եւ ամենայն արարած, վասն զի յայսմ հետէ ամենայն ազգք հաւատացելոց Քրիստոսի ի խաւար շրջելոց են. զի այսուհետեւ խաւարին կարգք եկեղեցւոյ Քրիստոսի յամենայն ազգաց հաւատացելոց, թուլանան ի պահոց եւ յաղօթից, պակասին յոյս հանդերձելոց, երկիւղ դատաստանին Աստուծոյ արհամարհի, բառնայ ճշմարիտ հաւատք յամենայն ազգաց, տկարանայ աստուածպաշտութիւն ատեն զպատուիրանն Աստուծոյ, դիմադարձ լինին բանից սուրբ Աւետարանին Քրիստոսի.

Then, when the vardapet of the Armenians discerned the lamentation of all the visitors, he opened his mouth and commenced speaking with sighs and many tears, and began weeping for all the nations of believers. He wept too for the orders of clerics, for the corruption of the sanctity of the holy sacrament. [He wept also] for the Church of God and for the dissolution of the divine precepts which had been preserved by the Church. Then he began to speak to the Armenian princes as follows:

"O, my glorious sons, listen to these words of the wounded and grieving Yovhanne's. For behold, today completes the thousand years from the [time of the] torments of the crucifixion of Christ, and the freeing of Belial, whom the Savior had bound in the Jordan River. This is what was revealed to us forty years ago by that first omen, as we said then. Now, again, it has reoccurred as first the heavens were torn apart and the world darkened. Behold, in this year the luminaries became dark as did all creation, and henceforth all the nations of believers in Christ will go about in darkness. Hereafter the blessed orders of the Church of Christ will be darkened among all the nations of believers. They will grow lazy about fasting and prayers, belief in a future life will be reduced, fear of God's judgment will be scorned, and true faith will disappear from all the nations. Piety will grow weak. [People] will loathe the precepts of God and turn away from the words of the blessed Gospel of Christ.

«Ամենայն ոք հակառակ գտանին սրբոց պատուիրանաց Աստուծոյ, արհամարհեն զբանս սուրբ վարդապետացն, անգոսնեն եւ զհրամանս կանոնաց սրբոց հայրապետացն, եւ այնու բազումք անկանին ի բարձրութենէ հաւատոց եւ ատեն զդրունս սուրբ եկեղեցւոյ, եւ ի ծուլութենէ պահոց եւ յաղօթից՝ կուրանան յաստուածպաշտութեանցն. բազումք մտանեն ընդ լծով անիծից, վասն զի ոչ հաւանին խրատու աստուածեղէն բանիցն սուրբ առաջնորդացն: Որդիք անիծանին ի ծնողաց իւրեանց առ ի յոչ հնազանդութենէ զաւակաց, ծնողքն չարչարին ի ծննդոց իւրեանց. ցամաքեցաւ գութ սիրոյ բարեկամաց ի հարց եւ ի զաւակաց:

«Եւ ահա յայսմ հետէ բազում հերձուածք մտանեն յեկեղեցի Աստուծոյ ի ծուլութենէ հայրապետացն, վասն զի թուլամորթին եւ տկարանան եւ հաւատոյ քննութիւն ոչ առնեն եւ կան յիմարեալք: Յաղագս արծաթոյն թողուն ի բաց զհաւատն, եւ պակասին օրհներգութիւնք ի տանէն Աստուծոյ. երկիւղն եւ ահ սոսկալի դատաստանին Աստուծոյ յաւուրն ահաւորի որ լինելոցն է՝ փարատեալ խափանին յամենայն մտաց. Մոռանան զհատուցումն արդարոցն եւ մեղաւորացն, վասն զի մեղսասէրք եւ ցանկացողք լինելոց են չար ճանապարհին. փափաքանօք երթան ի մեղաց ժողովարանն, զի ահա ի թագաւորաց եւ յիշխանաց եւ յառաջնորդաց ապականելոց է երկիր:

"Everyone will be found in opposition to the holy commandments of God. They will scorn the words of the blessed vardapets and will ignore the canons of the blessed patriarchs, and thereby many will fall from the heights of faith and loathe the doors of the blessed Church. Through laziness [in keeping] the fasts and prayer they will become blind to the worship of God. Many will fall under the yoke of curses, since they do not heed the advice of the divine words of the holy leaders. Sons will be cursed by their parents for lack of submission, and parents will be tormented by their children. The mercy of loving friendship between fathers and sons will dry up.

"Behold, hereafter many heretics will enter the Church of God from the laziness of the patriarchs, because they grow feeble and weak and will not examine the faith. They will become as fools. They will abandon the faith for love of silver, and prayers will diminish from the House of God. The fear and dread of the terrible judgment of God on that fearful [Day of Judgment] which is to come will vanish and be blocked out of every mind. They will forget the recompense of the righteous and the sinners, because they will become lovers of sin and desirous of the path of evil. With longing, they will go to the assembly houses of sin, for the country will be polluted by kings, princes, and prelates.

27. «Առաջնորդքն եւ իշխանքն լինելոց են կաշառասէրք եւ ստախօսք եւ սուտերդմունք եւ ի ձեռս կաշառացն թիւրեն զդատաստանս իրաւանցն աղքատին, եւ յաղագս այսորիկ առաւել բարկանայ Աստուած ի վերայ նոցա, զի զառաջնորդութիւնն եւ զիշխանութիւնն ընդ երեսաց վարեն եւ ոչ ըստ Աստուծոյ. եւ տիրեալ իշխանաբար ի վերայ վիճակին եւ ոչ ահիւն Աստուծոյ հովուել եւ ուսուցանել, որպէս պատուիրեաց սուրբ առաքեալն Պօղոս: Իշխանք եւ դատաւորք պոռնկասէրք առաւել քան աստուածասէրք եւ ատեցողք լինին սուրբ ամուսնութեան եւ փակին ընդ պոռնկութեան ախտին եւ սիրեն զկորուստ նմանեաց իւրեանց. մեծարեն զմատնիչսն եւ զգողսն, յափշտակեն անիրաւաբար զաշխատողաց զինչսն, անողորմ ի վերայ ուղղել դատաստանացն:

«Որդեակք իմ, ահա յայսմ հետէ ի հակառակութենէ առաջնորդաց փակելոց են դրունք սուրբ եկեղեցւոյ եւ վերանան սրբութեան կարգք յամենայն ազգէ. եւ յաղագս արծաթսիրութեան տան ձեռնադրութիւն բազում անարժանից եւ զամենայն պղծեալսն ածեն ի կարգ քահանայութեան. եւ յայնժամ պատարագի Քրիստոս ի ձեռն անարժան քահանայիցն եւ բազումք անարժանութեամբ հաղորդին ի նմանէ, ոչ եթէ ի փրկութիւն՝ այլ ի դատապարտութիւն եւ ի կորուստ հոգւոյն: Եւ ուր ուրեք կայ ճշմարիտ պատարագող Քրիստոսի սուրբ Խորհրդոյն յաղագս ազգիս, որ ի ձեռն նոցա ողորմի Աստուած աշխարհի:

27. "Prelates and princes will become lovers of bribes, liars, and oath-breakers. Through bribes they will pervert their judgments of the rights due to the poor. Therefore, God will become even angrier at them as they conduct their prelacies and principalities willfully and not according to God. They rule like princes over their dioceses, not shepherding and teaching through fear of God, as the blessed apostle Paul commanded. Princes and judges will love prostitutes more than God and will become haters of holy matrimony. They will closet themselves with the disease of prostitution and will enjoy the ruination of people like themselves. They will honor traitors and thieves and unjustly ravish the belongings of workers and be merciless when making judgment.

"My sons, henceforth, because of conflicts among prelates, the church doors will be closed while the ranks of holiness will disappear from all nations. Through the love of silver they will ordain many unworthy people and all manner of abominable [folk] will be brought into the ranks of the priesthood. Then the divine liturgy of Christ will be conducted by unworthy priests and many will take communion from them unworthily—not for the salvation of their souls but with the result of damnation and loss of them. In some places, among diverse peoples, there still will be found true celebrants of the holy Mystery of Christ and, through them, God will have mercy on the land.

«Որդեակք, զուրբսն եւ զառաքինիսն վիրաւորեն եւ զանարատն դարձուցանեն ի քահանայութենէ առ ի չունելոյ արծաթ, ոչ տան զձեռնադրութիւն: Եւ որպէս ասացաք՝ յառաջ քան զչորեքտասան ամն ի լինելոյ միաւումն նշանին, եթէ պակասին բազումք ի հաւատոց աստուածպաշտութեանց, վասն զի բազումք ի քահանայից եւ ի կրօնաւորաց թուլամորթին ի կրօնից իւրեանց. լինելոց են ցանկասէրք, ախտից փափագողք, որոճալով որոճեն զերգս դիւական. կրօնաւորքն փախչին յանապատէն եւ ատեն զուրբ երամս ճգնաւորացն եւ զվարս առաջին կրօնաւորացն ատեալ անարգեն. լինիցին խանգարիչք կարգաց եւ կրօնից, փախչին ի ձայնէ սաղմոսերգութեանցն Աստուծոյ:

«Այս ամենայն լինելոց է, որդեակք իմ. յազգս այս յըղփանան առաջնորդք աշխարհի արծաթսիրութեամբ եւ զամենայն անկեալս եւ զորոշեալս ի շնորհաց Որդւոյն Աստուծոյ յառաջ կոչեն եւ ածեն զնոսա ի կարգս քահանայական եւ զամենայն մերժեալսն գլուխ եւ առաջնորդ կացուցանեն ի վերայ ժողովրդեանն Աստուծոյ. եւ ոչ գիտեն զինչ գործեն, վասն զի կուրանան ի սաստկութենէ արծաթսիրութեանն: Եւ առաւել ունիմ ասել զայս. զի ահա յայսմհետէ մեծաւ խոցմամբ վիրաւորելոց է Քրիստոս յանարժան քահանայիցն, քան զխաչիլն եւ զչարչարիլն ի Հրէից. զի պական ի նոցանէ վճարելոց է ի սոցանէ, եւ լսելոց է՝ եթէ «Ընկեր, վասն որո՞յ մտեր յայս հարսանիսս»: Յայնժամ կապեալ ոտիւք եւ կապեալ ձեռօք հանեն զնա ի խաւարն արտաքին եւ զոր ժողովեացն՝ կուտի կորստեամբ ի վերայ նորա: Որդեակք իմ, ահա այս ամենայն լինելոց է ի յետին ժամանակս. զի արձակեցաւ սատանայ ի հազար ամէ կապանացն, զոր կապեաց Քրիստոս խաչիւն իւրով.

"My sons, the saintly and virtuous will be wounded and the pure will be turned away from the priesthood, for lack of silver and [the unjust clerics] will not ordain them. As we said 14 years ago when the other sign appeared, many will fall from their faith in divine worship because many priests and clerics will grow slack in their worship. They will become lecherous, people who desire disease, and people who delight in diabolical songs. Clerics will flee from the desert [retreats], loathe the blessed flock of ascetics and, hating the conduct of the first clerics, will disrespect their ways. They will become obstructers of the orders and of religion. They will flee from the sound of the singing of psalms to God.

"All this will come to pass, my sons, because the spiritual leaders of the land will be filled with the love of silver. They will promote all those fallen and separated from the grace of the Son of God, and will bring them into the priestly order. All the rejected ones they will establish as heads and prelates over the people of God. Nor will they know what it is they are doing, since they will be blinded by the strength of [their] love of silver. Furthermore, let me say this: behold, Christ will be pierced by a great wound by the unworthy priests even more so than by His crucifixion and suffering at the hands of the Jews. What [the Jews] omitted will be supplied by these [unworthy priests]. And one will hear: 'Friend, why have you come to this wedding?' Then binding [that person] hand and foot, they will remove him to the outer darkness, and that which he gathered will be heaped up on him for his destruction. My sons, behold, all this will come to pass in the latter times. For Satan has been released from [his] thousand years' bondage, [he] whom Christ bound with His Cross.

«Եւ երերեսցին ճշմարիտ հաւատացեալքն Քրիստոսի՝ կալով ընդդէմ նորա ի պատերազմն, զի ունի պատերազմել ընդ սուրբսն, որք պատուիրանաւն Աստուծոյ պահպանեալ կան ի կարգս ճշմարիտ խոստովանութեան Քրիստոսի Աստուծոյ մերոյ, որք կան յազգս ազգս: Այսուհետեւ լինին յարձակմունք այլազգեաց՝ պիղծ զօրքն Թուրքաց անիծեալ որդւոցն Քամայ ի վերայ ազգաց քրիստոնէից, եւ ի սուր սուսերի մաշի ամենայն երկիր. սովով եւ գերութեամբ անցանէ ամենայն ազգ հաւատացելոցն Քրիստոսի. յանմարդ դառնան բազում գաւառք, բառնալոց է զօրութիւնք սրբոց յերկրէ, քակտին բազում եկեղեցիք ի հիմանց, խափանեսցի խորհուրդ խաչին Քրիստոսի. ի բազմանալ անօրէնութեանցն խափանին տօնախմբութիւնք սրբոցն: Գրգռին որդիք ընդ հարցն, ատեցողք լինին հարք առ որդիս, յարիցեն եղբարք ի վերայ միմեանց, սպանութեամբ եւ արեան հեղութեամբ ջանան կորուսանել զիրեարս, ուրանան զգութ եւ զսէր եղբայրութեանն, ցամաքեսցի արիւն եղբայրութեան նոցա, եւ այսպիսի գործովք հաւասարակից լինին անօրինացն. եւ յազգաց անօրինաց ծփի երկիր, եւ ցօղ արեան զգենուն բոյսք անդաստանաց, եւ զամս վաթսուն սրով եւ գերութեամբ աւերելոց է երկիր:

"Nonetheless, true believers in Christ will appear to battle against him [Satan] since [Satan] must war against saints who are preserved by the commandments of God and stand in the ranks of the true confession of Christ our God and who exist in different nations. Hereafter there will occur invasions of foreigners—the loathsome troops of the accursed Turks, sons of Ham—[who will come] against the Christian nations and put all countries to the sword. With sword and slave-taking they will pass through all nations believing in Christ. They will depopulate many districts. The might of the saints will be removed from the country. They will demolish to the foundations many churches. The mystery of Christ's Cross will be suppressed. In extending their impious [religion], they will suppress celebrations of the feast-days of the saints. They will incite son against father; fathers will hate their own sons; brothers will rise up against each other; and, with killing and shedding of blood, they will try to destroy one another. They will forget kindness and brotherly love, and the blood of their brotherhood will dry up. Through such deeds they will become equal to the impious [invaders]. They ground itself will become harmed by the nations of invaders, as a dew of blood will clothe the plants and for 60 years the earth will be desolated through the sword and captive-taking.

28. «Եւ յայնժամ ելցեն ազգն արիականք, որք են Փռանգ, եւ բազմութեամբ զօրօք առցեն զսուրբ քաղաքն Երուսաղէմ, եւ ազատի ի գերութենէն սուրբ գերեզմանն Աստուածընկալ: Եւ զկնի այսորիկ զամս յիսուն տագնապի երկիր ի զօրացն Պարսկաց սրով եւ գերութեամբ, եւ եւթնապատիկ առաւել քան զորս յառաջ կրեցին հաւատացեալք, եւ ահաբեկին ամենայն ազգք հաւատացելոց Քրիստոսի. եւ ի բազմութենէ նեղութեանցն յուսահատին զօրք Հռովմայեցւոց, բազում անցումն եւ կոտորած կրեն ի յազգէն Պարսից. եւ ընտիր ընտիրս ի քաջ զօրականացն խողխողեն սրով եւ գերութեամբ, մինչեւ ի փրկութենէ յուսահատին զօրքն Հռովմայեցւոց: Եւ զկնի ամացն սկիզբն առնուն ի զօրանալ առ սակաւ սակաւ եւ ուր ուրեք լինի մնացեալ յառաջին գնդէն. եւ ամ յամէ յառաջ գան եւ հաստատին իբրեւ տեղապահ զոլով աշխարհաց եւ գաւառաց:

«Յայնժամ որպէս ի քնոյ զարթուցեալ լինի թագաւորն Հռովմէացւոց եւ հասանէ որպէս զարծիւ ի վերայ զօրացն Պարսից ահագին բազմութեամբ՝ որպէս զաւազ առ եզր ծովու. ելցէ որպէս զհուր բորբոքեալ, եւ յաղէ նորա դողան ամենայն արարածք, եւ Պարսիկք եւ ամենայն յայնկոյս մեծ գետոյն Ջահունեաց: Եւ յայնժամ թագաւորն Հռոմայեցւոց տիրելով տիրէ ամենայն աշխարհի զամս բազումս. եւ նորոգումն առնու ամենայն երկիր եւ շինութեան հիմն արկանէ եւ այնպէս նորանայ որպէս զկնի ջրհեղեղին. բազմանան ծնունդք մարդկան եւ անասնոց, բղխեսցեն աղբեւրք զգնացս ջրոց: Պտղաբերին անդաստանք առաւել քան զառաջինն.

28. "Then a nation of braves will arise, who are the Franks. With a multitude of troops they will take the blessed city of Jerusalem and free from captivity the holy Sepulcher which held God. After this the country will be in crisis for 50 years, from the sword of the Persian troops and captive-taking, while believers will suffer seven times more than before. All the nations of believers in Christ will be terrified. From the multitude of tribulations, the troops of the Byzantines will despair and will suffer much death and destruction from the Persian nation. The most select and choice fighters will be pierced with the sword and led into captivity, until the Byzantine forces despair of salvation. After 50 years they will gradually strengthen and remnants of former troops all over will advance and establish themselves as rulers of lands and districts.

"Then, as though awakening from sleep, the emperor of the Byzantines will advance like an eagle against the Persian forces with a frightening multitude [as numerous] as sand on the seashore. He will arise like a blazing fire and, from fear of him, all creatures will tremble, while the Persians and all troops of the foreigners will flee to the other side of the great Jahun River. Then the emperor of the Byzantines will rule over all lands for many years. The entire country will be renewed and a foundation for building will be laid. Things will be renewed just like after the Flood. Births will increase among humankind and animals. Fountains will gush forth water. Fields will yield more than before.

«Եւ այնուհետեւ անկանի սով ի յաշխարհն Պարսից զբազում ամս, մինչեւ յարձակեալ զմիմեանս ուտիցեն. եւ յահէ զօրութեան թագաւորին Հոռվմայեցւոց բազում իշխանք Պարսից ելցեն ի քաղաքաց եւ ի գաւառաց իւրեանց եւ առանց պատերազմի զփախուստ արասցեն յայնկոյս Ջահուն գետոյ, եւ զամենայն ժողովս մթերից իւրեանց զամաց բազմաց՝ զոսկւոյ եւ զարծաթոյ եւ զամենայն բազմութիւն գանձուցն որպէս զհող կամ զքարակոյտս անչափ համարով առցեն յաշխարհէն Պարսից եւ բարձեալ տարցեն յաշխարհն Հոռվմայեցւոց. եւ զամենայն մանկունս եւ զաղջկունս եւ զկանայս տարցեն ի գերութիւն յաշխարհն Հոռվմայեցւոց. աւերակս եւ անմարդ լինելոց է տունն Պարսից ի զօրացն Հոռվմայեցւոց եւ հաստատի ամենայն իշխանութիւն երկրի ի ներքոյ ձեռին թագաւորին Հոռվմայեցւոց»:

Զայս այսպէս ասաց սուրբ վարդապետն Յովհաննէս եւ արձակեալ յուղարկեաց զիշխանսն Հայոց խաղաղութեամբ, եւ գնացին յաշխարհն իւրեանց:

Յայսմ ժամանակի զօրաժողով արար իշխանն Հայոց Գանձի եւ գնացեալ էառ զքաղաքն Բերկրի յարեւելս՝ ի Պարսից եւ կոտորեաց առ հասարակ զամենայն քաղաքն եւ ի սուր սուսերի մաշեաց զօրսն Տաճկաց. եւ զբազում աւուրս պատերազմեցաւ ի վերայ կլային եւ ի մեծ վտանգ էարկ զնոսա. եւ բազումք սատակեալ լինէին ի ջրոյ: Եւ այսպիսի պատերազմաւ անհոգացեալ կային զօրքն Հայոց եւ էին ի մեծ գինարբութեան. եւ Խտրիկն, որ է ամիրայ քաղաքին Բերկրոյ, եւ սորա տեսեալ զանպատրաստութիւն զօրացն Հայոց, գրեաց ի քաղաքակիցսն իւր գալ ի յօգնութիւն իւր:

"Then famine will fall upon the land of the Persians for many years until [the people] attack and devour one another. From fear of the power of the Byzantine emperor, many Persian princes will arise from their cities and districts and flee to the other side of the Jahun River without battle. All their stores of gold and silver, accumulated over many years, and the entire multitude of their treasures, heaped up like earth or stones without number, will be taken from the land of the Persians and taken to the land of the Byzantines. All their boys and girls and women will be taken in captivity to the land of the Byzantines. The House of the Persians will be ruined and depopulated by the Byzantine troops, while rule over the entire world will be under the hand of the Byzantine emperor."

Thus spoke the blessed vardapet Yovhannēs. In peace he released and put on their way the Armenian princes, who returned to their own land.

In this period the Armenian prince Gandzi mustered troops and went and took from the Persians the city of Berkri in the East. He generally destroyed the entire city and put the Tachik troops to the sword. For many days he fought over the citadel, putting [the Tachiks] in great danger. Many perished in the water. Given this sort of fighting, the Armenian troops became careless and were in a state of great drunkenness. Xtrik, who was the emir of the city of Berkri, observed the unpreparedness of the Armenian troops and wrote to his citizens to come to his aid.

Եւ արարին ժողով այլազգիքն եւ եկեալ գտին զնոսա անպատրաստս. եւ ընդ առաւօտն յարձակեցան ի վերայ քրիստոնէիցն զօրաց եւ արարին սաստիկ կոտորածս զնոսա. եւ սպանաւ յաւուրն յայնմիկ մեծ իշխանն Հայոց Գանձի, եւ մնաց Տաճատ ի տան հայրենեաց իւրոց. որդի նորա եւ Գանձի եւ ամենայն զօրքն իւր անցին ի քաղաքին Բերկրի:

29. Իսկ ի փոխել թուականութեանս Հայոց յամս ՆՁՁ յարուցեալ Տէր Պետրոս կաթուղիկոսն Հայոց յաթոռոյ իւրմէ ծածկաբար եւ գնաց ի Վասպուրական խռովութեան աղագաւ, զի թագաւորն եւ ամենայն նախարարք եւ ազատագունդք զօրքն Հայոց ոչ լինէին ունկնդիր աստուածային պատուիրանացն: Եւ եղեւ Տէր Պետրոս ի Վասպուրական զամս չորս. եւ կացեալ էր ի Ձորոյ վանքն, զոր շինեալ էր սուրբ հայրապետն Ներսէս. եւ անչափելի տրտմութիւն եղեւ աշխարհին Հայոց ի թողուլն նորա զաթոռ հայրապետութեանն: Եւ յայնժամ թագաւորն Յովհաննէս եւ ամենայն նախարարք Հայոց գրեցին նենգութեամբ թուղթ առ Տէր Պետրոս՝ լինել ունկնդիր ամենայն հրամանաց նորա եւ ականջալուր լինել ամենայն լուսաւոր վարդապետութեան նորա. գրեցին զայս հանդերձ մեծամեծ երդմամբ եւ զիշխանսն Հոռոմց, որք եկեալ էին կողմնապահք՝ կացուցանէին զնոսա միջնորդս: Եւ լուեալ Տէր Պետրոս ստութեան երդմանց նոցա եւ դառնայր յաթոռ իւր:

The foreigners massed, arrived, and found them thus unprepared. At dawn they attacked the Christian troops and destroyed them severely. On that day there died the great prince of the Armenians, Gandzi. His son, Tachat, remained in his patrimonial House. And so it came about that Gandzi and all his troops died in the city of Berkri.

29. At the beginning of the year 486 of the Armenian Era [A.D. 1037] Lord Petros, Catholicos of the Armenians, arose from his throne and secretly went to Vaspurakan because of the commotion, for the king and all the *naxarars* and the *azatagund* troops of the Armenians did not heed the divine commandments. Lord Petros was in Vaspurakan for four months, staying at Dzoroy monastery, which had been built by the blessed patriarch Nerse's. There was immeasurable sorrow in the land of the Armenians at [Petros'] leaving his patriarchal throne. Then King Yovhanne's and all the naxarars of the Armenians wrote a deceitful letter to Lord Petros saying that they would be obedient to his commands and heedful of all his radiant teachings. They wrote this with very great vows and they also designated as intermediaries [some] Byzantine princes, who had come as lieutenants. Lord Petros heeded their false oaths and returned to his throne.

Եւ եղեւ յորժամ մտանէր ի քաղաքն Անի, հրամանաւ թագաւորին Յովհաննէսի արգելական արարին զՏէր Պետրոս զտարի մի եւ զամիսս հինգ. եւ առաքեաց թագաւորն ի վանքն ի Սանահին եւ ետ բերել զմեծն Դէոսկորոս զհայր վանիցն: Եւ եկեալ նա եւ կացեալ հակառակ Տէր Պետրոսի. եւ նստուցին զնա կաթողիկոս յաթոռ երկու, եւ ոչ ըստ Աստուծոյ հրամանացն. եւ ահա կարի յոյժ խաբեալ եղեւ մեծ հռատորն Դէոսկորոս եւ կորոյս զայնչափ պատիւն՝ զոր ունէր, եւ ոչ ոք էր որ ընդունէր զձեռնադրութիւն նորա որպէս օրէն է սուրբ Աթոռոյն. եւ ոչ քարոզեցաւ անուն նորա ի մէջ եկեղեցւոյ ընդ այլ հայրապետսն, վասն զի անարժան համարեցան զնա այնր պատուոյ. եւ եղեւ սուգ մեծ ի վերայ տանն Հայաստանեայց. եւ ի ձեռնադրութեանն նորա ոչ ժողովեցան եպիսկոպոսք եւ քահանայք եւ հայրապետք. այլ նա յանդգնեալ ըստ սրտին խորհրդոյն եւ զբազումս յանարժանիցն ձեռնադրեաց յեպիսկոպոսութիւն. այլ եւ որք վասն յայտնի յանցանացն իւրեանց մերժեալ էին յաթոռոյն յառաջին հայրապետացն, զամենեսեան զնոսա յառաջ կոչեաց:

Իսկ եպիսկոպոսքն եւ վարդապետքն Հայոց աշխարհին ընդ նզովիւք փակեցին զթագաւորն եւ զամենայն նախարարսն Հայոց վասն հակառակութեան, որ եղեւ ի մէջ եկեղեցւոյն: Եւ յայնժամ թագաւորն եւ իշխանքն Հայոց սարսեալք յահէ անիծիցն, կամեցան դարձուցանել զՏէր Պետրոս յաթոռ իւր, եւ նա զաւուրս բազումս ոչ առնոյր յանձն. եւ ամենեքեան խնդրէին զթողութիւն ի նմանէ, եւ նա պնդեալ կայր. եւ յայնժամ գրեաց թագաւորն թուղթ եւ ամենայն իշխանքն Հայոց ի յԱղուանք եւ կոչեցին զկաթողիկոս Աղուանից աշխարհին զՏէր Յովսէփ, զի գայցէ ի բարեխօսութիւն եւ ի հաստատութիւն Տէր Պետրոսին ի քաղաքն Անի:

By order of King Yovhanne's, as soon as he entered the city of Ani, they arrested Lord Petros [and held him] for one year and five months. Then the king sent to Sanahin monastery and had the abbot, the great De'oskoros, brought [to Ani]. When he arrived, they established him in opposition to Lord Petros, seating him as Catholicos on the throne of the patriarchate of the Armenians for one year and two months, not in accordance with God's commands. Behold, the great rhetorician, De'oskoros, was greatly tricked and lost the great respect which he had [commanded]. Nor did anyone accept as valid his ordination to the blessed throne. Nor did they mention his name with the other patriarchs during the church service, since they considered him unworthy of that honor. And thus great mourning descended on the House of the Armenians. At his ordination, bishops, priests, and patriarchs did not assemble. He, in turn, willfully ordained many unworthy [men] to the episcopacy, including those who had previously been rejected from their thrones by earlier patriarchs due to clear transgressions. [De'oskoros] called all of them back.

The bishops and vardapets of the land of the Armenians excommunicated the king and all the Armenian naxarars for the contention which had developed in the Church. It was then that the king and princes of the Armenians, terrified from fear of the anathemas, wanted to return Lord Petros to his throne. However, [Lord Petros] for many days did not agree to this. Everyone sought forgiveness from him, though he remained firm [in his refusal]. Then the king and all the princes of the Armenians wrote a letter to Aghuania, and called upon the Catholicos of the land of the Aghuans, Lord Yovse'p', so that he come and intercede and [re]establish Lord Petros in the city of Ani.

Եւ եղեւ ի թուականութեանս Հայոց ՆՁԷ լինէր մեծ ժողով ի քաղաքն յԱնի եպիսկոպոսաց, հայրապետաց, կրօնաւորաց եւ վարդապետաց, ազատաց եւ իշխանաց իբրեւ չորք հազարաց. որ էր գլուխ ժողովոյն ծերունին Յովսէփ՝ կաթուղիկոսն Աղուանից. եւ սուգ մեծ հասուցանէին Դէոսկորոսի եւ յոյժ պարտաւորեցին զնա եւ մերժեցին ի պատուոյ եւ ընկեցին յաթոռոյ հայրապետութեան. եւ զամենայն ձեռնադրեալսն ի նմանէ ընդ բանադրութեամբ փակեցին, եւ զի մի՛ ոք զնոսա ի կարգ քահանայութեան կոչեսցէ. եւ հաստատեցին զՏէր Պետրոսն յաթոռ հայրապետութեան իւրոյ, եւ եղեւ խաղաղութիւն սուրբ եկեղեցւոյն Հայաստան աշխարհին. եւ Դէոսկորոս գնաց ի Սանահինն ի վանքն իւր եւ կարի յոյժ ամաչելով ընդ գործս իւր:

Դարձեալ ի թուականութեանս Հայոց ի յամի ՆՁԹ եւ լանէր աստղ մի գիսաւոր՝ ջահաւոր կերպարանօք եւ երեւեալ նորա յարեւմուտս կոյս յերեկօրէն եւ յետս յետս սողալով գնայր. եւ եհար զբազմաստեղն եւ զլուսինն եւ ինքն աներեւոյթ եղեւ եւ յարեւմուտս դարձաւ:

Ի նմին ամի յարեան Բուլղարք ի վերայ Հոռոմոց. եւ զօրաժողով արար թագաւորն Հոռոմոց Միխայլն զամենայն աշխարհն Յունաց եւ անհամար բազմութեամբ գնաց ի վերայ Բուլղարաց. եւ մեծաաաատ բարկութեամբ արար աւար եւ գերութիւն զբազում գաւառս եւ սրով հասանէր մինչեւ ի թագաւորութիւնն Բուլղարաց. եւ զօրքն Բուլղարաց ժողով արարին ընդդէմ թագաւորին Յունաց: Եւ եղեւ սաստիկ կոտորած յաւուրն յայնմիկ. եւ յաղթեցին զօրքն Բուլղարաց զօրացն Հոռոմոց եւ փախստական արարին զնոսա առաջի իւրեանց եւ սրով յարձակեցան զհետ նոցա. եւ յաւուր յայնմիկ արեամբ ծածկեցաւ ամենայն երեսք դաշտացն. եւ թագաւորն Միխայլ փախստական անկանէր ի Կոստանդնուպօլիս: Եւ զօրացան Բուլղարք ի վերայ Յունաց եւ առին զամենայն աշխարհին իւրեանց եւ զերծան ի ծառայութենէ Հոռոմոց. եւ եղեւ խաղաղութիւն մեծ ի վերայ ազգին Բուլղարաց:

Now in 487 of the Armenian Era [A.D. 1038] there convened a great assembly of some 4,000 bishops, patriarchs, clerics, and vardapets, azats and princes in the city of Ani. The head of this gathering was the aged Yovse'p', Catholicos of the Aghuans. They brought much grief upon De'oskoros and greatly condemned him. They rejected him from the honor [of the position of Catholicos] and deposed him from the throne of the patriarchate, anathematizing all who had been ordained by him, so that none of them might be called to the ranks of the priesthood. They [re]established Lord Petros on the throne of his patriarchate and there was peace in the blessed Church of the land of Armenia. De'oskoros went to his monastery of Sanahin, greatly ashamed of his deeds.

In the year 489 of the Armenian Era [A.D. 1040] a comet appeared, looking like a torch. It appeared in the western part of the sky in the evening and crept along backwards. It struck the Pleiades and the moon, turned to the west, and disappeared.

In this same year the Bulghars arose against the Byzantines. The Byzantine emperor Michael massed an innumerable multitude of troops from all the Byzantine lands and went against the Bulghars. With great anger he looted many districts and took captives and killed, as far as the kingdom of the Bulghars. The troops of the Bulghars massed against the Byzantine empire. There was a great slaughter on that day when the forces of the Bulghars defeated the Byzantine forces, putting them to flight before them, and pursuing them with the sword. On that day the entire face of the plain was covered with blood, while Emperor Michael fled to Constantinople. The Bulghars grew stronger against the Byzantines and took all of their land, freeing themselves from service to them. And great peace came over the Bulghar nation.

30. Յայսմ ամի մեռաւ թագաւորն Հայոց Աշոտ Բագրատունի որդին Գագկայ եւ եղբայր Յովհաննիսի, եւ մնաց իւր տղայ որդի մի Գագիկ անուն ամաց հնգետասանից. եւ բերաւ Աշոտ ի քաղաքն Անի, եւ թաղեցին զնա ի տապանատունն առաջին թագաւորացն Հայոց. եւ վասն զի ի կենդանութեան իւրում Աշոտ ոչ մտաւ ի քաղաքն յԱնի մինչեւ յօր մահուն իւրոյ, զի յոյժ երկնչէր Յովհաննէս ի յԱշոտոյ, զի էր այր քաջ եւ հզօր: Եւ եղեւ զկնի մահուանն Աշոտոյ թուլամորթեցան զօրքն Հայոց եւ ատեցին զարուեստս պատերազմի, մտին ընդ լծով ծառայութեան ազգին Հոռոմց, նստան ի գինարբուսն, սիրեցին զբարբուտ եւ զերգս գուսանաց. հեռացան ի միաբանութենէ միմեանց եւ յօգնութիւն իրերաց ոչ հասանէին. եւ երկիր՝ զոր սրով անցանէր, նոքա լալականութիւն առնէին եւ զմիմեանց զկատարածն լային եւ զմիմեանս մատնելով ի սուր տանն Յունաց. եւ եղեն աւերիչք ազգականաց իւրեանց եւ ի կողմն հակառակաց իւրեանց դարձան:

Յայսմ ժամանակիս զօրաժողով արար մեծ ամիրայն Պարսից Ապուսուար իբրեւ հարիւր յիսուն հազար՝ զազգսն անօրինաց եւ մեծաւ սրտմտութեամբ յարձակեալ գայր ի վերայ քրիստոնէից եւ դառնաշունչ բարկութեամբ մտաւ յաշխարհն Աղուանից ի գաւառն Դաւթի Անհողին բազում վիշտս էած հաւատացելոց:

30. In this year there died Ashot Bagratuni, king of the Armenians, son of Gagik and brother of Yovhanne's. He was survived by his fifteen-year-old son, named Gagik. Ashot['s body] was brought to the city of Ani, where they buried him in the mausoleum of the first kings of the Armenians. It happened that during his lifetime, until his death, Ashot did not enter the city of Ani, since Yovhanne's greatly feared Ashot, because he was a brave and powerful man. After Ashot's death, the Armenian troops grew lazy and hated the art of warfare. They went under the yoke of servitude to the Byzantine nation and sat in drunkenness, enjoying the lute and minstrel songs. They distanced themselves from the unity they [once] had for each other, and no longer came to each other's aid. As for the country, which was being put to the sword, they just wept over it and wept over what they did to one another, meanwhile betraying one another to the swords of the House of the Byzantines. They became the destroyers of their own relatives and turned to the side of their opponents.

In this period the great emir of the Persians, Apusuar[36] massed troops from the impious peoples—some 150,000 troops—and came against the Christians, attacking with bitter anger the land of the Aghuans, and occasioning much grief in the district of Dawit' Anhoghin.[37]

36 *Apusuar:* Abu'l-Uswar, Kurdish emir of Dvin.

37 *Anhoghin:* "the Landless".

Եւ Դաւիթ երկուցեալ ի բազմութենէ զօրաց այլազգեացն ոչ ելանէր ի պատերազմ: Իսկ անօրէնն Ապուսուար էառ բազում գաւառս եւ թիմաբերդս չորս հարիւր. եւ տարի մի կացեալ անդ արար իւր հնազանդ զմեծ մասն աշխարհին եւ կամեցաւ գալ ի վերայ Դաւթի. յայնժամ անճարեալ Դաւթի եւ յուղարկէր առ թագաւորն Յովհաննէս, որ նստէր յԱնի, եւ ասէր՝ թէ «Էառ Ապուսուար զամենայն գաւառս Հայոց աշխարհիս եւ գայ ի վերայ իմ, եւ եթէ ինձ ոչ օգնէք, երթամ իւր ի հնազանդութիւն, եւ լինիմ իւր առաջնորդ եւ խաւար ածեմ գաւառիդ Շիրակայ»: Եւ լուեալ զայս Յովհաննէս, յուղարկէր Դաւթի արս չորս հազար. նոյնպէս եւ յուղարկեալ ի Կապանին թագաւորն. եւ նա տայր նմա արս երկու հազար: Եւ այսպիսի օրինակաւ սպառնացեալ Ափխազաց թագաւորին, եւ նա յուղարկէր յօգնութիւն Դաւթի արս չորս հազար:

Եւ ինքն Դաւիթ ժողովեալ զիւր զօրսն իբրեւ տասն հազար եւ յուղարկեաց առ կաթուղիկոսն Աղուանից եւ ասէր, թէ «Այս ազգ անօրինացն վասն քրիստոսական հաւատոցն գան ի վերայ մեր եւ կամին զօրէնս խաչապաշտացս խափանել եւ զհաւատս հաւատացելոցն Քրիստոսի ջնջել. եւ ահա արժան է եւ իրաւունս ամենայն հաւատացելոց ընդդէմ սոյն երթալ եւ մեռանիլ ի վերայ քրիստոսական հաւատոցն:

Dawit', who was frightened by the multitude of the troops of the foreigners, did not go forth to battle. Meanwhile, the impious Apusuar seized many districts and 400 fortresses. For a year he remained there, making a large part of the land obedient to him. Then he wanted to go against Dawit'. Dawit', with no other recourse, sent to King Yovhanne's, who sat in Ani, saying: "Apusuar has taken all the districts of the lands of the Armenians, and [now] is coming against me. If you do not help me, I will obediently submit to him. Then I will become his guide and ruin your district of Shirak." When Yovhanne's heard this, he sent 4,000 men to Dawit' and likewise sent 2,000 men to the king of Kapan. The king of the Abkhaz, threatened by this example, also sent 4,000 men to Dawit's assistance.

Then Dawit' gathered his own forces, some 10,000 men, and sent to the Catholicos of the Aghuans, saying: "This nation of impious people is coming against us because of our Christian faith. They want to destroy the laws of our Cross-worshipping people and to exterminate the faith of believers in Christ. It is fitting and proper for all the faithful to go against them and to die for the Christian faith.

«Արդ ժողովեա զամենայն եպիսկոպոսունսդ Հայոց աշխարհիդ որ յԱղուանսն են եւ ի բանակ այսր հասիր, զի ընդ մեզ մեռանիջիք»: Զոր եւ արար իսկ եւ երկերիւր եպիսկոպոսօք գնայր Տէր Յովսէփն ի բանակն քրիստոնէից: Եւ գրեաց եւ ի վանորայսն առ հարսն գալ միաբան ամենայն կրօնաւորօքն ի զօրս հաւատացելոց. եւ ժողովեաց զամենայն քահանայս Աղուանից աշխարհին եւ զսարկաւագունսն եւ քարոզ կարդաց ընդ ամենայն գաւառսն եւ ասէր. «Եթէ այր իցէ եւ եթէ կին, որ ցանկացող է մարտիրոսական մահուն, ահա հասեալ եղեւ յայսմ ամի ի վերայ մեր. ում պիտոյ է Քրիստոս, վաղվաղակի առ մեզ հասցէ»:

Եւ լուեալ զայս՝ հայր որդւովքն եւ մայր դստերօքն ի բանակն հաւատացելոցն հասին. եւ լցաւ դաշտն առ հասարակ անթիւ բազմութեամբ իբրեւ զհօտս հանդերձ գառամբք:

31. Եւ լուեալ զայս Ապուսուար՝ ծիծաղէր ի վերայ եղելոցս այս եւ խաղայր գայր ի վերայ զօրացն քրիստոնէից: Եւ յայնժամ հրամայեաց Դաւիթ քարոզ կարդալ եպիսկոպոսացն եւ կրօնաւորացն եւ քահանայիցն, զի ամենայն ոք իւր զէն պատերազմի խաչ առցէ ի ձեռս իւր եւ միայն զաւետարանն Քրիստոսի եւ այնիւ ընդդէմ թշնամեաց սրբոյն ընթացարուք: Եւ յայնժամ ամենայն բանակն խաչ եւ աւետարան դարձաւ. ահա մերձեցան զօրք անօրինացն եւ բազմութիւն քահանայիցն կային ընդդէմ նոցա: Իսկ Դաւիթ քան հազարաւ հասանէր ի վերայ այլազգեացն արանց քաջաց:

"Now gather up all your bishops from the land of the Armenians who are among the Aghuans and come here to the army, so that they die along with us." Lord Yovse'p' did that and went to the Christian army with 200 bishops. Furthermore, he wrote to the abbots of the monasteries to come along with all the clerics to the forces of the faithful. He gathered up all the priests and deacons of the land of the Aghuans and proclaimed through all the districts, saying: "If there is any man or woman who seeks a martyr's death, behold, this year it has come upon us. Let those who love Christ immediately come to us."

Hearing this, fathers with their sons and mothers with their daughters came to the army of the faithful. The plain filled up with an uncountable multitude, like flocks with their lambs.

31. Now when Apusuar heard about this, he laughed and approached the Christian forces. Then Dawit' ordered the bishops, monks, and priests to preach so that each one take a cross in hand as a weapon of war and, with only the Gospel of Christ, go against the enemies' swords. Then did the entire army turn to the Cross and the Gospel. The troops of the impious approached and the multitude of priests were opposite them. Then Dawit', with 20,000 brave men, came against the foreigners.

Իբրեւ ճակատ զճակատ հարան, ձայն բարձին քահանայական դասքն միաբան առ Աստուած լալով, որ եւ հնչեաց երկիրն ի ձայնէն, եւ ասէին. «Արի՛, Տէր, օգնեա մեզ եւ փրկեա զմեզ վասն անուանդ քում սրբոյ»: Իսկ զօրքն հաւատացելոցն իբրեւ ի ծով մխեցան ի մէջ բանակին անօրինացն, որ եւ ծածկեցան իսկ: Յայնժամ քահանայական դասքն շարժեցան միաբան զքրիստոսական սուրբ նշանն եւ ի վերայ թշնամեացն դիմեալ յարձակեցան. եւ հուր սաստկապէս ցոլացեալ ի նոցանէ եւ եհար զզօրսն այլազգեացն. եւ առ հասարակ ի փախուստ դարձան. եւ զօրքն Հայոց՝ սրով զհետ նոցա, զաւուրս հինգ ահագին կոտորածով վարեցին զզօրսն այլազգեացն, որ եւ արեամբք ծածկեցան դաշտք եւ լերինք. առին եւ անթիւ գանձս ոսկւոյ եւ արծաթոյ եւ աւարս բազումս, եւ մնացեալ զօրքն Պարսից մազապուրծ մերկ եւ բոկ անկան յաշխարհն իւրեանց. եւ հոտեցաւ Աղուանից աշխարհն ի պիղծ դիակացն իւրեանց: Եւ յաւուրս երիս տիրանայր Դաւիթ ամենայն զաւառացն, զոր էառ այլազգին, եւ մեծաւ պարգեւօք յուղարկեաց զամենայն զօրսն, որք եկին իւր յօգնութիւն. եւ բաշխէր բազում ինչս յաւարէն՝ եպիսկոպոսացն եւ քահանայիցն եւ ամենայն եկեղոցն առ նա եւ արձակեաց զնոսա. եւ եղեւ խաղաղութիւն:

When the armies clashed, the priestly orders in unison raised their voices to God, weeping, while the land resounded with the noise. They cried: "Arise, Lord, help us and save us for Your holy name." The troops of the believers plunged into the midst of the army of the impious as though into a sea. They were, in fact, covered by them. Then the priestly orders, united, raised the blessed Christian symbol [the cross] and attacked the enemy. A strong flame blazed forth from them and struck the troops of the foreigners. One and all [the enemy] turned to flight. The Armenian troops, sword in hand, pursued them for five days and killed the enemy forces so severely that the plains and mountains were covered with blood. They took innumerable treasures of gold and silver and much booty. The troops of the Persians, naked and barefoot, escaped to their own land by a hairsbreadth. The land of the Aghuans stank from their foul corpses. In three days Dawit' ruled over all the districts which the foreigners had seized. With grand gifts he sent home all the troops which had come to his aid. He divided up many goods from the loot, giving them to the bishops, priests, and to all who had come to him. Then he released them, and there was peace.

Եւ յայսմ ամի ոմն անօրէն եւ չար իշխան յազատացն Սենեքարիմայ գնաց առ թագաւորն Յունաց եւ չարաչար մատնեաց զԱտոմ եւ զԱպուսահլ զՍենեքարիմայ զորդիսն եւ ասէր, եթէ՝ Կամին ապստամբել ի վերայ քո եւ յարուցանել քեզ վիշտս եւ հալածանս: Եւ լուեալ զայս թագաւորն Միխայլ, հաւատաց ստախօս բանիցն եւ առաքեաց ի Սեբաստիա զակողութն իւր հնգետասան հազարօք՝ բերել զնոսա առ իւր, զի մի՛ փախիցեն. եւ հասանէր ակողութն զօրօքն ի Սեբաստիա քաղաքն: Եւ լուեալ զայս որդւոցն Սենեքարիմայ, հիացեալ զարհուրեցան. եւ տեսեալ ակողութն զիմաստութիւնն ոչ էր նման նոցա, բայց նոքա երկնչէին գնալ:

Յայնժամ Շապուհ իշխանն ասէր ցԱտոմ եւ ցԱպուսահլ. «Կամի՞ք զի զզօրսդ Հոռոմոց ցիր եւ ցան ածեմ ընդ երեսս դաշտացս»: Եւ արար զրահսն եօթն կրկնակի եւ զարկանէր թրով ի վերայ եւ ի վայր հեղոյր մանր զերկաթն: Եւ ասեն որդիք թագաւորացն Հայոց. «Մի՛ եղիցի այդպէս, այլ երթամք զհետ կոչնականացդ»: Եւ տուեալ զտուրս բազումս զօրագլխին եւ գնացին զհետ նորա ի Կոստանդնուպօլիս. եւ ի մտանել ի քաղաքն դիմեցին լալով ի գերեզման թագաւորին Վասլին եւ զերդման թուղթն իւրեանց ի վերայ գերեզմանին ընկենուին եւ ասէին՝ եթէ «Դու բերեր զմեզ յաշխարհս Հոռոմոց, եւ ահա մահու սպառնան մեզ: Դատ արար մեզ յոսոխէն մերմէ, ո՛վ հայր մեր»: Եւ լուեալ զայսպիսի իմաստութիւնս թագաւորն Միխայլ՝ հիանայր յոյժ եւ հրամայեաց զմատնիչն կորուսանել:

In this same year a certain impious and wicked prince from the azats of Senek'erim [Artsruni] went to the emperor of the Byzantines and maliciously betrayed Atom and Apusahl, Senek'erim's sons, saying: "They want to rebel against you and bring grief and trouble upon you." When Emperor Michael heard this, he believed these lying words and sent his acolyth to Sebastia with 15,000 men to bring them to him, so that they would not flee. The acolyth arrived at the city of Sebastia with his troops. When the sons of Senek'erim heard about this, they were astonished and frightened. They saw that the acolyth's wisdom was not equal to their own, and they were afraid to accompany him.

Then Prince Shapuh said to Atom and Apusahl: "Would you like me to scatter the Byzantine troops all over the face of the plain?" And he took seven layers of armor and struck it with his sword, causing small fragments of iron to break off. The sons of the Armenian king replied: "No. We shall go in answer to the summons." After giving many gifts to the military commander, they went with him to Constantinople. Entering the city, they went to the tomb of the emperor Basil in tears and appealed to it, throwing on it a letter [containing an oath] which had been given to them. And they said: "You brought us into the land of the Byzantines. Behold, now they threaten us with death. O, our father, vindicate us before our accuser." When such wisdom was heard by Emperor Michael, he was greatly surprised and commanded that their accuser should be destroyed.

32. Ի Հայոց տումարիս եւ ի թուականութեանս ամի ՆՂ մեռաւ թագաւորն Հայոց Յովհաննէս՝ եղբայրն Աշոտոյ, որդի Գագկայ, որդւոյ Աշոտոյ, որդւոյ Սմբատայ, որդւոյ Երկաթայ՝ Բագրատունի ազգաւ, եւ թաղեցին զնա ի քաղաքն յԱնի ի գերեզմանսն առաջին թագաւորացն Հայոց: Եւ եղեւ իբրեւ լուան զայս ազգն Հոռոմոց, ժողով արարեալ թագաւորն Հոռոմոց Միխայլն եւ հասանէր յաշխարհն Հայոց եւ աւար հարկանէր զտունն Հայոց սրով եւ գերութեամբ: Վասն զի Յովհաննէս ի կենդանութեան իւրում գիր էր տուեալ Հոռոմոց՝ եթէ զկնի մահուան իմոյ Անի Հոռոմոց լինի, եւ այնու առնոյր տուրս եւ իշխանութիւնս ի Հոռոմոց զամս հնգետասան: Եւ զկնի մահուանն Յովհաննիսի այր ոմն յիշխանաց տանն Հայոց, որ էր այր նենգաւոր, անուն Ազատ Սարգիս հայկազն, ազգ առնէր Հոռոմոց եւ ի տուր տայր զաշխարհն Հայոց եւ զգանձատունսն առաջին թագաւորացն Հայոց յափշտակեաց եւ տարաւ յԱփխազք, բերդամուտ եղեալ. եւ աւանս բազումս էառ ընդ ձեռամբ իւրով եւ կամեցաւ թագաւորել ի վերայ Հայոց, զոր ոչ ընդունեցին զնա ազգն Բագրատունեաց, վասն զի հայկազն էր:

Յայսմ ամի բազում անցումն եղեւ տանս Հայոց ի ձեռն Դաւթի Անհողինի՝ ազգապետին Յովհաննիսի Հայոց արքային: Սա յարուցեալ ի վերայ թագաւորութեանն Հայոց եւ մատնեաց ի սուր եւ ի գերութիւն զգաւառս բազումս եւ գայր անցանէր զօրօք բազմօք յաշխարհն Հայոց. թողեալ զաշխարհն Աղուանից եւ գայր ի վերայ աշխարհին Հայոց. բազում նեղութեամբ եւ անթիւ կրակով այրեցան ի զօրաց նորա. եւ դարձաւ ի յԱղուանից յաշխարհն ի տուն իւր:

32. In 490 of the Armenian era [A.D. 1041], the king of the Armenians, Yovhanne's, of the Bagratid line, died. He was the brother of Ashot, son of Gagik, son of Ashot, son of Smbat, son of [Ashot, who was called] the Iron. They buried him in the city of Ani, in the mausoleum of the first kings of the Armenians. As soon as word of this reached the Byzantine nation, Michael, emperor of the Byzantines, assembled troops. He reached the land of the Armenians and subjected the House of the Armenians to the sword and to captive-taking. This was because Yovhanne's, during his lifetime, had given a document to the Byzantines [stating that] "after my death Ani shall be [the property] of the Byzantines." In return for this [promise, Yovhanne's] had received gifts and authority from the Byzantines for 15 years. Following Yovhanne's death, a certain individual who was one of the princes of the House of the Armenians, a treacherous man named Azat Sargis Haykazn, informed the Byzantines that he was giving the land of the Armenians to them as a gift. He ravished the treasury of the first kings of the Armenians and took it to Abkhazia, and he himself holed up in a fortress. He brought many hamlets under his control and wanted to rule as king over the Armenians. However, the line of the Bagratids did not accept him because he was a Haykazn [descendant of the line of Hayk].

In this year Dawit' Anhoghin, a relative of [the late] Yovhanne's, king of the Armenians, brought much travail to the House of the Armenians. He arose against the Armenian kingdom and subjected many districts to the sword and to captive-taking by coming to the land of the Armenians with many troops. He left the land of the Aghuans and came against the land of the Armenians. His forces caused much hardship and started many fires. Then [Dawit'] returned to his home, in the land of the Aghuans.

Յայսմ ամի յարեան Հոռոմք կրկնակի ի վերայ աշխարհին Հայոց՝ եւ առ ի չգոյէ գլուխ զօրացն Հայոց, բազում տեղիք հաւանեցան Հոռոմոց, եւ վասն զի էր կատարած մեծ ի վերայ աշխարհին Հայոց: Եւ յայնժամ ժողովեցան զօրք Հոռոմոց ի վերայ թագաւորաբնակ քաղաքին Անւոյ հարիւր հազարաց եւ բանակ հարկանէին ի դուռն քաղաքին Անւոյ: Յայնժամ ժողովեցան մնացեալք զօրքն Հայոց առ մեծ սպարապետոն Վահրամ Պալհաւունին եւ խնդրէին ելանել ի պատերազմ ի վերայ զօրացն Հոռոմոց, վասն զի զօրքն Հոռոմոց սաստիկ հայհոյութեամբ եւ բազում նախատանօք գային ի վերայ պատերազմել: Յայնժամ մեծաւ սրտմտութեամբ լցեալ լինէին զօրքն Հայոց, եւ բարկութեամբ որպէս զգազանս զայրացեալք եւ առ հասարակ ելեալ ի պատերազմ արք երեսուն հազար հետեւակք եւ ձիաւորք ընդ դուռն, որ Ծաղկոյի ասի, եւ որպէս զկայծակն հեղան ի վերայ զօրացն Հոռոմոց եւ զայնքան զհպարտացեալ եւ զամբարտաւանեալ զօրսն ընդ կրունկն դարձուցանէին ի փախուստ եւ անողորմ ի բերան սրոյ կոտորէին զնոսա. եւ Ախուրեան գետոն որ գայր՝ ի յարիւն դարձաւ. եւ ի ձայնէ գազանացեալ զօրացն Հայոց փախստականքն ոչ կարէին փախչել, այլ կային յիմարեալք եւ մատնեալք ի ձեռս սրոյ: Եւ անդ էր տեսանել զահեղ եւ զմեծ օրն ի վերայ զօրացն Հոռոմոց, որ ի քսան հազարէն հարիւր լինէր մնացեալ: Յայնժամ ընդ մէջ անցեալ սրբասնեալն եւ մեծ սպարապետոն Վահրամ Պալհաւունին եւ բազում ողոքանօք աղաչէր պատգամաւորութեամբն առ զօրսն Հայոց եւ հազիւ կարաց հաւանեցուցանել՝ որ զօրքն Հոռոմոց սակաւիկ յետ ելանէին եւ այնու զերծեալք լինէին զօրքն Հոռոմոց որք մնացին. եւ այլ ոչ եւս խնդրեցին զօրքն Հոռոմոց զքաղաքն Անի, այլ դարձան ամօթով եւ գնացին ի Կոստանդնուպօլիս առ Միխայլն:

In this year the Byzantines again arose against the land of the Armenians and, since there was no head of the Armenian forces, many places accepted the Byzantines and, therefore, great destruction was visited on the land of the Armenians. Then some 100,000 Byzantine troops massed against the royal capital of Ani and encamped before its gates. Then the remaining troops of the Armenians assembled by the great sparapet Vahram Pahlawuni and sought to battle against the Byzantine forces, for the Byzantine troops had come against them in warfare with great insults and curses. Filled with great anger and rage, the Armenian troops were like frenzied animals. Some 30,000 infantry and cavalry arose to fight. They passed through the gate called the Tsaghots' Gate, and fell upon the Byzantine troops like lightning. They put to flight those troops which had been so proud and insulting, mercilessly pursuing and putting them to the sword. The Axurean River, which flowed there, became red with blood. The fugitives were unable to escape from the sounds of the frenzied Armenian troops, but remained stupefied and were betrayed to the sword. [The results of that] great and awful day could be seen there as it was visited upon the Byzantine troops, for out of 20,000 [troops], only 100 survived. Then Vahram Pahlawuni, the great sparapet, who had been raised in holiness, interceded and through many entreaties and messengers sent to the Armenian forces, was barely able to convince them to leave alone the few surviving Byzantine soldiers they were pursuing. Thereafter the Byzantine forces did not seek [to rule over] Ani. Rather, in disgrace, they returned to Michael in Constantinople.

33. Յայնժամ զարթուցեալ մանուկ մի ութ եւ տասն ամաց՝ Գագիկ անուն, ի նոյն շառաւիղէն Բագրատունեաց, որդի Աշոտոյ արքային, որդւոյ Գագկայ՝ որդւոյ Աշոտոյ՝ որդւոյ Աբասայ՝ որդւոյ Սմբատայ՝ որդւոյ Երկաթայ: Եւ մանուկս այս Գագիկ էր յոյժ իմաստուն եւ երկիւղած եւ աստուածասէր. եւ ժողովեցան ամենայն նախարարքն Հայոց առ հայրապետն Տէր Պետրոս եւ օծին զԳագիկ թագւոր ի վերայ ամենայն տանն Հայոց շնորհօք Հոգւոյն սրբոյ եւ հրամանաւ մեծի իշխանին, որով եւ օծեաց զնա սրբակեացն մեծն Մարգէն, որ էր ազգաւ հայկազնեան եւ հայրենեօք Պալհաւունի, որոյ անուն ըստ նախնոյն իւրոյ Գրիգոր ճանաչի, եւ էր յազգէն սրբոյն Գրիգորի: Սա երկրորդ Սամուէլ երեւեալ, որ յօծ զԴաւիթ արքայ ի վերայ տանն Իսրայէլի. սա թագաւորեցոյց զԳագիկ ի վերայ տանս Հայաստանեայց, յոյժ բարեպաշտ եւ աստուածասէր եւ անպարտելի յիմաստասիրական ջոկսն. սա ջանայր իմաստութեամբն իւրով հաստատել զաթոռ թագաւորութեանն Հայաստան ազգիս եւ հայցէր յԱստուծոյ օժանդակ լինել նմա եւ ազգին Պալհաւունեաց:

Յայնժամ Գագիկ ի ձեռն զօրաց իւրոց ըմբռնեալ զՍարգիս եւ ի խոշտանգանս ազգի ազգի արկանէր զնա, մինչեւ յոչ կամացն նորա տիրանայր բերդից եւ գաւառաց եւ քաղաքաց եւ ամենայն գանձատանն հայրենի իւրոյ, զոր յափշտակեաց:

33. In this period there arose a lad of eighteen years, named Gagik. [He was] from the same Bagratid line: the son of King Ashot, son of Gagik, son of Ashot, son of Abas, son of Smbat, son of [Ashot] the Iron. This youth, Gagik, was extremely wise, devout, and pious. All the naxarars of the Armenians assembled near the patriarch, Lord Petros, and anointed Gagik king over the entire House of the Armenians. [This was] by the grace of the Holy Spirit and by order of the great prince [Grigor Magistros], who anointed him. [Grigor Magistros] was of the Haykazean line and Pahlawuni by descent [from whom came] the blessed [Catholicoi] of great Egypt. He was named Gregory after his ancestor and was descended from the line of Saint Gregory. He appeared as a second Samuel, who had anointed David over the House of Israel. [Grigor Magistros, who] enthroned Gagik as king over the House of the Armenians, was an extremely devout and pious man, and invincible among the ranks of the philosophers. Through his wisdom he tried to establish on a firm basis the throne of the kingdom of the Armenian nation, looking to God to help him and the Pahlawunid line.

At this time Gagik with his troops seized Sargis and subjected him to various tortures until—against his will—[King Gagik] came to rule over the fortresses, districts, and his entire patrimonial treasury, which [Sargis] had seized.

Յայնժամ կամօք բարերարին Աստուծոյ խաղաղանայր զօրքն Հոռոմց, եւ այլ ոչ յաւելան ի խնդրել զքաղաքն Անի եւ ոչ այլ պատերազմ յարուցանել ընդ Հայք: Յայնժամ եղեւ յաջողեալ երկու ամ թագաւորութիւնն Գագկայ շնորհօք Հոգւոյն սրբոյ: Իսկ յաւուրս յայսոսիկ ժողով արար թագաւորն Գագիկ եւ գնայր խաղայր ընդ աշխարհս հայրենեաց իւրոց եւ զամենայն անհնազանդսն ի հնազանդութիւն ածէր եւ գթշնամիսն մեծաւ բարկութեամբ դարձուցանէր եւ երթեալ բազմութեամբ զօրօք, բանակ հարկանէր յԱյրարատեան գաւառին՝ առնուլ զվրէժխնդրութիւն յազգէն հարաւայնոյ: Յայնժամ սպառազինեալ մեծի իշխանին Գրիգորի որդի Վասակայ Պալհաւունւոյ եւ երթեալ զօրօք բանակս հարկանէր ի վերայ գետոյն Հուրաստանի մերձ ի Բջնի մեծի ամրոցին: Յայնժամ զօրք այլազգեացն գան ի վերայ զօրացն Հայոց. եւ եղեւ պատերազմ սաստիկ, եւ զօրքն Հայոց յաղթեցին զօրացն Պարսից, եւ արարին կոտորած մեծ ի վերայ Հուրաստանի գետոյն եւ զիշխանս թուրք զօրացն ձերբակալ արարին, եւ մնացեալքն փախստական գնացին ի Պարսիկս:

Յայնժամ յազդմանէ չարին կրկին շարժումն լինէր Յունաց դաւաճանութեամբ եւ կեղծաւորութեամբ սուտ քրիստոնէին Դաւթի Անհողինին, զոր հարկ եղեւ մեզ զանուն նորա փոխել եւ ասել թէ Դաւիթ, վասն զի ի վիհն տառապանաց էած զազգս քրիստոնէից. եւ ինքն հոգւովն տանջեալ եղեւ ի բանսարկուէն եւ ի վիհն կորստեան յաւիտենից տանջանացն մատնեալ լինէր:

At the same time, through the will of benevolent God, the Byzantine troops had become pacified and no longer sought the city of Ani, nor did they stir up warfare against the Armenians. And thus, through the grace of the Holy Spirit, two years of Gagik's reign as king passed successfully. Then King Gagik assembled troops and went throughout the land of his ancestors, bringing all the disobedient [elements] into obedience and, in great anger, turning back all his enemies. He went with a multitude of troops and encamped in the Ayraratean district, taking vengeance on the nation of the South. Then the great prince Grigor, son of Vasak Pahlawuni, arrived and went with his troops [to an area] close to the great fortress of Bjni. He encamped by the Huraztan River. Then the troops of the foreigners came against the Armenian troops, and a fierce battle ensued. The Armenian forces defeated the Persian forces, making a great slaughter by the Huraztan River. They arrested the Turkish princes, while the survivors fled to the Persians.

At that time, through the influence of the Evil one, once more the Byzantines made a move. This was through the treachery and falseness of that fake Christian, Dawit' Anhoghin. Indeed, we should change his name to Abyss,[38] since he drove the Christian people to the pit of perdition. He himself, spiritually tortured by Satan, betrayed himself to the eternal torments of that pit of perdition.

38 A play on words.

Յայսմ ամի զօրաժողով արար թագաւորն Հոռոմց Միխայլն զամենայն աշխարհն Յունաց եւ այլ ի Հայոց զօրացն, որք ընդ Հոռոմց իշխանութեամբն էին՝ Սեբաստիա եւ Տարօն եւ ամենայն Վասպուրական. եւ անթիւ բազմութեամբ հասանէր թագաւորն Միխայլ յարեւմուտք եւ գերի առեալ զամենայն աշխարհն Գթաց եւ զապստամբսն ածէր ի հնազանդութիւն եւ արար իւր հնազանդ զամենայն աշխարհն եւ դարձաւ ի Կոստանդնուպօլիս. եւ մերձ ընդ մերձ մեռանէր թագաւորն Միխայլ:

Եւ թագաւորեաց ի վերայ Հոռոմց փոխանակ նորա քուեր որդին իւր, որ Կեսառոսն էր, եւ զամիսս չորս կալեալ զթագաւորութիւնն եւ այլ ոչ եւս, վասն զի խորհեցաւ խորհուրդս չարս եւ անձամբն անձին իւրոյ որոգայթս պատրաստեաց, ըստ այնմ եթէ՝ «Որ փորէ խորխորատ ընկերին իւրոյ, անձամբ իւրով լցցէ զնա»: Իսկ սորա այնչափ հպարտացեալ՝ որ զգործն իւր ոչ իմացաւ. վասն զի զԿիւռազոյի զդուստրն Կոստանդեայ կայսերն իբրեւ զբոզ խուզել համարձակեցաւ եւ կապանօք աքսորեաց զնա ի կղզւոջ. եւ զպատրիարգն Կոստանդնուպօլսի բռնեաց եւ եդ զնա կապանօք ի բանդ, վասն զի կամեցաւ ազգաւն իւրով ժառանգել զաթոռ թագաւորութեանն, վասն զի էին պիղծք եւ անօրէնք եւ ապականիչք աշխարհի:

In this year Michael, emperor of the Byzantines, massed troops from the entire realm of the Byzantines, including Armenian troops who were under Byzantine rule—from Sebastia, Taro'n, and all of Vaspurakan. With an uncountable multitude, Emperor Michael moved westward, enslaving the entire land of the Goths. He brought the rebels into submission, made obedient to himself the entire land, and then returned to Constantinople. Soon thereafter, Emperor Michael[39] died.

Then, in [Michael's] stead, his sister's son,[40] who was a Caesar, ruled over the Byzantines. He ruled for four months, and no more. This was because he had evil intentions and prepared a snare that he himself got caught in, as is said: "He who digs a pit for his friend, falls into it himself."[41] He became so arrogant that he himself did not realize what he was doing. He dared to cut off the hair of Zoe, daughter of Constantine, as though she were a whore, and then exiled her to an island, in chains. He seized the patriarch of Constantinople and placed him in jail, in fetters. This was because [Michael] wanted to bequeath the throne of the realm to his own family. They were a foul, impious people, and polluters of the land.

39 *Michael* IV, the Paphlagonian, 1034-1041.
40 *Michael* V, the Calfat, 1041-1042.
41 Proverbs 26:27; 28:10.

Եւ յետ աւուրց ինչ օգնութիւն հասանէր յԱստուծոյ պատրիարգին, եւ այլափոխեալ զինքն զերծեալ ի կապանաց բանդին եւ փախստական լեալ անկանէր ի սուրբն Սոփի եւ շարժեալ զամենայն քաղաքն Կոստանդնուպօլսի ի վերայ Կեսառոսին, եւ եղեւ ահագին պատերազմ ի մէջ քաղաքին Կոստանդնուպօլսի: Եւ լինէր յայնմ աւուր սաստիկ պատերազմ եւ կոտորած ի յերկուց կողմանցն եւ յարեան ճապաղին լինէր ամենայն քաղաքն, եւ յաւուրն յայնմիկ կայր սուրբն Սոփի ի մէջ բազում արեանց. եւ յաղթեաց պատրիարքն Կեսառոսին, կալան զնա եւ զաչսն նորա խաւարեցուցին եւ զազգին իւրոյ զամենեցուն տունն հիմն ի վեր արարին եւ զթագուհին զԿիւռազոյի մեծաւ փառաւորութեամբ դարձուցին ի Կոստանդնուպօլիս:

34. Յայսմ ամի սպանաւ մեծ իշխանն Հայոց Խաչիկ եւ տղայ որդի նորա Իշխան անուն՝ ի Վասպուրական գաւառին: Ժողովեցան Հեր եւ Սամուսատ եւ ասպատակ արարին զԹուռնեւան գաւառն. եւ համբաւն հասանէր առ Խաչիկ. որպէս թէ զօրքն այլազգեաց մտին ի գաւառն քո: Եւ նա էր այր քաջ եւ յաղթող ի պատերազմօղ, յազգէ ի վերոյն յառիւծ ջոկէ. բայց ծերացեալ էր եւ թողեալ զգործ պատերազմին եւ հառաչելով ապաշաւէր, քանզի աւագ որդին նորա քաջն Հասան եւ Ճնճղուկն հանդերձ զօրօքն ի յարեւմուտքն էին զհետ թագաւորին Միխայլի:

But after some days aid came to the patriarch from God. [The patriarch] escaped from the bonds of prison, disguised himself, and fled to [the church of] Saint Sophia. Then the entire city of Constantinople moved against this Caesar, and there was a frightful battle inside the city of Constantinople. On that day there was a fierce battle with killings on both sides. Blood flowed throughout the city, including inside Saint Sophia. The patriarch['s partisans] defeated the Caesar. They seized [Michael V] and blinded him, completely destroyed his family, and returned the [former] empress Zoe to Constantinople in great glory.

34. In this year in the district of Vaspurakan there died the great prince of the Armenians, Xach'ik, and his young son. [Fighters had] assembled from the districts of Her and Salmast and raided the district of T'or'newan. News reached Xach'ik that "the troops of the foreigners have entered your district." Now [Xach'ik] was a brave man, successful in warfare, and from a line of lions. However, he had grown old and had left off the business of warfare. [Now] he was sighing and lamenting that his sons with their troops—the senior son, Hasan, as well as Chnchghuk—had gone west with Emperor Michael.

Եւ յայնժամ իշխանն Հայոց Խաչիկ ոչ կարաց համբերել սրտին, յարուցեալ եօթանասուն արամբք հասանէր այլազգեացն, եւ զորդին իւր ի տանն արգելական արար զԻշխան անունն, զի տղայ էր հնգետասնամեայ: Եւ իբրեւ հասաւ Խաչիկ այլազգեացն, տեսաւ բազում զօրս: Զայն ետ արանց իւրոց եւ ի պատերազմ մտանէր եւ բախէր սաստկապէս զայլազգիսն եւ յերկիր թաւալեցուցանէր: Եւ ահա տեսանէր զի տղայ որդի նորա զերծեալ լինէր յարգելանոցէն եւ գայր ի պատերազմ. իբրեւ ետես Խաչիկ՝ բեկաւ նորա, քանզի տղայ էր եւ գեղեցիկ. եւ գայր Իշխան անունն իբրեւ զկորիւն առիւծոյ եւ ուժգին բախէր զպատերազմն. Եւ հասեալ Խաչիկ կալաւ զնա եւ յուղարկէր ի տուն. իսկ նորա զերծեալ մտանէր ի պատերազմ եւ առ տխմարութեանն քաջապէս մտանէր: Եւ իմացան զնա՝ թէ որդի առն քաջին է, փակեցին զնա ի մէջ եւ կալան եւ սպանին: Եւ տեսեալ Խաչիկն՝ բեկաւ ողն նորա, եւ անկաւ սուսերն ի ձեռաց նորա. եւ տեսեալ զայն զօրաց այլազգեացն՝ դիմեցին ի վերայ նորա, կալան զնա եւ սպանին. եւ մնացեալքն փախստական գնացին ի տունս իւրեանց:

Եւ զկնի աւուրց ինչ գային որդիք Խաչիկայ յարեւմըտից. եւ լուեալ էին զմահն հօրն իւրեանց եւ զտղայ եղբօրն, գային սեւ զգեստիւք եւ լացին բազում լալիւնս: Եւ յայնժամ Հասան կոչեաց ռայիս մի Քուրթ, որ էր իւր սահմանակից, եւ տայ նմա հազար դահեկան եւ ասէր. «Մուտ ի Հեր եւ ի Սաղմաստ, եւ ասա՝ թէ Թոռնեւան եւ ամենայն աշխարհն անմարդ է, զի՞ կայք պարապ. բազում հօտս ոչխարաց եւ ծառայս ընդ վայր շրջին»: Եւ արար ռայիսն այնպէս:

Xach'ik, prince of the Armenians, was unable to restrain his heart, and went against the foreigners with 70 men. Meanwhile, he had confined to the house his son Ishxan, who was a fifteen-year-old boy. When Xach'ik reached the foreigners, he saw their many troops. He called out to his men and entered battle, fiercely striking at [the enemy] and felling them to the ground. But then, behold, he spotted his son, who had escaped his confinement, and had entered the battle. When Xach'ik saw his handsome young son there, his heart broke. Ishxan, like a lion's cub, came and vehemently joined the battle. Xach'ik reached him, seized him, and sent him home. But [Ishxan] got free and reentered the fray, bravely, but foolishly. When [the enemy] learned that he was the son of brave Xach'ik, they surrounded, seized, and killed him. Seeing this, Xach'ik lost his strength, and the sword fell from his hand. When the troops of the foreigners saw this, they moved against him, seized, and killed him. The survivors fled to their homes.

After some days Xach'ik's sons came back from the west. Hearing about the deaths of their father and young brother, they came back wearing black mourning clothes and weeping profusely. Then [Xach'ik's son] Hasan called upon a Kurdish chief who was their neighbor. [Hasan] gave him 1,000 dahekans and said: "Go to Her and Salmast and say: 'T'or'nawan and the whole land is depopulated. Why are you sitting idle? Many flocks of sheep and servants are wandering about.'" The chief did this.

Եւ ժողովեցան այլազգիքն արս հնգետասան հազար, եկին մտին ի նոյն տեղին. եւ գայր ռայիսն եւ պատմեաց Հասանայ եւ Ճնճղուկին. եւ ժողովեալ Հասանայ զօրս իւր արս հինգ հազար եւ մեծաւ զայրացմամբ իբրեւ զխոցած գազան հասանէր ի վերայ բանակի անօրինացն: Եւ ձայն տուեալ Հասան արտասուալից գոչմամբ ի ճակատ այլազգ-եացն եւ ասէր. «Ո՞ւր է այրն այն, որ եսպան զհայրն իմ զԽաչիկ. յառա՛ջ եկեսցէ»: Եւ ահա գայր մի ոմն յայլազգ-եացն սեաւ մի եւ հզօր, եւ ձայնեալ ասէր՝ «Ես եմ, որ սպանի զառիւծն զԽաչիկ, եւ ահա իւր պատերազմու ձին եւ զգեստն եւ իւր նշանակն եւ թուրն, զոր ունիմ ես»: Եւ տեսեալ Հասանն որդի նորա ելաց եւ հանեալ զթուրն ի պատենիցն՝ որպէս զառիւծ հասանէր ի մէջ այլազգեացն եւ հարեալ զնա՝ ընդ երկուս պատառեաց, յերկիր ընկենոյր եւ առեալ զձին եւ զնշանակն անվնաս ելանէր: Այսպիսի օրինակաւ ձայն բարձեալ Հասանայ Ճնճղուկն եւ ասէ. «Ո՞վ է, որ եսպան զեղբայրն իմ զԻշխան անուն. ելցէ՛ յա-տենի զի տեսից զնա»: Եւ գայր Պարսիկ մի քաջ, ձայն տըւ-եալ եւ ասէր. «Ես եմ, որ սպանի զԻշխան անունն, եւ ահա իւր սպիտակ ձին եւ իւր վառ նշանակն եւ թուրն»: Եւ որ-պէս կայծակն հասաւ Ճնճղուկն ի վերայ նորա եւ սատակ-եաց զնա եւ առեալ զձին եւ զնշանակն գայր առ Հասան. եւ ձայն տուեալ Հասան զօրացն եւ քաջապէս բախեալ ի պա-տերազմ՝ դարձուցին ի փախուստ եւ կոտորեցին ի նոցանէ արս չորս հազար. եւ դարձան խաղաղութեամբ եւ մեծաւ ուրախութեամբ եւ փոխեցին զսեւ զգեստն իւրեանց:

The foreigners assembled 15,000 men, came, and entered that very area. The [Kurdish] chief came and explained [what was happening] to Hasan and Chnchghuk. Hasan assembled some 5,000 of his men and, in great rage, like a wounded beast went against the army of the foreigners. Hasan gave an anguished cry, addressed to the brigade of foreigners: "Where is the man who killed my father, Xach'ik? Let him come forth." Then, behold, a man emerged from the foreigners, dark and strong, and called out: "I am he who killed the lion Xach'ik, and here are his war horse, garment, standard, and sword, which I have with me." When [Xach'ik's] son, Hasan, saw this, he wept. Then, unsheathing his sword, he advanced through the foreigners like a lion, struck [the man] and cleaved him into two parts, [and he] fell to the ground. Then he took the horse and standard and emerged unharmed. Following the same example, Hasan's [brother,] Chnchghuk, cried out: "Who is the one who killed my brother, Ishxan? Let him come forth that I may see him." Then a brave Persian, shouted out: "I am he who killed the one named Ishxan. Behold, here are his white horse, standard, and sword." Chnchghuk advanced on him like lightning, killing him, and, taking the horse and standard, went back to Hasan. Then Hasan signalled to his troops, who valiantly entered the battle, turning [the enemy] to flight and killing 4,000 of them. Then [Hasan and Chnchghuk] turned back in peace with great joy, and changed out of their black [mourning] clothes.

35. Իսկ ի բարձրանալ թուականութեանս Հայոց ՆՂԲ թագաւորեաց ի վերայ Հոռոմոցն Մոնոմախն, որ ասէին անուն Կոստանդին: Յայսմ ամի եղեւ պատերազմ սաստիկ ի վերայ Հոռոմոց, զի իշխանն Մանիակ, այն որ յառաջ էառ զՈւռհա քաղաք, զօրաժողով արարեալ ի վերայ Մոնոմախին եւ կապեաց թագ ի գլուխն եւ արար ժողով զամենայն արեւմուտս եւ օգնական կալեալ իւր զաշխարհին Հռոմայեցոց. եւ յահէ եւ յերկիւղէ նորա ժողովեցան առ նա ամենայն արեւմուտք, վասն զի էր յաղթանդամ եւ քաջ ի պատերազմ: Յայնժամ թագաւորն Մոնոմախն արար ժողով զամենայն ազգն Յունաց եւ զայլս ի զօրաց Հայոց աշխարհին եւ յարուցեալ գնաց յաշխարհին արեւմտից ընդդէմ Մանիակայ՝ որ ի ձեռն քաջութեան իւրոյ խնդրէր զաթոռ թագաւորութեանն. եւ էր երկիւղ մեծ ի վերայ զօրացն Հոռոմոց: Իսկ յառաջ քան զխմբել պատերազմին՝ բարկութիւնն Աստուծոյ հասանէր ի վերայ արեւմտից զօրաց, եւ յաղթողն Մանիակ յանկարծամահ լինէր, եւ բարձաւ չարն ի միջոյ եւ եղեւ խաղաղութիւն մեծ. եւ ամենայն ապստամբքն փախեան, եւ զոմանս հնազանդեցոյց, եւ թագաւորն դարձաւ ի Կոստանդնուպօլիս:

Յայսմ ժամանակիս սկսաւ անօրէն Սարգիս յառաջ բերել զչար նենգութիւնն իւր եւ ազգ արարեալ Մոնոմախին եւ ասէր, եթէ «Կոչեա առ քեզ զԳագիկ ի Կոստանդնուպօլիս սիրոյ պատճառանօք եւ յայնժամ խաբէութեամբ առցես ի նմանէ զքաղաքն Անի»:

35. Now at the start of the year 492 of the Armenian Era [A.D. 1043], Monomachus ruled over the Byzantines. He was also called Constantine.[42] In this year there was a severe war among the Byzantines. This was due to Maniakes, the one who previously had captured the city of Edessa. [Maniakes] massed troops against Monomachus, put a crown on his own head, and assembled the entire West, and he also had support from [other parts of] the Byzantine realm. Out of fear and dread of him, [Maniakes] assembled by him the entire West, since he was victorious and brave in combat. Then Emperor Monomachus massed all the Byzantine troops and other troops from the land of the Armenians. He arose and went to the western lands against Maniakes who, through his bravery, sought the throne of the realm. There was great fear of him among the Byzantine forces. However, before they even massed for battle, the wrath of God struck the western troops and the triumphant Maniakes died suddenly. And thus this evil man was removed from their midst and great peace reigned. All the rebels fled and some were brought to submission. Then the emperor returned to Constantinople.

In this period the impious Sargis [Vest Sargis of Siwnik'] started to bring forth his treachery. He notified Monomachus, saying: "Summon Gagik to you in Constantinople on the pretext of friendship and then take the city of Ani from him by trickery."

42 *Constantine* IX Monomachus, 1042-1055.

Եւ լուեալ զայս թագաւորն՝ Մոնոմախ, ուրախ լինէր յոյժ, բուսաւ ի սիրտ նորա բոյս չարութեան առ ի բառնալ զթագաւորութիւնն Հայոց։ Եւ գրեաց թուղթ առ Գագիկ արքայ Հայոց հանդերձ մեծամեծ երդմամբ եւ այնչափ մոլեգնեալ՝ մինչեւ զքրիստոսական աւետարանն եւ զնշանն սուրբ խաչին Քրիստոսի միջնորդս եւ երաշխաւորս յուղարկեալ է Հայք եւ այսպիսի օրինակաւ կոչէր զթագաւորն Հայոց վասն սիրոյ եւ տեսութեան։ Եւ լուեալ զայս՝ Գագիկ ոչ էառ յանձն գնալ զհետ ստութեանն, վասն զի գիտէր զՀոռոմոց նենգութիւնն։ Յայնժամ նենգաւորն Սարգիս եւ այլ ոք յազատացն յառաջ մատեան, որք բանատուք էին առ Մոնոմախն, եւ քաջալերէին զնա գնալ եւ ասէին. «Ո՛վ թագաւոր, վասն է՞ր երկնչիս եւ ոչ գնաս վասն այսպիսի երդմանցս եւ միջնորդութեամբ Աւետարանիս եւ սրբոյ Նշանիս Քրիստոսի. եւ յաղագս մեր մի՛ երկնչիր, զի ահա անձինք մեր մեռանին ի վերայ քո»։ Եւ կացուցին միջնորդս զՏէր Պետրոս եւ արարին երդմունս սաստիկս յաւուր յայնմիկ. եւ բերին զսուրբ խորհուրդն մարմնոյ եւ արեան Որդւոյն Աստուծոյ եւ թանային զգրիչս յարիւն Կենարարին, եւ արարին երդման գիր հայրապետոն եւ ամենայն իշխանքն Հայոց. եւ յայնժամ գնաց Գագիկ արքայն Հայոց ի Կոստանդնուպօլիս առ թագաւորն Մոնոմախն։ Եւ ամենայն քաղաքն բախեալ ելանէին ընդ առաջ Գագկայ Հայոց արքային մեծաւ փառաւորութեամբ եւ տարան զնա առ թագաւորն՝ որպէս վայել է թագաւորի, եւ աւուրս ինչ մեծարեաց զնա Մոնոմախն։ Յայնժամ աստուածուրաց նենգաւորքն որք արեամբն Աստուծոյ կապեցին զերդումն սուտ կալի, առաքեն քառասուն բանալիս զքաղաքին Անւոյ առ թագաւորն Մոնոմախն եւ ի հետ թուղթ՝ թէ Անի քաղաքն եւ ամենայն արեւելքն քեզ եղեւ։

When Emperor Monomachus heard this, he was greatly pleased, while in his heart an evil plant had taken root—to eliminate the kingdom of the Armenians. He wrote a letter to Gagik, king of the Armenians, with great vows [for his safety] and, so much had [Monomachus] strayed that he sent to the Armenians the Christian Gospel and a relic of the holy Cross of Christ to serve as an intermediary and guarantee. And thus did [Monomachus] summon the king of the Armenians in friendship for an interview. When Gagik heard about this, he did not agree to follow after falseness, since he knew about the treachery of the Byzantines. Then the traitor Sargis and others from the azats who had encouraged Monomachus, came forth and urged [Gagik] to go, saying: "O king, why do you fear and why do you not go after such an oath—confirmed by the sending of the Gospel and the blessed relic of Christ—has been given? Fear not for us, for we will die for you." As an intermediary they designated Lord Petros, and on that day they swore a strong oath. The holy sacrament of the body and blood of the Son of God was brought forth and a pen was dipped into the life-giving blood [wine]. The patriarch and all the princes of the Armenians signed this written oath. Then Gagik, king of the Armenians, went to Emperor Monomachus in Constantinople. The entire city arose and in great glory came before Gagik, king of the Armenians, and took him to the emperor as was fitting for a king, and Monomachus exalted him for a few days. Then, the apostate traitors who swore a solemn oath with the blood of God, sent 40 keys of the city of Ani to Emperor Monomachus, with a letter that said: "The city of Ani and the entire East belongs to you."

36. Եւ կոչեաց թագաւորն զԳագիկ եւ զբանալիս տանն եւ զթուղթն առաջի նորա եդեալ՝ եւ ասէր ցԳագիկ, եթէ զԱնի եւ զամենայն արեւելք ետուն ի ձեռս իմ: Եւ ծանեաւ Գագիկ զնենգութեան գործն, յոգւոց եհան արտասուօք եւ ասէր. «Դա՛տ արասցէ Քրիստոս ընդ իս եւ ընդ նենգաւորսն իմ»: Եւ ասէր Գագիկ ցՄոնոմախն, եթէ «Տէր եւ թագաւորն ես եմ տանն Հայոց. ահա ես ոչ տաց զՀայք ի ձեռս քո, զի դու զիս խաբէութեամբ ածեր ի Կոստանդնուպօլիս»: Եւ զաւուրս երեսուն պնդեալ ոչ հաւանէր Գագիկ, եւ յորժամ զելս իրացն ոչ գտանէր, յայնժամ տայր զԱնի ի ձեռս Հոռոմոց. եւ տայր Գագկայ Մոնոմախն զԿալօն-Պեղատն եւ զՊիզու եւ ոչ յուղարկեաց զԳագիկ ի քաղաքն Անի, եւ զտունն հայրենի իւրոյ տայր բերել ի Հոռոմս. Եւ կայր պանդխտեալ ի մէջ անողորմ եւ չար ազգին Յունաց: Բայց ուր եւ հասանէր Գագիկ, նեղութիւն մեծ արկանէր ի վերայ ազգին Յունաց պէսպէս խայտառակութեամբ, վասն զի որպէս թագաւոր ահարկութեամբ կայր ի մէջ Հոռոմոց. բայց սուգ սաստիկ ունէր ի սրտի իւրում վասն հայրենի աթոռոյն իւրոյ, զոր նենգութեամբ յափշտակեցին աստուածուրաց եւ նենգաւոր ազգն հերետիկոսացն:

Արդ յորժամ փոխեցաւ թուականութիւնն Հայոց ի յամս ՆՂԳ զօրաժողով արար թագաւորն Մոնոմախ զամենայն աշխարհին Յունաց եւ ահագին բազմութեամբ յուղարկեաց զնոսա յարեւելս խնդրել զքաղաքն Անի եւ կացուցանէր զօրագլուխ զՊառակամանոսն՝ զայր ներքինի կուրտ գոլով, եւ գայր զօրօք բազմօք հասանէր ի դուռն Անւոյ: Եւ զայր կին կամէր դնել պահապան աշխարհին Հայոց փոխանակ հզօր քաջին Գագկայ. եւ Գագիկ այլ ոչ թողաւ ելանել յարեւելք:

36. The emperor summoned Gagik and placed before him the keys and the letter and said to Gagik: "You have given Ani and all the East into my hand." Then Gagik realized the treachery of the deed. In tears he said: "Let Christ judge between me and my traitors." Then Gagik said to Monomachus: "I am lord and king over the House of the Armenians. Behold, I do not give the Armenians into your hand. For you brought me to Constantinople by treachery." For 30 days [the Byzantines kept] insisting, but Gagik would not agree. However, when he could find no way out, he gave Ani over to the Byzantines. Monomachus gave to Gagik [the areas of] Kalon-Peghat and Pizu [in Cappadocia], but he did not send Gagik back to the city of Ani; and he had his family brought to Byzantine land. And thus was [Gagik] an exile among the cruel and evil nation of the Greeks. However, wherever Gagik went, he brought great treachery and various disgraces upon the nation of the Greeks since, as a king, he was regarded with awe among the Byzantines. However, he nurtured an intense sorrow in his heart because of his paternal throne, which the apostate and treacherous nation of heretics had ravished from him.

At the start of the year 493 of the Armenian Era [A.D. 1044], Emperor Monomachus massed troops from the entire realm of the Byzantines. He sent this enormous multitude to the East to demand the city of Ani. [Monomachus] designated as their military commander [a] parakoimomenos [named Nicholas], who was a eunuch. He arrived at the gates of Ani with many troops. [Monomachus] wanted to install this eunuch as a defender of the land of the Armenians, in place of the mighty and brave Gagik. As for Gagik, [Monomachus] did not allow him to return to the East.

Իսկ ազգք Հայոցն, որք էին ի քաղաքն յԱնի, ոչ հաւանեցան տալ զքաղաքն, այլ յուզելով յուզէին զթագաւորն իւրեանց եւ հայհոյեալ նախատէին զամենայն ազգն Հոռոմոց: Եւ յայնժամ ելանէին ամենայն քաղաքն միաբան ի պատերազմ ի դուռն քաղաքին Անւոյ եւ դարձուցին ի փախուստ զզօրսն Հոռոմոց եւ կոտորելով արարին զնոսա հալածականս, եւ լափեցին առ հասարակ զամենայն բանակն նոցա. եւ դարձան զօրքն Հայոց ի քաղաքն Անի մեծաւ յաղթութեամբ. եւ գնացին զօրքն Հոռոմոց ամօթով յաշխարհն իւրեանց, եւ Պառակամանոսն ձմերեաց յԱղթիքն: Եւ իբրեւ իմացան զօրքն Հայոց՝ թէ թագաւորն Հայոց այլ ոչ է ելանելոց յարեւելս եւ ծանեան զնենգութիւն նախարարացն Հայոց առ հասարակ ամենայն տունն Հայոց. եւ արարին ամենայն քաղաքն ժողով ուր էին գերեզմանն ամենայն Հայոց առաջին թագաւորացն եւ անդ լացին զանտիրանալն ազգին Հայոց. լային եւ զաթոռ թագաւորութեանն իւրեանց եւ կոծ եդեալ առ հասարակ լային զթագաւորն իւրեանց զԳագիկ. լային եւ զամենայն ազգն Բագրատունեաց եւ անէծս ցաւագին կարդային նենգաւորացն Գագկայ: Եւ յորժամ անճարեալ հաւանեցան քաղաքն եւ ամենայն զօրքն, եւ գրեցին առ զօրապետն Հոռոմոց ի Պառակամանոսն եւ երդմամբ կոչեցին զնա ի քաղաքն Անի եւ ետուն զքաղաքն Անի ի ձեռս Հոռոմոց, եւ խախտեալ փըլաւ տէրութիւն ազգին Բագրատունեաց:

Now the Armenian people in Ani did not agree to give over the city. Rather, they longed for their own king and insulted the entire nation of Byzantines with swears. The entire city, united, arose to fight at the gates of the city of Ani, turning the Byzantine troops to flight, killing and pursuing [fugitives]. The Armenian troops destroyed the entire [Byzantine] army and then r turned in great triumph to the city of Ani. The Byzantine troops returned to their own land in disgrace, while the parakoimomenos wintered in Aght'ik'. When the Armenian troops realized that the king of the Armenians would not be returning to the East, and when they learned about the treachery of the Armenian lords, the entire city assembled near the mausoleum of the first kings and wept over the lordless nation of the Armenians. They also wept over the throne of their kingdom and, especially, they mourned for their king, Gagik. They wept for the entire line of the Bagratids and severely cursed Gagik's traitors. When the city and the entire army accepted the fact that there was no [other] way out, they wrote to the Byzantine military commander, to the parakoimomenos, and, with an oath [of safety], called him to the city of Ani, and gave the city into the hands of the Byzantines.Thus did the lordship of the Bagratids, pulled apart in this way, collapse.

Դարձեալ ի թուականութեանս Հայոց յամի ՆՂԴ ե-ղեւ մեծաասատ բարկութիւն Աստուծոյ ի վերայ արարա-ծոցս. քանզի հայեցաւ տէր Աստուած բարկութեամբ յարա-րածս իւր, եւ եղեւ շարժ ահաւոր եւ սոսկալի, եւ դողաց ա-մենայն տիեզերք առ հասարակ ըստ բանի մարգարէին՝ որ ասէ. «Ո՞ հայի յերկիր եւ տայ դողալ սմա»: Արդ այս-պիսի նմանութեամբ շարժեցաւ ամենայն արարածքն, եւ բազում եկեղեցիք խախտեալ փլաւ ի հիմանց եւ յԵկեղեաց գաւառին. եւ քաղաքն՝ որ յԵրզնկան կոչի՝ փլաւ առ հասա-րակ. եւ պատառեցաւ երկիրն եւ արք եւ կանայք ընկղմե-ցան ի խորս անդնդոց, եւ զաւուրս բազումս գայր ձայն աղաղակի նոցա ի խորս անդնդոց. եւ էր յամառնային ժա-մանակին եւ յաւուր աւուր շարժէր երկին յամին յայնմիկ, որ ոչ բաւեմք պատմել վասն բարկութեանն եւ խռովու-թեանն, զոր էած Աստուած ի վերայ արարածոցս վասն մեղաց մերոց. եւ զամառնային ժամանակն խաւար եւ մութն լինէր ի վերայ երկրի, մինչեւ արեգակն եւ լուսին ի կերպս արեան երեւէին, եւ յորժամ կամարն ելանէր՝ յիս-տակ էր:

37. Յայսմ ամի եւ յաւուրս աշնանային խաղաց զօրքն Հոռոմոց եւ գնացին ի վերայ քաղաքին Դվնայ. եւ ի խմբել պատերազմին՝ բարկութիւն հասանէր յԱստուծոյ ի վերայ զօրացն Հոռոմոց եւ լինէին պարտեալք յերեսաց այլազգ-եացն եւ դարձան ի փախուստ. եւ եղեւ կոտորած մեծ ի վե-րայ քրիստոնէիցն, եւ բազումք ի զօրացն Հոռոմոց անկան ի սուր եւ ի գերութիւն, ընդ որ եւ մեծ սպարապետն Հայոց Վահրամ հանդերձ որդւովն իւրով Գրիգորիւ սպանաւ ի մեծ պատերազմին ի Դուին քաղաքին:

Also [occurring] in the year 494 of the Armenian Era [A.D. 1045], the great wrath of God fell upon [all] creatures. For the Lord God looked upon his creations in anger, and a frightful, terrifying earthquake occurred. The entire universe shook, just as the words of the prophet put it: "He looks upon the earth and makes it tremble."[43] It was just in this manner that all creation was rocked. Many churches collapsed to their foundations in the district of Ekegheats', while the city called Erznka completely collapsed. Men and women sank into the depths of the abyss, and in many districts the sound of their cries, coming from the depths, could be heard for many days. It was summertime, and every day that year the earth shook. I am unable to narrate the anger and disturbance that God visited upon us creatures because of our sins. During the summer there was darkness and dimness over the earth, to the point that the sun and the moon had a bloody appearance, yet when the vault of the sky appeared, it was clear.

37. During the autumn of that year Byzantine troops advanced against the city of Dvin. When they massed for battle, the wrath of God fell upon the Byzantine troops. They were defeated by the foreigners and fled. There was a great destruction of Christians: many of the Byzantine soldiers were taken captive or fell to the sword, including the great sparapet of the Armenians, Vahram, along with his son, Grigor, who were killed in the great battle at the city of Dvin.

43 Psalms 114:7.

Յայսմ ամի շարժեալ եղեւ բարկութիւն մեծ ի տանէն Պարսից, եւ ելեալ գային արք երեք ի դիւանէն՝ ի Տուղրէլ սուլտանէն՝ Պօղի, Պուկի, Անազուղլի՝ եւ հասանէին բազում զօրօք յաշխարհն Տաճկաց. եւ անհամար գերութեամբ գայր բանակ հարկանէր ի վերայ Արեան գետոյ ի սահմանս Մօււլայ: Եւ յայնժամ զօրապետն Մօւլայ, որ աւէին Խուրէշ, տէրն Մօւլայ, զօրաժողով արարեալ գայր ի վերայ նոցա արապիկ զօրօքն. եւ արարին պատերազմ սաստիկ յերկուցունց կողմանցն. եւ յայնժամ Թուրքն յաղթեաց արապիկ զօրացն եւ արար փախստական զնոսա եւ զկանայս եւ զորդիս նոցա էառ ի գերութիւն: Եւ յայնժամ ամիրայն Տաճկաց Խուրէշն կապեաց սեւ նշանակ եւ մտաւ ճիչկան յարապիկք եւ արար ժողով մեծ եւ գայր ի վերայ Թուրքին. եւ սաստիկ պատերազմաւ յաղթեաց նոցա եւ առեալ զգերութիւնն իւր եւ զնոցայն. եւ գնաց Թուրքն փախստական մինչեւ ի Պաղին եւ արարեալ բազում կոտորածս ի բազում տեղիս եւ ի գաւառն Թլմխոյ եղեւ բազում արհինհեղութիւնս քրիստոնէից: Եւ այսպիսի անհամար գերութեամբ զօրքն Թուրքաց դիմեալ երթային յաշխարհն Պարսից եւ հասանէր մինչեւ յԱրճէշ քաղաքն Հայոց:

In the same year, great anger arose and moved from the House of the Persians. Three men from the divan of Sultan Tughril—Po'ghi, Puki, and Anazughli—arose and came with many troops to the land of the Tachiks. Taking countless captives, they came and camped by the river Arean, by the borders of Mosul. Then the military commander of Mosul, whom they called Xure'sh, lord of Mosul, assembled troops and came against them with Arab troops. A fierce battle was waged by both sides. Then the Turks triumphed over the Arab troops, putting them to flight and taking into captivity their women and children. At this point Xure'sh, the emir of the Tachiks, put a black sign [of mourning] on himself and went as a bringer of bad news among the Arabs. He assembled a large force and went against the Turks. He conquered them in a severe battle and took back his captives and captured others [of the Turks]. The Turks fled as far as Paghin[44] and wrought much destruction in many places. In the district of T'lmux there was a great shedding of Christian blood. And thus, with innumerable captives, did the Turkish troops head for the land of the Persians, reaching the Armenian city of Archesh.

44 A canton of Sophene.

Եւ էր անդ զօրավար մի Հոռոմց՝ որում անուն ա-սէին Ստեփան կատապան. եւ ամիրայքն Պարսից յուղար-կեցին բազում աւարս Հոռոմց զօրավարին՝ զի տացէ նոցա անց, զի գնասցեն յաշխարհն իւրեանց: Իսկ նորա հը-պարտացեալ ելանէր ի պատերազմ ի վերայ զօրացն Թուրքաց. եւ յայնժամ յաղթեցին զօրացն Հոռոմց Թուրքն եւ արարին սաստիկ կոտորածս եւ կալան զՍտեփան կա-տապանն եւ տարան ի Հեր քաղաք. եւ զկնի բազում չար-չարանացն մեռանէր ի ձեռաց անօրինացն. եւ քերթեցին զմորթ մարմնոյ նորա եւ լցեալ զնա խոտով եւ կախեցին զպարսպէն, զոր լուեալ ազգի նորա, եկեալ գնեցին զմար-մինն եւ զմորթն ի տասն հազար դահեկան:

38. Դարձեալ ի թուականութեանս Հայոց ՆՂԵ ամին զօրաժողով արարեալ Մոնոմախ թագաւորն Հոռոմց եւ կացուցեալ զօրագլուխ զմեծ իշխանն Հոռոմց՝ որում ա-նուն ասէին Տելիար կուրտ եւ ներքինի գոլով, եւ գայր ա-հագին բազմութեամբ եւ անթիւ զօրօք ի վերայ քաղաքին Դվնայ, եւ բանակ հարկանէր ի դուռն քաղաքին. եւ էր ի ձմերային ժամանակն. եւ ի սաստկութենէ սառնաման-եացն եւ ի բախմանէ առատաբուղխ անձրեւացն ոչինչ կա-րաց առնել, այլ դառնայր անյաղթելի եւ խաղայր գնայր ի Հոռոմց աշխարհն:

Located there was a Byzantine general named Step'an the captain. The Persian emirs sent [messages] to this Byzantine general for many days, so that he allow them to pass and go on to their own land. He, however, pridefully arose to battle the Turkish troops. The Turks conquered the Byzantine troops. There was a great killing and [the Turks] seized the catapan Step'an and took him to the city of Her. After many torments, he died at the hands of the impious ones. They flayed the skin from his body, filled it with straw, and hanged it from the gate. When his family heard about this, they came and purchased his body and skin for 10,000 dahekans.

38. In the year 495 of the Armenian Era [A.D. 1046], Monomachus, emperor of the Byzantines, assembled troops and appointed as their military commander a great Byzantine prince, [who was also] a *telarches* and a eunuch. He came against the city of Dvin with an enormous and uncountable multitude of troops. He camped by the city's gates. Now it was wintertime and, because of the severity of the cold and the down-pouring of abundant rain, he was unable to accomplish anything. Rather, withdrawing without a triumph, he turned back to Byzantine territory.

Իսկ յորժամ փոխեցաւ թուականն Հայոց յամս ՆՂՁ, դարձեալ գայ Տեյիարն զօրօք բազմօք եւ իջանէր ի վերայ քաղաքին Դվնայ. եւ բազում չարչարանս եւ տագնապս գործեաց այնմ գաւառին եւ սրով եւ գերութեամբ ապականեաց զամենայն ազգն Տաճկաց եւ դարձաւ յաշխարհին Յունաց խաղաղութեամբ:

Յայսմ թուականութեանս Հայոց պատրիկ ոմն՝ անուն Թոռնիկ, ապստամբեաց ի վերայ Մոնոմախին, որ է ի քաղաքէն Անբռնապօլսէ, այր քաջ եւ հզօր եւ պատերազմող. եւ սորա ժողով արարեալ ամենայն աշխարհին արեւմտից եւ զԳնդից, եւ ահագին բազմութեամբ գայր ի վերայ Կոստանդնուպօլսի եւ ի մեծ տագնապ եւ ի նեղութիւնս արկանէր զքաղաքն.

Եւ թագաւորն ոչ իշխեաց ելանել ի պատերազմ, եւ այնչափ ձանձրացաւ քաղաքն Կոստանդնուպօլիս ի պատերազմէն, մինչեւ քարուկրով կալան զդուռն քաղաքին. եւ այնչափ ահագին արարեալ Թոռնիկ զպատերազմն, մինչեւ զսուրբ Անարծաթքն, որ կայ արտաքոյ քաղաքին՝ քարայատակ արարեալ եւ զամենայն քարն առ հասարակ յՈվկիանոս ընկէց՝ զմեծ եկեղեցւոյն զսուրբ վկայիցն: Իսկ թագաւորն Մոնոմախ եւ ամենայն իշխանք քաղաքին Կոստանդնուպօլսի յահ եւ յերկիւղ լեալ եւ ելս իրացն ոչ կարէին գտանել եւ ընդդէմ քաջութեան Թոռնկայ ոչ կարէին կալ: Իսկ պատրիարգն եւ ամենայն իշխանքն եւ թագաւորն խորհեցան չար խորհուրդս վասն Թոռնկայ եւ գրեցին երդմունս ահավորս եւ սուտ եւ խաբանօք երդուան Թոռնկայ դնել զնա Կեսառ եւ թէ զկնի մահու Մոնոմախին Թոռնիկ լիցի թագաւոր. եւ այսպիսի գրեցին եւ երդմամբ հաւատարմացուցին զիրեանց նենգութիւնն. եւ ասէին թէ՝ Գտաք ի գիրս զի զկնի մահուան Մոնոմախին դու նստցիս յաթոռ թագաւորութեանս:

At the start of the year 496 of the Armenian Era [A.D. 1047], the telarches again arrived with many troops and descended on the city of Dvin. He wrought many evils and disasters in that district and, with the sword and by taking captives, polluted the entire nation of Tachiks. Then he peacefully returned to the land of the Byzantines.

In the same year, a certain Armenian patrician named T'or'nik [Leo Tornices] rebelled against Monomachus. [T'or'nik] was from the city of Adrianopolis, a brave, mighty, and martial man. He had massed troops from the entire western territories and from the Goths and, with an enormous multitude, came against Constantinople. He put that city into a grave crisis and dire straits.

Now the emperor did not dare to go forth to battle. The city of Constantinople had so wearied of warfare that they blocked the city's gate with stones. T'or'nik pursued the fight with such fury, that he completely demolished the [church of the] blessed Anargyri, which was located outside the city, and then threw all the stones of this great church of the holy martyrs into the Ocean. Now Emperor Monomachus and all the princes of the city of Constantinople were terrified and could not find any way out, nor were they able to resist T'or'nik's bravery. It was then that the patriarch, all the princes, and the emperor hatched a wicked plot against T'or'nik. They wrote powerful oaths that were also false and treacherous, swearing that T'or'nik would be made a Caesar and that after Monomachus' death, T'or'nik would be emperor. Thus did they write to him and by oath confirmed their treachery, saying: "We have found in books that after Monomachus' death you shall be seated on the throne of the realm."

Եւ ելեալ պատրիարգն առ Թոռնիկ եւ քահանայքն եւ իշխանքն եւ երկրորդեալ զերդումն առաջի Թոռնկայ, եւ եղեւ սէր եւ խաղաղութիւն. եւ միաբան ածին զնա ի Կոստանդնուպօլիս. եւ յետ սակաւ աւուրց ուրացան զերդումն իւրեանց եւ ուրացան զմիջնորդն Աստուած՝ որպէս եւ սովոր են ազգս Հոռոմց երդմամբ կորուսանել զամենայն մեծամեծսն աշխարհի. եւ յայնժամ խաւարեցուցին զաչսն Թոռնկայ զառն քաջի:

39. Յայսմ թուականութեանս Հայոց ՆՂԸ, յաւուր Մոնոմախի կայսերն, որ նենգութեամբ եւ երդմամբ եբարձ զթագաւորութիւնն Հայոց ի յազգէ Բագրատունեաց, յայսմ թագաւորութեանս եւ ի հայրապետութեանն Տէր Պետրոսի Հայոց կաթուղիկոսի զարթեաւ աստուածասաստ բարկութիւնն ի տանէն Պարսից հրամանաւ Տուղրէլ սուլտանին. եւ ելեալ երկու զօրապետքն բազում զօրօք ի դիւանէ անտի, որք անուանեալ ասէին Աբրէիմ եւ Գթլմուշ, եւ անթիւ բազմութեամբ գան ի յաշխարհին Հայոց, վասն զի ի ձեռացն Հոռոմց գիտացին անտէր եւ անպահապան զամենայն աշխարհին Հայոց. զի զարս քաջս եւ զհզօրս քակեալ հանին յարեւելից Հոռոմք եւ կուրտ զօրապետօք ջանային պահել զաշխարհին Հայոց եւ զամենայն տունն արեւելից:

The patriarch went before T'or'nik, and [with] the priests and princes they confirmed the oath in T'or'nik's presence. Then there was friendship and peace, and they brought him into Constantinople in unity. However, after a few days they violated their oath and betrayed God's intercession, as is the custom of the nation of the Romans—to ruin all the grandees of the land through [false] oaths. Then they blinded the eyes of that brave man, T'or'nik.

39. In 498 of the Armenian Era [A.D. 1049-1050] in the days [of the reign] of Emperor Monomachus—who treacherously and by a [false] oath took the kingdom of the Armenians from the line of the Bagratids—during the patriarchate of Lord Petros, Catholicos of the Armenians, divine wrath was aroused from the House of the Persians by the order of Sultan Tughril. Two military commanders, named Ibrahim and Qutlumush, arose with many troops from the divan there. With a countless multitude of troops they came to the land of the Armenians, since they knew that the entire land of the Armenians was lordless and undefended by the actions of the Byzantines. This was because the Byzantines had removed from the East brave and mighty men and, employing eunuch military commanders, tried to hold the land of the Armenians and the entire House of the East with them.

Եւ ահա յայսմ ամի զօրք անօրինաց հասանէին ի հռչակաւորսն եւ ի բազմամբոխ քաղաքն Հայոց՝ որ կոչի Արծն. եւ գտեալ անպարիսպ զքաղաքն եւ անթիւ բազմութեամբ լցեալ զարանց եւ զկանանց եւ անհամար չափս ոսկւոյ եւ արծաթոյ: Եւ քաղաքացիքն տեսեալ զզօրս այլազգեացն միաբան ի պատերազմ ելեալ, եւ խմբեցաւ շուրջ զեզերօք քաղաքին սաստիկ եւ ահաւոր պատերազմ. եւ եղեւ զվեց ժամ աւուրն զմիմեանս կոփէին եւ արեամբ լցաւ անդաստանքն, վասն զի ոչ գոյր տեղի փախստեան եւ ոչ օգնական, միայն զմահն ունէին յոյս.

Եւ ի բազմութենէ անօրինացն ձանձրացան զօրքն քաղաքին եւ ի փախուստ դարձան. եւ այլազգիքն սրով յարձակեցան ի վերայ քաղաքին եւ սաստիկ կոտորածով առ հասարակ ի ներքոյ սրոյ անցուցին զամենայն քաղաքն իբրեւ զբիւրս հնգետասան: Այլ զոսկւոյ եւ զարծաթոյ եւ զդիպակաց աւելորդ է ասել, վասն զի ոչ արկանի ընդ գրով. բայց զայս բազում անգամ լուեալ է մեր ի բազմաց յաղագս քորեպիսկոպոսին՝ որ ասէին Դաւթուկ, եթէ զգանձատունն նորա Աբրիհիմն էառ եւ քառասուն ուղտ բարձան զգանձարանն նորա, ութ հարիւր վեցկի եզանց ելանէին ի տանէ նորա: Եւ կայր յայնժամ ութ հարիւր եկեղեցի ընդ պատարագով: Եւ այսպիսի դառն կատարածիւ եւ չարաչար մահուամբս սրով անցաւ վայելուչ եւ փառաւոր քաղաքն Արծն, եւ կամ որպէս լալով ասացից՝ զանցումն իշխանացն եւ զքահանայիցն, որք անթաղք եւ կերակուր գազանաց լեալ, եւ փառաւոր կանայք հանդերձ տղայօքն վարեցան ի գերութիւն յաշխարհն Պարսից յանգին ծառայութիւն: Եւ ահա այս սկիզբն եղեւ Հայոց կորստեանս. լուր՝ միտ դիք կատարածիս եւ անցմանս արեւելից մի առ մի ամ յամէ, վասն զի այս է առաջին քաղաք, որ առաւ սրով եւ գերութեամբ ի Հայոց:

Behold, in this year the troops of the impious reached the renowned and populous city called Artsn. They found the city unwalled and filled with an innumerable multitude of men and women and countless quantities of gold and silver. When the citizens saw the troops of the foreigners, they arose in unison and went to fight. A fierce and dreadful battle took place on the outskirts of the city. Until the sixth hour of the day [the two forces] struck at one another and they filled the plain with blood, for there was nowhere to flee and no aid. Their only hope was death.

After being worn out by the multitude of the impious ones, the forces from the city turned and fled. The foreigners turned upon the city with their swords and wrought a severe destruction, putting the entire city to the sword, some 150,000 people. It is superfluous to mention the quantities of gold, silver, and brocades [they seized], because it cannot be estimated. However, we did hear this many times from many people concerning [the great wealth of] the chorepiscopus [rural bishop] Dawt'uk, when Ibrahim seized his treasury: that it took 40 camels and 800 oxen [yoked] in groups of six to bear the treasure away from his home. At the time [of the raid] there were 800 active churches. Thus was the glorious and lovely city of Artsn put to the sword with such bitter acts and wicked slaughter. In tears, how can I relate the deaths of princes and priests who remained unburied and the food for beasts; or the glorious women with their children who were led into slavery to the land of the Persians. Behold, this was the start of the destruction of the Armenians. Listen and heed what transpired and [an account of] the destruction of the East which took place year after year. For [Artsn] was the first city which was taken by the sword and the enslavement of the Armenians.

Իսկ յորժամ լուաւ զչար համբաւս զայս թագաւորն Մոնոմախ, առաքեաց զօրս յարեւելս եւ կարգեաց զօրագլուխ զօրացն զԿամենն, զԳրիգոր Վասակայ որդին եւ զԼիպարիտն զեղբայրն Ռատին առն քաջին, եւ բազում զօրօք հասանէին յաշխարհին Հայոց առ ի պատերազմել ընդ զօրսն Պարսից:

Յայսմ ամի գրեաց Մոնոմախ թագաւորն Յունաց թուղթ առ Տէր Պետրոս Հայոց հայրապետն, զի եկեսցէ առ նա ի Կոստանդնուպօլիս: Եւ Տէր Պետրոսն կամաւ իւրով յօժարեաց գնալ. խորհեցաւ ի միտս իւր եւ ասէ. «Գուցէ այլ ոչ թողուն զիս Հոռոմք ելանել յարեւելս», անուանեաց զաթոռ հայրապետութեան իւրոյ զամենագովելին զՏէր Խաչիկ: Նոյն օրինակաւ խորհեցաւ եւ յաղագս միւռոնին օրհնեալ ձիթոյն՝ օծմանն հաւատոյ Հայաստանեայց. պահեաց յԱհուր գետն երկաթի ամանօք իբրեւ լիտր չորս հարիւր, վասն զի մի՛ գուցէ անկանիցի ի ձեռս Հոռոմոցն. եւ կայ պահեալ մինչեւ ցայսօր ժամանակի. ի գիշերի արարեալ զայս՝ մերձ ի դուռն քաղաքին Անւոյ:

40. Եւ ինքն իւր տանեցի ազատօքն փառաւոր արամբք երեք հարիւր՝ վառեալ զինուք, եւ վարդապետս եւ եպիսկոպոսունս եւ երաժիշտս եւ կրօնաւորս, քահանայս հարիւր եւ հեծեալս ի փառաւոր ջորւոջ, հետեւակ պաշտօնեայս երկերիւրս:

Now when Emperor Monomachus heard this wicked news, he sent troops to the East, designating as military commanders Kamen [Kekaumenos], Grigor, son of Vasak, and Liparit, brother of that brave man, R'at. With many troops they reached the land of the Armenians to fight against the Persian forces.

In this same year Monomachus, emperor of the Byzantines, wrote a letter to Lord Petros, the patriarch of the Armenians so that [Petros] come to him in Constantinople. As it happened, Lord Petros was quite willing to go. However, he thought to himself: "Perhaps afterwards the Byzantines will not allow me to return to the East." Therefore, he named the most praiseworthy Lord Xach'ik [as locum tenens] to his patriarchal throne. In the same way [Petros] considered the matter of the chrism, the holy oil used for consecration in the rites of the Armenians. He stored the chrism in the Ahurian River in iron vessels weighing as much as 400 ltrs, so that it would not fall into Byzantine hands. To this day it is preserved there. Now [Petros] did this at night. [The hiding place was] close to the gates of the city of Ani.

40. Then he himself [set out on his journey to Constantinople] accompanied by azats from his household: 300 glorious armed men, one hundred vardapets, bishops, musicians, monastics, and priests, mounted on splendid mules, as well as 200 domestics on foot.

Եւ էր զհետ Տեառն Պետրոսի նախնականն եւ լաւն ի բնաւից Բուլղար վարդապետն, եւ ամենագովելին Խաչատուր դպրապետն եւ Թադէոս՝ որ էր այր անպարտելի գրչութեամբ, Գէորգ Քարնեղեցին եւ Յովհաննէս Քարնեղեցին եւ Մատթէոս Հաղբատացին եւ Մխիթար Բնայրեցին եւ Տիրանուն եւ իմաստասէր Կապանեցին, Մխիթարիկն, Վարդան Սանահեցին, Բարսեղն Բաշխատացին եւ համավայելուչն եւ շքեղն Տէր Եղիսէն եւ Բարսեղն նորին եղբայրն, Գէորգ՝ ջուլահակ ձագն եւ Տէր Եփրեմն եւ Տէր Անանէ եւ Տէր Խաչիկն: Արդ այս ամենայն վարդապետք եւ իմաստասէրք եւ հմուտք հին եւ նոր Կտակարանացն Աստուծոյ: Եւ ինքն ամենագովելին Տէր Պետրոս սոքօք հետեւեալ ճանապարհորդութեամբ հասանէր ի Կոստանդնուպօլիս:

Եւ յորժամ լուան զգալն նորա, դղրդեցաւ ամենայն քաղաքն Կոստանդնուպօլսի ընդ առաջ Տեառն Պետրոսի, հանդերձ մեծամեծօք եւ ահաւոր փառօք տարան զնա ի սուրբն Սոփի, եւ անդ հանդիպեալ թագաւորին եւ պատրիարգին եւ իջուցին զնա ի փառաւոր տան: Եւ հրամայեաց տալ ծախս Տեառն Պետրոսի. յառաջին աւուրն ետուն կենդինար մի. իսկ յերկրորդ աւուրն գնաց Տէր Պետրոս ի պաղատն առ թագաւորն. եւ լուեալ թագաւորն զգալն՝ ել ընդ առաջ նորա եւ հրամայեաց նստուցանել զՏէր Պետրոս յոսկի սէլին, զոր ի ժամ գնալոյն Տէր Եղիսէ յինքն առեալ. իսկ սպասաւորք թագաւորին ջանային առնուլ, եւ նա ուժգին ոչ տայր.

Accompanying Lord Petros were [the following persons]: First and best was Vardapet Bulghar; then the most praiseworthy Xach'atur, the chief scribe; and T'ade'os, who was invincible in writing; Ge'org K'arneghets'i, and Yovhanne's K'arneghets'i, and Matt'e'os Haghbatats'i, and Mxit'ar Bnayrets'i, and Tiranun and the philosopher Kapanets'i, Mxit'arik, Vardan Sanahnets'i, Barsegh Bashxatats'i, and the universally revered and magnificent Lord Eghise' and his brother, Barsegh, Ge'org Julahakdzag and Lord Ep'rem and Lord Anane' and Lord Xach'ik. All these men were vardapets and philosophers and well-versed in the Old and New Testaments of God. The most praiseworthy Lord Petros, accompanied by them on his journey, arrived in Constantinople.

When [the residents of Constantinople] heard about his arrival, the entire city was motivated to come out before Lord Petros and, with grandees in attendance and in stunning splendor, they took him to Saint Sophia. There he was met by the emperor and the patriarch[45] and then he was taken to a glorious residence. The emperor ordered that Lord Petros should be given a stipend for expenses. On the first day, they gave one *kentenarion*. On the second day, Lord Petros went to the palace, to the emperor. When the emperor heard of his arrival, he arose and went before him and ordered that Lord Petros be seated on a golden throne. At the time of departure, Lord Eghise' took [the throne]. Now the emperor's attendants tried to take it from him, but he, forcefully, would not give it up.

45 *Patriarch* of Constantinople, Michael I Cerularius (1043-1058).

Եւ տեսեալ թագաւորն հարցանէր զպատճառս չտալոյն: Եւ յայնժամ պատասխանի ետ Տէր Եղիսէ եւ ասէր. «Ո՛վ թագաւոր, հայրապետական աթոռ է, եւ ոչ ոք է արժանի ի սմա նստիլ, բայց միայն Տէր Պետրոսն»: Եւ լուեալ զայս թագաւորն՝ իրաւունս համարեցաւ զբանն, զոր ասաց Տէր Եղիսէ. եւ ասաց թագաւորն. «Թոյլ տուք զառաքելական աթոռդ ի դմա»: Յայնժամ ասէ թագաւորն Տէր Եղիսէի. «Հազար դահեկան է աթոռդ, պահեսցես զդա տեառն քում, զի մի՛ այլ ոք ի դմա նստցի»:

Եւ այսպիսի փառաւորութեամբ կացեալ Տէր Պետրոսին ի Կոստանդնուպօլիս ի մէջ Հոռոմց զամս չորս, եւ աւուր յաւուր յաւելէր փառօք եւ պատուօք ի մէջ Յունաց. եւ յորժամ երթայր ի պաղատ թագաւորին, նախ զհայրապետական գաւազանն յառաջ տանէին. եւ յորժամ տեսանէր թագաւորն՝ երկրպագանէր եւ հրաման տայր թագաւորն մեծամեծաց իւրոց ելանել ընդդէմ Տեառն Պետրոսի: Եւ զկնի չորից ամաց բաշխէր թագաւորն եւ պատրիարգն Տէր Պետրոսի բազում ընծայս՝ գանձս եւ դիպակս ոսկւոյ եւ արծաթոյ եւ ազգի ազգի զարդարանս եւ իշխանութիւնս տայր ազատաց նորա եւ զքուրորդին իւր զՏէր Անանէ աբար Սենզելոս. եւ զամենայն պատուական զգեստս տրուեալ հայրապետին Հայոց, եւ յուղարկեցին զնա խաղաղութեամբ հանդերձ մեծամեծ տրօք. եւ ի քաղաքն Անի ոչ ժամանեաց, այլ երթեալ բնակէր ի Սեբաստիա քաղաքն առ ազգն Սենեքարիմայ մեծաւ փառաւորութեամբ:

When the emperor saw this, he asked the reason for not giving it. Then Lord Eghise' responded, saying: "O Emperor, it is [now become] a patriarchal chair and no one is worthy of sitting on it except for Lord Petros." When the emperor heard this, he thought that what Lord Eghise' said had merit, and he said: "Let the apostolic throne remain with him." Then the emperor said to Lord Eghise': "That chair is worth 1,000 dahekans. Keep it for your lord, so that no one else may sit on it."

In such glory did Lord Petros stay in Constantinople among the Byzantines for four years, daily increasing in grandeur and honor. Whenever he went to the palace, the patriarchal scepter was carried before him. Whenever the emperor saw him, he would kneel before him and the emperor also ordered his grandees to arise and go before Lord Petros. After four years, the emperor and the patriarch had given to Lord Petros numerous gifts: treasures and brocades [woven with] gold and silver, as well as diverse types of ornaments. [The emperor] gave authority to [Petros'] azats and also made a *syncellus* of his sister's son, Lord Anane'. All sorts of venerable garments were given to the patriarch of the Armenians, and they sent him off in peace with very magnificent gifts. However, he did not go to the city of Ani. Rather, he went to dwell in the city of Sebastia in great glory, by the family of Senek'erim.

41. Արդ յորժամ հասանէր զօրքն Յունաց ի յարեւելք, Կամենն եւ Առօնն եւ Գրիգոր Վասակայ որդին կոչեցին զհետ իւրեանց զԼիպարիտն զՎրաց իշխանն, եւ հասեալ նոցա ի բերդն՝ որ կոչի Կապուտռու, ի տեղին՝ որ Արջովիտ ասի. եւ լուեալ Թուրք զօրացն՝ զտեղի առին. եւ բընակեցան Հոռոմ զօրքն ի յԱրջովիտ: Եւ յայնժամ եկին զօրք այլազգեացն ի վերայ Լիպարիտին՝ առն քաջին. եւ նորա հանեալ զպահապանս ի գիշերի զքուրորդին իւր զՉորտուանէլն՝ զայրն հզօր եւ պատերազմող, եւ յայնժամ սկսան զօրք այլազգեացն ի գիշերին պատերազմիլ. եւ հասանէր ձայն պատերազմին առ Լիպարիտն՝ եթէ «Հասիր, զի զօրք այլազգեացն պատեաց զմեզ»: Եւ ասէր Լիպարիտն՝ եթէ «Շաբաթ է, եւ ոչ է օրէն Վրացեացս ելանել յաւուր շաբաթու ի պատերազմ»: Յայնժամ Չորտուանէլն որպէս զառիւծ ի գիշերին բախէր զճակատ այլազգեացն. եւ մինչդեռ վարէր զնոսա, դիպեալ եղեւ նետ մի ի բերան նորա եւ ընդ ծոծրակն ելանէր, եւ այնպէս մեռանէր Չորտուանէլն՝ այր քաջ եւ հզօր: Եւ յորժամ լուաւ Լիպարիտն զմահ Չորտուանէլին, որպէս զգազան զայրացեալ ելանէր ի պատերազմ եւ վարեաց զամենայն այլազգիսն ընդ երեսս դաշտացն եւ արեան ճապաղիս արարեալ զնոսա:

41. Now when the Byzantine forces reached the East, Cecaumenus, Aaron, and Grigor, Vasak's son, called for the Georgian prince, Liparit, to join them. They reached the fortress called Kaputr'u in the place called Arjovit. When the Turks heard about this, they halted, while the Byzantine forces camped in Arjovit. Then the troops of the foreigners came against that valiant man, Liparit. He had removed his sister's son, Ch'ortuanel', a mighty and martial man, as night watchman, and it was then that the troops of the foreigners began to fight, at night. Battle cries reached Liparit, saying: "Hurry, the troops of the foreigners have surrounded us." Liparit replied: "It is unlawful for us Georgians to go to battle on Saturday." At that moment Ch'ortuane'l, like a lion, struck at the front [brigade] of foreigners in the night. As he was putting them to flight, an arrow hit him in the mouth and emerged from the back of his neck. Thus did that brave and mighty man, Ch'ortuane'l, die. When Liparit heard about Ch'ortuane'l's death, he went to battle, like a crazed beast, and drove all the foreigners across the face of the plain, turning it into a bloody swamp.

Եւ յորժամ տեսանէր զօրքն Հոռոմոց զքաջութիւն Լիպարիտին, ի տուր ետուն զնա եւ թողին զԼիպարիտն ի մէջ այլազգեաց եւ փախան, զի մի առցէ զանուն քաջութեան: Եւ տեսեալ զայն զօրաց անօրինացն, դարձան միաբան ի պատերազմ ընդ Վրաց զօրացն. եւ յորժամ սաստկացաւ պատերազմն, եւ գոչէր որպէս զառիւծ Լիպարիտն ի մէջ անօրինացն, եւ յայնժամ մի ոմն ի զօրաց Վրացն յետոյ կացեալ եւ թրով հարեալ հատանէր զերկուս ջիլս ձիոյ Լիպարիտին. զոր իմացեալ Լիպարիտն՝ ի շտապս լեալ յետ կոյս դարձեալ եհար զնա եւ սատակեաց. եւ ինքն Լիպարիտն իջեալ նստէր ի վերայ գետնոյն յասպարիսին վերայ եւ ձայն տուեալ ասէր՝ թէ «Ես եմ Լիպարիտն»: Եւ յայնժամ զբազումս ի զօրաց Վրացեացն կոտորեցին եւ զայլն արարին փախստական. եւ զԼիպարիտն առեալ գերի եւ տարան զնա ի Խորասան առ Տուղրէլ սուլտանն, վասն զի յառաջագոյն լուեալ էր զանուն նորա եւ զամենայն քաջութիւն նորա գիտէր: Եւ կացեալ առ սուլտանն զամս երկուս եւ արար ի տեղիս տեղիս քաջութիւնս. եւ զխափշիկն՝ զայր հզօր եւ քաջ, հանին զերկուքն առաջի սուլտանին ի պատերազմ. եւ Լիպարիտն յաղթեալ սատակեաց զայլազգի զխափշիկն. եւ յայնժամ սուլտանն ազատեաց զնա եւ մեծ պարգեւօք յուղարկեաց զնա ի Հոռոմք: Եւ յայնժամ եկեալ Լիպարիտն ի Կոստանդնուպօլիս. եւ տեսեալ զնա թագաւորն Մոնոմախ՝ ուրախ լինէր յոյժ. եւ մեծամեծ պարգեւօք յուղարկեաց զնա ի տուն առ կինն իւր եւ առ որդիքն: Լիպարիտնս այս եղբայր էր Ռատին եւ Ջոյատին՝ վրացի ազգաւ՝ ի հզօր ջոկէ:

Now when the Byzantine troops observed the bravery of Liparit, they departed and abandoned him in the midst of the foreigners, and they fled—so that he would not attain a name for valor. When the forces of the foreigners saw this, they unitedly turned to battle the Georgian troops. When the battle grew more fierce, Liparit roared like a lion amidst the impious ones, and then someone from the Georgian troops, who had remained behind, cut Liparit's horse's tendons. When Liparit realized this, he quickly turned around and killed [the perpetrator]. Then Liparit himself dismounted and went and sat on his shield by the banks of the river and shouted: "I am Liparit." Then many of the Georgian troops were killed and others fled. [The Saljuqs] took Liparit captive and took him to Sultan Tughril in Khurasan. For [Tughril] previously had heard his name and knew about all his valorous deeds. [Liparit] remained near the sultan for two years, performing brave deeds here and there. Now there was a mighty and valiant Qipchaq [at Tughril's court]. The two of them were brought before the sultan to fight. Liparit defeated and killed that foreign Qipchaq. And then the sultan freed him and sent him to the Byzantines with grand gifts. When Liparit arrived in Constantinople and Emperor Monomachus saw him, he was delighted. With very great gifts [Monomachus] sent him to his home, to his wife and children. This Liparit was the brother of R'at and Zoyat, of Georgian nationality,[46] and from a vigorous line.[47]

46 *i.e.,* of Chalcedonian confession.

47 *A vigorous line:* the Orbeleans.

Դարձեալ ի թուականութեանն Հայոց յամի ՆՂԹ եղեւ սաստիկ խռովութիւն ի տունն Հոռոմոց, եւ բազում գաւառք մաշեցան ի սուր սուսերի: Եւ եղեւ կատարածք մեծամեծք եւ աւուրք դառնաշունչք ի ձեռն գիշակեր եւ անօրէն պիղծ ազգին Պածենկաց՝ չար եւ արեանարբու գազանացն. վասն զի ազգք օձիցն էլին եւ հարին զԽարտէշքն, եւ Խարտէշքն էլին եւ հարին զՈւզն եւ զՊածինակն, եւ միաբան բորբոքեցան ի վերայ տանն Հոռոմոց, եւ բազում նեղութիւնս անցուցին ընդ Կոստանդնուպօլիս. եւ փառաւոր իշխանք մատնեցան ի գերութիւն, զորս ոչ կարեմ պատմել զաղէտս թախանձանացն, զոր կրեաց տունն Հոռոմոց յամին յայնմիկ. վասն զի գազանապէս եւ անողորմ գերեցին զազգն Յունաց. եւ թագաւորն զարհուրեալ ոչ իշխեաց ելանել ի պատերազմ, զի անթիւ եւ անհամարք էին զօրք թշնամեացն. եւ զբազում աւուրս կացեալ՝ գնացին յաշխարհն իւրեանց. եւ ապա այնուհետեւ եղեւ խաղաղութիւն յաշխարհին Հոռոմոց:

42. Իսկ յորժամ բարձրացեալ աւարտեցաւ թուականս Հայոց ազգիս ի յամս Շ, մատեան առ թագաւորն Մոնոմախ չարաթոյնք եւ լեզուք նենգաւորք եւ մատուցանէին չարախօսութիւն վասն փառաւոր իշխանաց Հայոց, որք ի գաւառն Պաղնայ բնակեալ կային, եւ ասացին՝ թէ Անհնազանդ կան հրամանաց քոց եւ կամին ապստամբ լինել ի քէն:

Again in the year 499 of the Armenian Era [A.D. 1050-1051], there were severe disturbances in the House of the Byzantines, and many districts were put to the sword. These were bitter days full of major events brought on by the rapacious, impious, and filthy Pecheneg people, those evil and blood-thirsty beasts. For the nation of serpents arose and struck the Xarte'shk'.[48] The latter, in turn, arose and struck at the Uzes and Pechenegs and, all together, they were aroused against the House of the Byzantines and brought many tribulations upon Constantinople. Glorious princes were taken captive. I am unable to relate the sorrowful disasters which the House of the Byzantines was subjected to during that year. Like merciless wild beasts [the invaders] enslaved the nation of the Byzantines. The terrified emperor did not dare go out to battle, since the troops of enemies were innumerable and countless. After remaining there for many days, they returned to their own land. After that there was peace in the land of the Byzantines.

42. At the end of the year 500 of the Armenian Era [A.D. 1051], some poisonous people with lying tongues went before Emperor Monomachus and spoke evil words about the glorious princes of the Armenians who dwelt in the district of Paghnatun. They said: "They disobey your orders and want to rebel from you."

48 *Xarte'shk':* "fair-haired" (possibly, the Magyars).

Եւ առաքեաց զօրապետս հանդերձ զօրօք ի Պաղին եւ անհրաւաբար հեղոյր զչարութեան թոյնս իւր ի վերայ անմեղաց. եւ բարկութեամբ սկսաւ ապականել զամենայն գաւառն. եւ զամենայն իշխանսն սկսաւ ի փառաց ընկենուլ, վասն զի էր այր պիղծ եւ չար, որ էր զօրագլուխ սատանայի, որոյ անունն նորա Պեռոս ճանաչի. եւ կամեցաւ որ զմեծ իշխանսն զորդիսն Հաբէլի ձերբակալս առնել, զՀարպիկն այր քաջ եւ զհզօր եւ զԴաւիթ եւ զԼեւոն եւ զԿոստանդին՝ զչորս եղբարսն, այսմ օրինակաւ եւ զայլ իշխանսն: Յայնժամ իշխանքն ծածկաբար խորհուրդ արարին զի ամենայն ոք զիւր ամրոցն բռնեսցէ՝ մինչեւ ծանուցանեն թագաւորին զաւերումն գաւառին յանօրէն Պեռոսէ. եւ միաբան արարին երդումն միաբանութեան՝ զի յայգ շաբաթու առցէ ամենայն ոք զիւր ամրոցն:

Եւ յայնժամ մի ոմն ի միաբանելոցն՝ Թորոսակ անուն՝ տէրն Թլպաղայ, ուրացաւ զերդումն եւ ազդ արարեալ անօրէն Պեռոսին, թէ ամենայն իշխանքն միաբանեցան չգալ ի կոչումդ քո. եւ զայս ամենայն ոչ գիտացեալ Հաբելի որդւոցն, եւ որպէս յառաջն ասացեալ էին՝ յաւուր շաբաթուն առին զմեծ ամրոցն՝ որ կոչի Արկնի, որ էր մերձ ի գաւառն Թլխոյ. եւ այլ ամենայն միաբանքն գնացին ի կոչն Պեռոսին:

[Monomachus] sent a military commander with troops to Paghin who unjustly spewed his venom on the innocent. In fury this man, whose name was Per'os, began to pollute the entire district, and to deprive the princes of their glories, since he was a loathsome and evil man, and Satan's military commander. He wanted to arrest the great princes, the four brothers who were Abel's sons: the brave and mighty Harpik, Dawit', Lewon, and Kostand. He also wanted to do the same to the other princes. Then the princes secretly made a plan that all of them would keep to their own fortresses until the emperor could be informed about the destruction of the district by the impious Per'os. They made an oath of unity that on Saturday morning each of them would [begin to] remain in his own fortress.

And then one of the conferees, who was named T'orosak, the lord of T'lpagh [Paghnatun], broke his oath and notified the impious Per'os that "all the princes have united to not respond to your summons." Harpik's sons knew nothing about this [betrayal]. As previously decided, on Saturday they took the great fortress called Arkina, which was close to the district of T'lkhum. Meanwhile, all the other [princes], united, went to Per'os' summons.

Եւ լուաւ զայն, զոր արարին որդիքն Հաբելի, արար ժողով ի վերայ բերդին Արկնոյ զօրս բազումս. եւ տեսանէր զամրութիւն բերդին՝ հիանայր յոյժ եւ ոչ կարէր պատերազմել, վասն զի բարձր էր յոյժ եւ անառ էր ի թշնամեացն. եւ ոչ կարաց մերձենալ ի նա: Եւ յայնժամ խորհեցաւ զայս ինչ չար եւ ասաց. «Եթէ ոք բերցէ զգլուխ Հարպկանն առ իս, առցէ զանձ ոսկւոյ եւ արծաթոյ բազում եւ իշխանութիւնս եւ մեծութիւնս ի թագաւորէն»:

Եւ լուեալ զայս սննդակիցք եւ նախածանօթքն իւր, որք առ ինքն էին ի բերդն, եւ խորհեցան խորհուրդ անօրէնութեան զՅուդայի եւ զԿայենի եղբայրասպանին: Եւ էր մօտ ի բերդն տեղի հակառակ, եւ Հարպիկն առեալ արս եւ ելեալ պահէր զտեղին. եւ զաւուրս երեք ոչ իշխեաց ննջել ամենեւին. եւ ասեն նենգաւորքն. «Վասն է՞ր ոչ ննջես, տէր մեր, զի ահա այսօր անձինք մեր մեռանին ի վերայ քո անձինդ»: Եւ հաւատացեալ նոցա՝ ննջեաց, զի ձանձրացեալ էր յոյժ. եւ իբրեւ քաղցրացաւ ի քունն, յարուցեալ ազգականն իւր հատանէր զգլուխն Հարպկանն՝ զառն հզօրի եւ քաջի, եւ ի նոյն գիշերին հասուցանէին զգլուխն առ Պետռոս կատապանն. եւ սպանողքն ոչինչ օգտեցան՝ բայց միայն անէծս:

When [Per'os] heard what Abel's sons had done, he massed numerous troops by Arkina fortress. However, when he observed the fortification of the stronghold, he was greatly astonished and was unable to fight, since it was very lofty and unassailable by enemies. He was unable to approach it. Then he conceived a wicked plan and said: "Should someone bring Harpik's head to me, he will receive a treasure of gold, much silver, as well as authority and greatness from the emperor."

When [Harpik's] childhood friends and those close to him, who were with him in the fortress, heard this, they came up with an impious plan [resembling those] of Judas and the fratricidal Cain. Near the fortress, and facing it, was a place that Harpik had gone to guard, taking some men with him. For three days he did not dare to sleep at all. The traitors said to him: "Our lord, why don't you sleep? Behold, today we would die for you." Believing them, he slept, since he was extremely weary. While he was deeply asleep, one of his relatives arose and cut off the head of Harpik, that mighty and valiant man. That same night he took the head to the captain Per'os. But the killers did not profit at all from this. All they received were curses.

Եւ հրամայեաց Պեռոս ի ձոր ցցեալ զգլուխ Հարպկանն եւ տանել ընդդէմ դրան բերդին. եւ ի լուսանալն տեսեալ եղբարցն նորա՝ ծանեան եւ վաղվաղակի բացեալ զդուրսն եւ արկեալ հող ի վերայ գլխոց իւրեանց եւ լալով գային երեք եղբարքն եւ անկանէին առաջի հատեալ գլխոյ Հարպկանն. եւ այնչափ կոծ առեալ նոցա, մինչեւ ողբս առեալ լային ամենայն զօրք բանակին: Եւ այսպիսի օրինակաւ տիրանայր Պեռոսն ամուր բերդին Արկնոյ եւ զեղբարսն Հարպկանն՝ զորդիսն Հաբելի տարաւ ի Կոստանդնուպօլիս առ թագաւորն Մոնոմախն: Եւ տեսեալ զնոսա թագաւորն եւ ամենայն տունն Յունաց, հիանային ընդ սոսկալի տեսիլ կերպարանցն նոցա, վասն զի ահաւոր էին տեսլեամբ եւ թիկամբքն հանդերձ բարձր էին քան զամենայն տունն Յունաց. եւ յաղագս գեղեցիկ տեսլեանն ոչինչ արար խրատ նոցա, այլ հրամայեաց անցուցանել զնոսա ի կղզի՝ զԴաւիթ եւ զԼեւոն եւ զԿոստանդին, զայր քաջք եւ հզօրք եւ երեւելի իշխանք Հայոց:

Per'os ordered that Harpik's head be stuck on a pole and taken opposite the entrance to the fortress. At daybreak, his brothers saw and recognized it. They immediately opened the gate and, throwing dirt on their own heads and crying, the three brothers came and fell down before Harpik's severed head. So much did they mourn him, that all the troops in the army also wept. And in such a fashion did Per'os come to rule over the secure fortress of Arkina. He took Harpik's brothers, Abel's sons, to Emperor Monomachus in Constantinople. When the emperor and the entire House of the Byzantines saw them, they were astounded at their formidable and awesome appearance, for they were taller and had broader shoulders than all the Greeks. Because of their good looks, [the emperor] ignored the advice [of the Byzantines to kill them] and instead commanded that they should be taken to an island—these brave, mighty, and prominent princes of the Armenians.

INDEX

INDEX

INDEX

INDEX

SOPHENE

www.ingramcontent.com/pod-product-compliance
Ingram Content Group UK Ltd.
Pitfield, Milton Keynes, MK11 3LW, UK
UKHW041636190726
13854UKWH00006B/2533

9 781925 937701